Trading Steel for Stone

Tales of a Rustbelt Refugee

Trading Steel for Stone

Turned Rocky Mountain Rescuer

Tom Wood

JOHNSON BOOKS
AN IMPRINT OF BOWER HOUSE
DENVER

Cover design and text composition: D.K. Luraas
Cover image: by Tom Wood; car image from Istock
Trading Steel for Stone logo design: Angie Lucht
Author photo: Amy Johnson Photography
Back cover photo: Adam Perou Hermans

Library of Congress Control Number: 2016938145
ISBN: 978-1-55566-467-1

Portions of the chapter "Forever Lost to the Mountain: They Died Doing What They Loved Best and Other Lies from RescueWorld" originally appeared in *5280: The Denver Magazine.*

The story of Heaton Amalgamated in the chapter "Rustbelt Recollections: My Dad the Devil, Ice Age Prophecies, and the Orange Bears" was originally published as "Ice Age Prophesies and the Dead Killer" in *Car Bombs to Cookie Tables: The Youngstown Anthology,* 2015, Belt Publishing.

Portions of the chapter "Suicide: The Low Side of That Rocky Mountain High" previously appeared in the Spring and Summer 2013 editions of the Mountain Rescue Association's Online Publication *The Meridian.*

Printed in the U.S.A.

9 8 7 6 5 4 3

"Mountains don't care, but we do."
—Dee Molenaar,
early member of the Mountain Rescue Association

"You can give credit to God or Darwin when someone survives
an ordeal in the mountains. That's your business."
—John Dill,
Yosemite National Park Ranger

"Volunteers are the only human beings on the face of the earth
who reflect this nation's compassion, unselfish caring, patience,
and just plain love for one another."
—Erma Bombeck,
humorist and fellow Rustbelt Refugee

"Dear God, please don't let me fuck up."
—Alan Shepard, Apollo Astronaut and
Tom Wood, Mountain Rescuer, Rustbelt Refugee

Contents

Prelude

The pitiful shape illuminated in the circle of my headlamp's light barely looked human. My first impression, after revulsion, was that someone was mistaken. There was no way this thing was alive.

My practiced technique of pre-visualizing worst-case scenarios didn't prepare me for what lay at the foot of that giant rock. The fact that this mangled mess of a man lying at my feet was alive somehow made it more difficult to cope with than if he'd been dead when we discovered him. It somehow seemed … unnatural and wrong that someone could be so horribly disfigured, y et still draw breath a full three days after his accident.

His colorful BASE jumper's chute (and some of those colors weren't from the parachute manufacturer, they originated from the chute's owner) was partially draped across his body. At first, I couldn't put my finger on what looked so out of place about his bloody visage. Then I realized with a start that his entire face was smashed flat as a board, with both eyes swollen completely shut. His mouth, partially open, revealed the jagged pieces of the few teeth that survived the impact.

His arms, legs, hands, and feet were frozen at impossible angles. Akimbo is the word, I believe. At each bend, splintered, yellowish-green knobs of bone poked out through tattered and blood-encrusted clothing.

My fellow mountain rescuers and I guessed that his chute had partially deployed after the jump from the top of Mt. Evans' Black Wall, nearly 1,000 feet above us, and slowed his fall enough to allow the possibility for survival. Based upon his injuries, it was likely that he had smashed into the colossal tombstone rock that now loomed above us with his arms and legs out in front of him, as if to ward off the tremendous and inescapable impact. His chute had covered him after he fell to the ground, keeping his core temperature high enough to prevent him from freezing to death. But the same freezing temperatures that threatened to kill him by hypothermia had paradoxically prevented him from bleeding out. His body had reserved most of his circulation for warming his core, thus robbing his arms and legs of blood that would have simply run out of him and onto the frozen ground.

His friends (there were now two of them on scene) huddled close and spoke hushed and tense words of encouragement in his bloodied ears that still oozed what looked to be cerebral-spinal fluid. Occasionally their heartfelt exhortations elicited a weak, gurgled moan of pain-wracked acknowledgment.

Stepping back from the halo of light encircling the BASE jumper, the enormity of what now lay ahead of us struck me full force. It hadn't even occurred to me (or anyone else) that we might have to devise an evacuation plan for a living, breathing human being. I had expected to find a battered body at the base of the cliff, take some photos for the coroner, scoop it into a bag and carry it out. Now we had a he to deal with, not an it.

This man needed a paramedic with a bag full of drugs, a litter, and lots of oxygen. We had none of those things on-site, so we requested them via radio. We were about four-and-a-half miles uphill from Mission Base, at an elevation of roughly 12,000 feet, and we didn't expect the cavalry to arrive anytime soon.

It was now one in the morning, and a crystal clear night. We guessed temps were in the teens. Many of us, expecting that we could be out searching for the entire night, had brought bivy sacs and sleeping bags. We huddled together under them, and took turns monitoring our subject's condition. All we could offer him was a space blanket and choked words of comfort until the sun arrived, hopefully bringing a medical helicopter with it.

Taking my turn at his side at around 3:00 a.m., it was impossible to detect the rise and fall of his chest under the silvery space blanket. I was genuinely concerned that he would simply stop breathing while I knelt there and I'd never know. So every ten minutes or so, I nudged his shoulder lightly and called his name. He responded by letting a low moan escape his clotted throat, and slightly turning his head toward me.

It was impossible for me to escape a creeping sense of guilt-ridden déjà vu. The poorly planned, foolish, and downright dangerous thrill-seeking pursuits of my youth should have ended like this.

That should be me lying there.

Introduction

Welcome to RescueWorld. My name is Tom, and I'll be your tour guide today. Be careful where you step, ladies and gents, it can get kind of messy here in RescueWorld.

And parents, you may want to leave the kids at home for this trip, as some of the things that go on here in RescueWorld blow right past PG 13, zip by Rated R, and dive straight into the realm of Not Rated.

If you expect to find this RescueWorld populated by fearless, hulking, strong-chinned, and totally ripped heroes aided by buxom blonde snow bunnies led into the mountains by faithful Saint Bernards sporting little barrels of schnapps around their thick furry necks as a fleet of helicopters piloted by crazy-but-somehow-capable veteran pilots spouting pithy one-liners that must all learn to work together in order to overcome their seemingly insurmountable differences and beat the odds to effect spectacular, death-defying mountain rescues ... sorry.

That's Planet Hollywood RescueWorld. It's down the road on the left, just listen for all the explosions and look for all the flashing lights.

And if you are looking for rousing tales of sooty, mustached protagonists rushing into burning buildings to save the day—again, sorry. There are no buildings to burn here in Mountain RescueWorld. You are probably looking for *Fire* RescueWorld. It's down the hill in the city. Nice bunch of folks, though.

This is Volunteer Mountain RescueWorld. Things are a little different here. A little more free-spirited. A lot more low budget. Kinda weird.

Volunteer Mountain Rescuers are a breed apart from their firefighting or ambulance-driving counterparts. No more or less professional. No more or less dedicated. No more or less heroic—though most of us shun that word. Just ... different.

I've been a Volunteer Mountain Rescuer for nearly eighteen years now. I've participated in more than four hundred calls in that time, and to this day it still amazes me that John and Susie Q. Public have virtually no idea how Search and Rescue (SAR) takes place in our country's high or remote places. Or why.

And just who are these people who dedicate so much of their time, energy, personal finances, and sometimes their lives "so that others might live?"

Well, first of all, we're pretty informal here in Volunteer Mountain RescueWorld. So let's just drop the Volunteer Mountain part and just stick with RescueWorld from here on out.

Here in the RescueWorld I know and love, all the "heroes" are everyday folk: high school teachers, housewives, pizza delivery guys, journalists, ex-military, rocket scientists, cowboy poets, full-time firefighters, welders, small business owners, carpenters, engineers, landscapers, liquor store cashiers, retirees, nurses, and even … roofers.

Miracles are performed on the cheap here in RescueWorld, often in between dropping the kids off at school and finding the time to pick up a pizza for dinner on the way home from a SAR mission.

Although popular fiction and film might lead you to think otherwise, mountain rescue in America is carried out by thinking, feeling human beings with humility and grace. Human beings whose primary commitments are to their families, churches, and their jobs. They are a far cry from the stoic, Stallone-like daredevils that single-handedly carry out fantastic rescues without lasting physical or emotional scars (again, if that's the sort of story you crave, Planet Hollywood RescueWorld is down the road).

Most of us are just regular folks who want to help other regular folks who are having a bad day in the mountains. Our love of the outdoors and an obsessive drive to help others is what draws us to this demanding line of work.

But the trail leading to a career in mountain rescue is far from straight. It is twisted and not without more than a few switchbacks. Case in point: Me. I am a born and bred Buckeye/part-time Kentuckian who stumbled into mountain rescue while I was busy running full-speed away from myself.

Mountain rescuer was not a career choice offered up to a skinny kid like myself growing up in northeastern Ohio by Mr. Bullock, our guidance counselor at Niles McKinley High School. Back then (in the early '80s) your career choices were rather limited. You may have wanted to grow up and be a fireman, an astronaut, or maybe president (if you had either sadistically driven parents or delusions of grandeur), but if you planned on sinking some roots and raising a family, you settled for a job at Republic Steel (like my mother's father), Chrysler (like my father's father) or General Motors (like MY father).

I've never been much for settling, so after a lot of moving up and down the Ohio River, I headed west and ended up here. In Colorado. Doing mountain rescue.

Ten years, two wives, and three children later, I stopped, took a breath and visited my local big-box bookstore. I noticed that the shelves were chock full of books that chronicled the daring exploits and harrowing adventures of both professional adventurers and amateur adrenaline junkies. Everyone who attempted Mount Everest, played golf at the South Pole, had a climbing partner die on them, or cut off their own arm had a thrilling tale to tell within the pages of books with really swell dramatic titles. The words: "Death," "Disaster," "Tragedy," or "Edge" were usually found in the titles of these books—sometimes all of them.

Some were well written. Others detailed feats so amazing and extraordinary that they didn't have to be well written—a third-grader could have penned them and still had you sitting on the edge of your seat.

But most adventure or climbing narratives seemed to focus on one event, one mountain, or one expedition. I've read many, many of the aforementioned books. Some I liked a lot. Some I may not have liked, but I could appreciate their value as testament to the extremes to which we foolish mortals push ourselves. This is not one of those kinds of books. Not exactly.

Upon further investigation, I discovered that there were a few books out there that delved into the lesser-known side of what happens to these mountaineers, climbers, skiers, endurance athletes, peak baggers, BASE jumpers, snowboarders, snowmobilers, backcountry big game hunters, and mushroom hunters (yes, I said mushroom hunters) when things go awry. In short, books that detailed the nuts and bolts of backcountry rescue.

As I stated earlier, I am now a mountain rescuer, and as a mountain rescuer, these kinds of books were always of interest to me because I related to the subject matter. But I couldn't figure out why anyone who wasn't a mountain rescuer would want to read books about mountain rescue. And unfortunately, many of the mountain rescuers who put aside their ice axes and picked up their pens to try their hand at mountain rescue writing worked so hard to prove how selfless they were that too much of the rescuer's humanity and humor was lost in the process.

Without some backstory or a better understanding of just who these rescuers are, how could a housewife in Basking Ridge, New Jersey, appreciate the grisly humor involved in the recovery of a sixty-nine-year-old hunter's frozen body from the Colorado backcountry? Why would a cab driver in Jacksonville, North Carolina, give a rat's ass about the desperate prayer whispered by a rookie rescuer suddenly put in charge of the rescue of a fellow rescuer who tumbled 900 feet down an avalanche chute after driving his snowmobile off a cliff with a rescued Texan on the back? These situations may as well happen on Mars if there is no relevance to the average person's daily life or empathy for the rescuers or the victims needing rescue. I realized that I wanted to make the average person give a rat's ass about mountain rescue.

In my efforts to write a book about the inner workings of mountain rescue, I came to the conclusion that it was impossible for me to do so objectively. I could not delve into the inner workings of mountain rescue without delving into the inner workings of the mountain rescuer. I just couldn't step back and remove myself from the story.

This book is my attempt to let the world know that mountain rescuers are *not* heroes. They are just regular people volunteering to put themselves into extraordinary situations. Regular people struggling to keep their jobs and homes in a crazy economy. Regular people worrying about the toll gravity and age—and maybe cancer—are taking on their bodies.

Regular people desperately trying to hold their marriages and families together. Regular people spending a lot of their present trying to make sense out of their past. Regular people juggling all of these efforts while doing their level best to prove that Darwin was wrong. Regular people like me.

Apologies in advance for any errors or omissions. Memoirs/non-fiction narratives like the one you now hold in your hands, more than anything else, rely on memory. And as we all know, our memories are often mercurial and fractured in nature. To that end, I've done my best to make certain that any dates, places, and events I mention are accurate to the best of my research and recollections. As for everything else, I can only say that my perceptions of the events I recount are true as best as I can honestly recall. In other words, this is my story, and I'm sticking to it.

My sincerest hope is that these recollections are not viewed by John and Susie Q. Public as being yet another collection of "mountain rescue war stories." War stories, in just the mere telling of them, tend to glorify the events described. I am not interested in glamorizing anything that either I or any other mountain rescuer has done. Quite the opposite, in fact.

When we perform rescues or searches in the backcountry, we sometimes make mistakes. We sometimes get scared. We sometimes laugh when we should cry, and cry when we should be laughing. Or struggle to feel anything when faced with so much trauma. And as volunteer mountain rescuers, we have a whole lot of living going on in between missions. There are almost never any individual heroes in mountain rescue, in spite of what popular media tells us. Rather, we are all but cogs in the rescue machine.

This book is not an attempt to air any dirty (or bloody) mountain rescue laundry. There have been a few books published about mountain rescue that played upon the conflicts that surrounded certain teams at certain points in time. Given the life-and-death nature of some of the work performed by mountain rescuers, it is not surprising that it draws huge egos like moths to a flame. It's practically an occupational hazard.

In relating some of my foibles and failures as a human being and as a mountain rescuer, some members of my family (both biological and rescue) may get caught in the crossfire. When someone within these pages is reflected in a less-than-flattering light, it must be understood that there is no malice intended. And I mean that with all my heart. We are all of us flawed, and to pretend otherwise goes against my nature.

I'll do my best to keep the rescue-speak and all the militaristic acronyms that SAR (I mean, Search and Rescue) work entails to a minimum. Although one can't speak of mountain searches and rescues without them, my goal here is to chart a more personal course as I set out to explain mountain rescue in the twenty-first century from the inside out. So please bear with me when I go on about potential MRA Code 4's who lost contact with the RP at 0700 hours and are now likely SOL because their PLB beacon alerted NOAA and then the AFRCC in FLA …

I feel I must be upfront about the fact that there are many events woven into the fabric of this book that have absolutely nothing to do with mountain rescue for anybody but me. Life stuff. As far as I'm concerned, it's all related. No one is born to be a mountain rescuer. There's always a backstory. There is always stuff in the middle that got us here.

As rescuers, we often lug around the emotional baggage that everyday life has saddled us with as we climb the mountain. We do not ply our trade in a void, and often the things that affect us most deeply on the mountain or in the forest have their roots deep in our past. Or they lie in wait, patiently, to pounce on our backs when we get back home.

Like most of the folks who perform mountain rescue for any length of time, I try my best not to judge those who need our services. As you will doubtless learn in the following pages, simple dumb luck (or divine providence) was all that kept me from becoming a victim needing rescue. Or a body in a bag.

Although I wouldn't say I was the King of Stupid, I could easily have been appointed the Duke.

Fair warning: There is a good bit of gallows humor in the pages of this book. As most nurses, doctors, cops, firefighters, and mountain rescuers will tell you, humor is a coping mechanism that many of us employ to deal with situations that would otherwise be unbearable. American literary critic Lewis Mumford summed it up very well when he said, "Humor is our way of defending ourselves from life's absurdities by thinking absurdly about them."

I've also heard it said that gallows humor is the type of humor most often needed by people when they must laugh at the fact that *nothing* is really all that funny. As professional rescuers, sometimes our sense of humor is the only weapon we have at our disposal to combat the brutal effects these tragic situations can have on our psyche.

Usually, this kind of humor is only witnessed by our fellow rescuers during the rescue and away from the general public. There are some situations that I will describe in this book that shed some light on these private moments of humor we share, but I would respectfully request that they be judged within their context. My heart goes out to *everyone* who has either been hurt or lost someone to the mountains. I am not one bit ashamed to admit I have shed tears over the losses and injuries of complete strangers in the mountains.

By including both the lighter moments on very dark missions and the more personal revelations of what we say and do in the thin air of Colorado's high country, I only mean to convey the humanity of the rescuers. No disrespect is *ever* intended to the memories of our subjects, their friends, or families.

It goes without saying that the feelings, impressions, opinions, and beliefs recorded within these pages are completely my own. They are not meant to reflect the opinions of my fellow rescuers on the Alpine Rescue Team, the sheriff's departments we work under, or the Mountain Rescue Association. It's all me.

My sincerest hope is that the documentation of a few of my experiences and impressions as a mountain rescuer do not alienate me from my comrades in arms. For the most part, what happens in RescueWorld stays in RescueWorld. We mountain rescuers are a fairly stoic, tight-lipped group of people who usually keep to ourselves and shun the limelight. We keep the discussions of our affairs in-house, and rarely share any behind-the-scenes glimpses with the general public.

So again, in breaking that self-imposed mountain rescuer code of silence, I hope it is understood by all those in the search and rescue community that this book is simply my attempt to put at least *one* human face to all those thousands of search and rescue volunteers who toil anonymously in service to their fellow humans.

My only apology is that it's my face—crooked grin and all—and not one that represents the wiser, smarter, and saner rescuers out there.

Meet the
Reporting Party

You can't take anything, including SAR, too seriously. Here, I'm spoofing a scene from the film Vertical Limit *on No Name Glacier near Juneau, Alaska. Photo by Marc Beverly.*

They Died Doing What They Loved Best and Other Lies from RescueWorld

"**They** died doing what they loved best." I hate when I hear someone say that. It's bullshit. Most of the time, anyway. It implies something that I'm not so sure I agree with. I think four out of five dentists surveyed would say *living* is what they loved to do best.

Based upon what I've witnessed, dying in the wilderness is not usually a gentle, transcendent experience. Most of the time, anyway. Death in the backcountry is not usually an event that typically allows one much time for introspection, reflection, or the opportunity to make peace or say goodbyes. Most of the time, anyway.

No, death in the backcountry is usually a bolt out of the blue (sometimes quite literally). I've observed that this backcountry brand of death (complete with that pine-fresh scent!) is not subtle, dignified, heroic, or pretty. It is random, brutal, completely unexpected, unfairly administered, chaotic, and sometimes quite messy. Again, most of the time. But not every time.

There's always the exception to the rule, and in my experience, the passing of Vern Rutledge might well be that rare exception. I suppose his death was the closest example I've come across of someone "doing what they loved best" when they kicked the bucket in the backcountry.

Sixty-nine-year-old Michigan native Vern Rutledge had been making his annual pilgrimage to the frigid, shadowed valley of wilderness below the 14,120-foot-tall massif known as Mount Evans for many years with his pal and wilderness outfitter, Jim Kilgore, to camp and hunt elk. Their basecamp, some 5 miles in from the Echo Lake trailhead, was only accessible by a long, narrow, winding trail.

On a clear, sub-zero December night in 1999, Vern suffered a massive heart attack in his sleep and passed on. I doubt that when Vern said goodnight to his hunting buddies, closed the flap on his dirty canvas tent, and zipped up his sleeping bag that he had any clue it was to be his last and final goodnight. But it was.

I would hazard one guess about his situation, though. I'd be willing to bet that he could have imagined a host of far more unpleasant ways to write his final entry in the book of life than, after more than six decades of drawing breath, quietly slipping away in his sleep after bringing down a bull elk with his good friends in the wilds of Colorado.

If you believe that when a person dies, their soul leaves their body and they are free from pain, then what happened to Vern shortly after his passing shouldn't trouble you much. But if you feel that a person's aura, spirit, mojo— whatever—sticks around for a while after that person's heart beats its final beat … well, I guess the rest of Vern's story might be a bit more troubling.

After making their grim discovery when Vern failed to join them for breakfast the following morning, one of the hunters from Vern's camp saddled up two horses, jumping onto the lead animal and trailing the other behind. The world had to be notified that Vern was no longer in it.

Upon reaching the trailhead payphone at the Echo Lake Lodge a few hours later, the hunter (now known in SAR lingo as the RP, short for Reporting Party) notified the authorities of Vern's passing and awaited their arrival.

The Alpine Rescue Team was quickly notified by the Clear Creek County Sheriff's Office (CCCSO) that we had an MRA Code 4 (deceased party) to carry out of the wilderness. Sandy-haired and stoic Clear Creek County Sheriff Deputy Rick Safe, the bespectacled CCCSO Detective Mark Douglas, myself, fellow Alpine rookie Lisa Desmaris (a great amateur tennis player from Minnesota, you betcha), and fourth-year Alpine Rescue veteran and ultra-runner par extraordinaire Todd Holmes completed the small group charged with the sad task of eliminating the possibility of foul play. If we determined that the cause of death was natural (which we fully expected), we were to bring his mortal remains out of the woods and turn Vern over to the coroner, who would in turn release him to his family out of state.

Although it is unheard of in some parts of the country for three volunteer rescuers (two of the three being rookies at that) and two sheriff's department appointees to make such a pronouncement without a coroner present, death in the Rocky Mountains sometimes challenges the rules. The difficulty in accessing a deceased subject in the remote reaches of the backcountry sometimes makes it nearly impossible for a coroner to reach these subjects. So when we are confronted with these rare situations, we do our best to recall

all the episodes of *CSI* we've watched on TV for tips on what to look for in the unlikely event that foul play took place.

It was nearing noon when we finally finished our briefing with the sheriff's deputies, slung our packs over our shoulders and set off toward the hunters' base camp, somewhere in the Metz Creek drainage below us. Our route in, the Captain Mountain Trail, was a narrow, snow-packed path that dropped into the vast wilderness below from a starting elevation of about 10,200 feet.

Sheriff Deputy Rick Safe mounted the extra horse that the RP had saddled and trailed behind him. With the horses walking single file down the eerily quiet, winding trail and the four of us hiking behind them, we set off.

The sense of urgency usually present for a rescue is mostly absent when we are heading in on a known recovery. It is simply not worth injuring or risking the life of a rescuer when bringing the deceased out of the backcountry. Not to say we won't do the best job we can to effect a recovery, it's just that we understand all too well that urgency can often lead to mistakes in the backcountry. And to be brutally honest, dead is dead. No one gets less dead by us hurrying unnecessarily.

We do our best to preserve the dignity of a Code 4, but this can be a tall order given the circumstances that we sometimes face. Vern would soon illustrate this point.

We arrived at the hunting camp in relatively good time, as most of the trip in was downhill. It was a pretty good-sized camp. There were a few dirty white canvas tents with stovepipes poking from holes in their roofs. Sizeable piles of freshly cut and blocked firewood were piled near them.

A large, brown-stained table in the center of the camp was devoted to the gutting and cleaning of the harvested elks. A short distance from the camp, I could see the steaming gut pile that was testament to the success of the hunters thus far. A half-dozen horses were tethered to a rope tied horizontally between a couple snow-covered pines, and the smell of the campfire was both welcoming and inescapable.

Jim, the owner of the outfitting and guide service, approached us and introduced himself as we unslung our packs and Deputy Safe and the hunter/RP dismounted. The other hunters in the camp went about their business, sneaking hurried glances at all of us as the deputy and the detective pulled out their small notebooks and rummaged through their jacket pockets in search of the small cameras they had brought.

After they asked Jim a few rudimentary questions, he led them over to the tent that was now Vern's final resting place. The deputies, grim-faced and businesslike, asked the three of us mountain rescuers who would like to volunteer to accompany them into the tent and assist them with their inspection of Vern's corpse. Both Lisa and I had been on the team for less than two years at that time, so we turned to Todd, who had been on the team longer than us, and was likely the most medically qualified. Todd, a man of few words, simply shrugged his shoulders, parted the flap, and disappeared into the tent.

About half an hour later, a much paler Todd emerged from the tent. I later asked Todd what had gone on in the tent. He told me that his job was to act as photographer and document the condition of Vern's body. Todd explained that the grizzled hunter was indeed still in his sleeping bag, wearing only the insulated union suit–style long johns he had retired in. As the deputy rolled the body onto its side and pulled down Vern's pants to check for how much blood had pooled on his bottom side (an indication of how long ago Vern expired), Todd snapped away.

After several more photos and many hurriedly scribbled notes (it was still very cold), Todd said their investigative work was done. No signs of foul play, just as we had expected.

I asked Todd, who worked as a flight simulator programmer for United Airlines and was one of the premier endurance racing athletes in the United States, if any of his medical training had been of use. "What medical training," he said with a shrug. With a wry grin, he informed me that he was only CPR certified, same as me. He confided that it was easier to just step forward than go through the hassle of drawing straws in front of the deputy.

It was now time to orchestrate Vern's return to civilization. But there was one slight problem … we had forgotten to bring a body bag. We had all assumed—erroneously, as it turned out—that one of the other members of our small group had grabbed one. Since we were too far down in the valley to communicate via radio with Operations up at the trailhead and there was no cell coverage, we were on our own.

Another trip out and back to retrieve a body bag would have taken too long, as the sun set in the valley around 3:00 p.m. We decided that two sleeping bags, one pulled from over his head and the other from his feet and tied in the middle, would have to do.

We all entered the tent to bundle him up according to our plans. The tent smelled of old canvas, old sweat, old farts, campfire smoke, and that accursedly sweet and earthy (but barely noticeable) scent that I can only describe as the odor of death.

After packaging his remains we carried him outside, carefully placed him on the ground, and held another pow-wow. Carrying the body up and out of the valley, using only manpower, was not an option. We had no litter to strap him into, and too few of us to carry him the 5 miles up the trail.

Helicopter evacuation was also out of the question, as most of the helicopters we work with will not do body recoveries by air unless the ground evacuation poses a significant risk of injury to the rescuers. And from the perspective of the mountain rescuer, no helicopter should ever be called into service for work in the mountains unless life and limb are at stake anyway. So that left horsepower.

We briefly entertained the idea of constructing a travois to hook up behind the horse, similar to the ones that hunters hastily construct with two long sticks connected by crisscrossed saplings to drag big game out of the backcountry. But given the dwindling daylight and the time needed to construct such a thing, we opted instead to simply strap Vern onto the back of one of the packhorses.

We quickly discovered two major flaws in this plan. First of all, as we were informed by Jim, horses are very intelligent creatures, and they don't like having dead people strapped to their backs.

Now, I spent no small amount of time around horses in my younger days (mostly getting thrown off of them and getting my teeth kicked out by them), and I had never heard such a thing. But seeing as how I'd never tried to strap a dead hunter onto the back of one, I was obliged to take the outfitter at his word.

So after Jim fitted a couple of side blinders onto the horse to restrict its field of vision to the trail in front of it, we gathered around Vern. Someone said a few words on Vern's behalf. This seemed the right time to do so. I wish I could remember what was said, and who said it, but that memory escapes me now.

After the short eulogy, we hoisted Vern's sleeping bag–shrouded corpse up onto the steed's back. And I'll be damned, the horse *did* freak out. The outfitter then informed us that this was the very same horse (let's just call him Trigger) that Vern had tended to and ridden all week. The freak-out was likely inspired by Trigger getting a nostril full of the recently deceased Vern's changed scent.

Hey, if I can smell death, who's to say horses can't? I think Trigger's reaction was perfectly acceptable, given the situation. I know I'd be a tad bit on edge if someone slapped a pair of blinders on my head and then forced me to carry the corpse of a person who'd been responsible for my care the last several days.

After calming the horse down, we set to our work once again. At this point in the sadly comedic saga that was unfolding, the second flaw in our hastily constructed plan became evident.

The temperature the night Vern died was well below zero, and had barely risen above single digits in the twenty or so hours since his heart had suddenly stopped beating. So whether from the bitter, freezing cold or the effects of rigor mortis, Vern was now as stiff as the proverbial board. Maybe even stiffer. We attempted to balance him across the middle of the animal's wide back, tie a rope around his neck and feet, and then run it under the horse's belly to the other side. But no matter how hard we tried, we could not keep him centered atop the horse ... he kept sliding off to one side or the other.

And worse, he stuck out too far from the sides of the horse. He'd act as a stopper wedge every time the horse encountered a tight squeeze or switchback on the trail. He might even get torn off of the horse's back entirely. Neither option would be very pleasant to deal with.

At this point, I think we all reached the same conclusion at the same time, but were hesitant to voice it. We all stood around Vern's rigid corpse, precariously balanced across Trigger's back, literally scratching our heads, absently toeing the ground and wondering who would be the first to broach the subject of what we all now knew we must do. The outfitter, sensing what we were contemplating, approached us.

"I am so sorry, but ..." I said awkwardly.

Although I can't remember his exact words, I believe it went something like, "Vern was a very good friend of mine. Do what you have to do. But I can't watch." He then stepped away a few paces and remained with his back to us as he fiddled distractedly with his horse's tack.

With a few quick and whispered words, we split up and got on either side of the horse. Two of us flanked Vern on each side. We couldn't tell which side was head, which was foot. I do think that he was facing up, although how I knew that I haven't a clue. While one of the deputies held the reins of the horse, and kept up a steady stream of soothing words to keep it calm, we counted to three.

On three, we all jumped up a little and pulled straight down on each end of Vern with all of our might. A wet cracking sound informed us that we had broken his spine. And maybe some ribs. After a couple more gut- and heart-wrenching pulls, we bent his form enough to tie his ends together under the horse. He was now molded into a horseshoe-shaped configuration over the nervous animal's broad back.

We were now ready to begin the slog back up the trail. The first couple miles passed without incident. But instead of the horse becoming more comfortable with the load strapped over its back as it climbed up the trail, it actually seemed to get more skittish the farther we went. As we stopped to allow the horses in front to negotiate one of the switchbacks, Vern's horse, the last in line, finally said, "The hell with this!"

It reared up and shook free of the person leading it. This, in turn, spooked the horse ridden by Deputy Rick Safe (nowadays we know him as Captain Safe, and we've had the honor and privilege of working with him on hundreds of calls). It also reared back, dumping the startled deputy unceremoniously into a snowbank on the uphill side of the trail.

As I ran up to make certain Rick was uninjured, Vern's horse took off like it had just glimpsed the proverbial barn. "SHIT!" we yelled in unison. In horror, we watched the spooked horse and its cargo disappear around the bend ahead. Todd and Lisa ran after the horse, while I stayed and helped Rick up out of the snow. His pride suffering the only injury, he quickly re-mounted his horse and we set off to find the others.

I had terrifying visions of the horse arriving at the trailhead well ahead of us, dragging what was left of Vern behind while the TV news crews caught the whole sordid affair on tape. Or almost worse, our party arriving back at the trailhead and confessing to the Clear Creek County sheriff, the coroner, Alpine's mission leader, and quite likely Vern's family that we had no clue where his body had gotten off to, and—by the way—had they seen a horse running around?

Luckily, Todd and Lisa and the other deputy located the spooked horse in a matter of minutes. I was flooded with relief till I heard Deputy Rick—a taciturn man usually of few words—behind me mutter, "Uh oh," followed by plenty of colorful words usually reserved for situations like this one. I turned around to see Rick, back astride his horse, lifting his pant leg to inspect the empty ankle holster strapped to his lower leg. He had apparently lost his weapon when he was tossed off the horse.

At this point, the sun was just about to drop over the mountain, and the temperature was plummeting as well. We were all pretty tired and irritable. We just wanted this ordeal to end. Now this. I think for a moment that the deputy actually considered following Trigger's lead by saying the hell with it, and then beating feet to the trailhead above. I'm sure he knew the resulting mountain of paperwork for a lost weapon may well have dwarfed Mount Evans, so he dismounted and we backtracked to search for his gun.

Although it took another twenty minutes, we located the pistol, which of course had been lost in the snow when Rick tumbled off the bucking horse. When we finally collected ourselves and got back to the business at hand, it was with renewed vigor and determination to escape the ever-weirdening situation that we set off for the trailhead.

Fortunately, neither Vern's family nor the media greeted us upon our return. His family was still en route from out of state. And apparently, the passing of an elderly hunter in the woods from natural causes was not newsworthy enough to warrant any cameras or reporters being dispatched to greet us at the trailhead.

Todd, Lisa, and I said nothing to our team members who greeted us at the trailhead about our morbid and back-breaking experience. But I'm pretty sure that the deputies alerted the waiting coroner there might be some … interesting post mortem injuries to our subject that were totally unrelated to a heart attack, and that they were our handiwork—not the result of any foul play.

We silently loaded Vern into the back of the coroner's Suburban. Vern's old hunting pal Jim sniffed a little and quickly wiped a tear away while he thought none of us were looking, but we were.

Driving home after our post-mission debrief, I both bemoaned and marveled at the fact that I had no tears to shed for Vern. I don't think myself a callous, thick-skinned man. So why did my reactions to the death of a fellow human being seem so matter of fact? Maybe it was because Vern was in the twilight years of his long life. Perhaps it was because his passing was almost instantaneous and caused him little pain. Or maybe it was something else— and I don't mean that it was because he died while doing what he loved best. Maybe—just maybe—I cared just enough to not care too much.

We are all wired differently. I've come to firmly believe that some of us handle the pain, suffering—and even death—of our fellow humans with fewer emotional scars than others might have to endure. In a strange way, maybe this is a gift. Just as we need to have people on this earth who feel empathy with and sympathy for the suffering of every living thing, so too is there a place in the universe for those of us who can help or aid those in pain or in need without allowing a tidal flow of grief to wash over and drown or paralyze us.

Nurses, doctors, firefighters, paramedics, police officers, and rescuers couldn't possibly carry out their life-sustaining work if they collapsed into a sobbing heap at the end of every workday. Not to say that these individuals don't care about the suffering of those charged to their care. You can't convince me that a hospice nurse tending to the weeping bedsores of a semiconscious, terminally ill cancer patient does so just because it's her job.

Some people are born to be plumbers. Some are born to be engineers. Others are born to drive a school bus. And some of us are just born to handle the grief of losing a fellow human that often goes hand in hand with the joy of saving a fellow human, without wanting to jump off the nearest cliff. Again, caring just enough to not care too much.

Not to say that we (and by we, I am referring to rescuers) are completely inoculated against feelings of despondency, depression, or anger when someone loses the battle for their own life on our watch. We are still very, very human, after all.

After speaking with fellow rescuers, I have since come to the conclusion that every fatality affects each of us in RescueWorld differently. A rescuer might respond to a dozen fatalities with nary a moment's lost sleep. Not a single tear shed, or moment lost in dark reflection as to the fleeting and fragile nature of our own existence. Of our own inescapable mortality.

But, I've come to understand that maybe the next time the pager chirps and prompts the mountain rescuer's Pavlovian call to action, death might well wear a face that resembles that of the rescuer's best friend from college. Or sister. Or brother. Or dad. Or mom. Or grandparent. Or the worst (so I'm told)—the rescuer's own child. Death is insidiously tenacious, and always itching to get under the skin of those of us who work in RescueWorld. We just can't predict which mission will get to us.

For those torturous times, the support of our teammates—our peers—is paramount. Even the comfort of our own spouses may not be enough to assuage the variety pack of emotions that can assault (or sneak up on) us after the mission that "really gets to you."

Case in point: the summer of 2010. Ten of my Alpine brothers and sisters and I helped recover three badly burned corpses from a plane that had crashed into the east side of the Continental Divide. I can say with complete honesty that I went about the grisly work with nary a second thought to the fact that only twenty hours earlier, the blackened skull I had just pulled from the still-smoldering wreckage and held in my rubber glove–encased hands had still been attached to a living, breathing human being. The plane was returning from an air show in the Midwest, and doubtless the pilot and two passengers were doing what they loved best—flying.

As we labored to remove the remains, I pitched in and helped with an almost giddy sense of detachment. We spent most of the morning and part of the afternoon working in concert with the county coroner, the Federal Aviation Administration and the National Transportation Safety Board. When our work was done, I marveled with a remoteness that surprised even me that what remained of the three corpses fit neatly into the small basket on the back of an ATV.

Before we began the 9-mile ride out on our ATVs, the sheriff brought us lunch. This lunch consisted of a delicacy that we refer to as jail sandwiches (lovingly made by inmates in county lockup for the consumption of hungry rescuers after a long day in the backcountry).

And while we ribbed the sheriff because this time around, the inmates had neglected to include any meat on our sandwiches (these "sandwiches" consisted of a single slice of processed cheese between two pieces of stale bread), we were grateful for the Doritos and small plastic packet of brilliantly yellow mustard that were included in each paper sack. I hungrily applied the condiment, and managed to get just as much mustard on my fingers as I did on my so-called sandwich. Absently, I licked the tart yellow mess from my fingertips as I sat cross-legged on the dirt next to the blue-bagged corpses strapped down to the ATV a few feet away. Just as I had cleaned the last of it from my finger, I froze, tongue to digit, as I looked sideways to fellow Alpine team member Angie Lucht. She regarded my finger-cleaning efforts with a look of amused disdain and disgust.

For although I had been wearing rubber gloves during the recovery, I still had smudges of ash, oil, and human remains on my hands and clothes. I slowly retracted my tongue, looking sheepishly at my filthy hands.

"Dude, that's *gross*," she said.

I taste dead people, I thought to myself, and then Angie (who must have had a similar thought) and I both burst into a fit of much-needed laughter. It wasn't exactly a therapy session on a couch with a licensed psychiatrist, but it would have to do for the time being.

I chuckled heartily at the awkward moment, but as soon as I thought no one was watching, I turned my head and discreetly spit and sputtered whatever I could get out of my mouth onto the ground and wiped my hands on my pants with a fastidiousness that would have done Lady MacBeth proud—for all the good *that* did—before finishing my so-called sandwich.

Shortly after that, we saddled up, rode down the mountain, and delivered our smallish blue bags to the coroner's assistants. Mission accomplished, right? But nearly two weeks later, I found myself in an odd state of mind.

I was edgy, and overly critical of myself, my wife, my kids, and my co-workers. Not raging like a postal worker, but maybe just enough off the scale for me (and of course my wife) to take notice that things that usually slipped by me unnoticed seemed to take on much larger proportions than I usually granted them.

I caught myself, more than a couple times, staring blankly into space, without being able to recall just what had so captured my attention. Unnervingly, this seemed to happen most often at stoplights in rush-hour traffic.

A simple goodbye hug from my youngest daughter suddenly resulted in a fierce reciprocal hug from me that suggested I was headed off to war rather than to work in Denver for the day. Food didn't seem to have enough flavor, and I was constantly in search of the salt shaker and the Tabasco to remedy that absence. Following this disturbing thread into the bedroom, the ol' libido took a nosedive. What's that, you say? Not supposed to talk about that part of the job, am I? Guess what boys and girls—it happens. A little-discussed occupational hazard.

Perhaps most inexplicably disturbing of all, I found myself embarrassingly fighting back tears with the back of my hand while watching, of all things, *Ferris Bueller's Day Off* with the kids. WTF indeed!?!

Putting the puzzle pieces together now on paper, it is no great mystery that I was in the early stages of PTSD. Better known as Post-Traumatic Stress Disorder. My issues, as it turns out, were "normal" reactions to the stressful situation I'd experienced. But had these symptoms continued untreated and undiagnosed, to the point that they'd become a full-blown disorder, professional help would have been needed. But back in the moment, I attributed my funk to the mundane aspects of life that somehow managed to pile up around me until they'd become a hill that prevented me from glimpsing happiness. Money problems, work problems, car problems—stuff like that. But it still didn't add up.

It wasn't until the night before I had to board a plane (just two weeks after the crash recovery effort) bound for Georgia, that I realized lifting burnt Thanksgiving turkey-sized torsos out of the ashes of that plane crash and putting them in labeled paper bags for the coroner might have had just a little to do with my recent funk. Let's not even discuss the sense of reluctance/anxiety I felt about climbing onto an airplane that next day.

Not sure why I didn't get that flash of inspiration earlier (especially since it had happened to a lesser extent after previous body recoveries), but that's how these things work, I guess. Sneaky little bastards, they are. That odd, tossed emotional salad of light depression, edginess, flatness, and listlessness sprinkled with a hint of bewilderment suddenly seemed like an understandable part of the mental menu I had been staring at.

Just knowing the root of these feelings went a long, long way toward releasing their hold over me. Never mind that I (mistakenly) thought I was savvy enough to recognize these warning signs—and therefore somehow immune to the effects of PTSD. So just how savvy did I imagine myself to be, you ask?

In my nearly eighteen years as a member of the Alpine Rescue Team, I've been directly involved in more than seventy body recoveries. As my much-better half, who is a homebirth midwife, and I sometimes joke, she helps brings 'em into the world, and I often help carry 'em out. Using this type of gallows humor as a way to cope with death and tragedy was a skill I learned long before I became a Rocky Mountain rescuer.

Back in the days when journalists were still tasked with reporting the news instead of creating the news, I worked as a reporter-slash-photographer for a small newspaper in rural West Virginia. It was during this mercifully brief stint at the *Parkersburg News* that I first discovered both my strong desire to relieve the suffering of others and my ability to care just enough to not care too much when forced to witness (and document) the incidental tragedies that were considered just part of the job. It was my first job out of college. It paid a whopping $6.75 an hour.

Parkersburg is a small blue-collar town situated at the intersection of the Kanawha and Ohio Rivers on the northwestern edge of Appalachia. One of my duties as a photographer/reporter was to interpret all the police codes when they came across the scanner on my desk and determine their newsworthiness. When something interesting came across the police band, I was to drop everything and rush to the scene of whatever was going on and be a good little photographer/reporter. Shoot first, ask questions later—like a good little soldier.

Now, domestic disputes didn't typically warrant space in our small newspaper unless they happened in public and a firearm was involved—which explains why I was the first reporter on scene for a domestic dispute call in a downtown bar in the early '90s. After picking up the call on the scanner, I grabbed my camera, raced out of the office, and was on scene in a matter of minutes. I was fast, but not fast enough to shoot first. Someone else had beaten me to that punch. But instead of a Nikon, it was a Smith and Wesson that fired the first shot that day. And the second, third, fourth, and fifth shots as well.

I arrived in time to see a topless (the paramedics had already cut away her shirt and bra to assess the extent of her wounds), slightly obese, unconscious, very bloody woman on a stretcher being wheeled out of the bar to an ambulance parked at the curb. As the frantic paramedic gave CPR, the woman's breasts lolled and heaved with each thrust of his arms as her lifeblood oozed out the multiple gunshot wounds peppering her chest and belly. I felt embarrassed and ashamed by both her nudity and the fact that I was there to exploit her death by getting a good photograph of the action.

So embarrassed, in fact, that I never even took the lens cap off, even though her handcuffed jealous boyfriend/murderer stood 15 feet away, witnessing the whole grisly scene play itself out through two swollen, blackened eyes. I'm sure it was just my imagination, but I felt that he was watching *me* more intently than his former partner—as if he was daring me to pick up the camera and snap a photo and thereby morally implicate myself in the crime. Become an accomplice of sorts.

I found myself secretly wishing that I had arrived in time to disarm the shooter and thereby save a life. Instead, I was stuck debating the ethics of photographing the grisly scene of a bloody, dying, half-naked woman that my editor would likely never run in our conservative newspaper in the first place.

And Parkersburg, being the politically conservative, blue-collar river town that it was, allowed me plenty of opportunities to witness its uglier (and sometimes tragic) side of life through the viewfinder of my camera.

One of the other duties I was charged with while serving as a photographer for the *News* was to shoot feature photography. This usually entailed driving around town for a couple hours a day in search of those wonderful slice-o'-life snapshots. Laughing kids chasing bubbles in the park. Two old toothless geezers playing checkers in front of the Five and Dime. A cute young couple sharing a milkshake in front of the Dairy Queen on a sweltering summer day. Those kinds of images. The kind people cut out of the paper and put on their refrigerators with little magnets or proudly glue into a scrapbook. While I can't say it was the most thrilling part of my job, it was a nice feeling to know that some of these images would be cherished by my subjects and their families for years to come.

As I said, in order to find these images, I had to spend a lot of time just driving around. On one of these feature photo hunts, I noticed a thick black pillar of billowing smoke in the distance. Recalling that worn-out old adage that where there's smoke, there's fire (and likely a good front-page photo of breaking news), I sped in that direction.

It was only a short distance away, and I was there in a matter of minutes. I think that what happened shortly after I arrived on scene may have been the beginning of the end of my career as a voyeuristic journalist (recording but never engaging), and my first baby step toward a career as a participant in preserving life as a volunteer rescuer.

I was again first on scene, this time beating out the fire department, the police, and the ambulances. I don't think there were really even any neighbors there yet. The scene was total chaos. The skeleton of a large steel-framed two-story building still remained (I later learned that it was a garage that housed race cars, and the blaze was the result of a cutting torch igniting some race car fuel), but the walls had been blown away, and everything inside was burning.

Then, I saw a figure stumble zombie-like from the haze of smoke. That's an impressive photo, I remembered thinking as I instinctively raised the camera to my eye and unconsciously ... <click>.

That day I learned a lesson that my journalism professors at Kent State University neglected to teach me. In photojournalism, you sometimes have to pick a side: Observer or Participant. A situation that I first pegged as being a great journalistic opportunity once again became a moral dilemma. When you keep that lens pressed to your cheek and look through the viewfinder, it's easier to pretend that you have no personal stake in the events swirling around you. Your job is to observe. And record.

But when you take the camera away from your face, you are no longer peering through the looking glass. You are no longer detached. The filter is gone. The mask is off. Lowering my camera, I suddenly realized that my front-page photo was a living, breathing human being shambling toward me. In mortal agony. With perhaps moments to live.

And he was still on fire. And there was absolutely no one else around. Fuck observation, it was time to participate. The poor smoldering creature (for he barely looked human, I sickly realized as I got closer) had had most of his clothes blown off, and his reddish-pink skin hung off him in ropes. He had no hair on his head, but somehow his tighty-whitey underwear was still white and intact. It's strange the details that stick out in your mind when things like this happen.

He just stood there as I ran across the grass, my camera bag bouncing uselessly against my hip. As I reached him, I asked the stupidest question I would ever ask anyone in my entire life. "Are you okay?" Of course he wasn't okay. He was as far away from okay as he could be. Even if he lived, he would never be okay again. I felt like a complete ass, but had no clue what else to say. Or do.

This is commonly known as "Deer in the Headlights Syndrome," and it is actually a more common reaction to unexpected emergencies than its better-known cousin, "Running Around Like a Chicken with its Head Cut Off Syndrome." I just stood there with him, encouraging him to remain standing because I was afraid that what was left of his skin would remain on the grass if he were to lie down and try to get back up. He nodded mutely in response to my words of encouragement and support until we both heard the blessed sound of approaching sirens. After that, I helped the paramedics lay out something that looked like cheesecloth on the stretcher before they allowed him to finally lie down. We carted him off to the waiting ambulance, and I don't recall much else.

I have no recollection of whether he lived or died. I didn't want to know. I gave my editor some swell shots of the building engulfed in flames, but I never even printed the first couple shots I took of the Burned Man. I think if I believed in hell, I would have been on the fast track to that Lake of Fire if those negatives had ever seen print.

I wish I could say I decided to quit journalism right then and there, in search of a higher calling. But the world being the way it is, it took me several more months to realize that I hated to document suffering like that. That, and even worse, photographing beauty pageants for little kids.

I fully understand that journalism, when functioning as it should, can play a part in righting wrongs and informing the general public. Photojournalists, especially, have traditionally played a huge role in capturing images that sparked public outcry or defined a generation, thereby leading to sweeping social and political change. Hell, I went to Kent State. If you want to talk about generation-defining photos, take a look at the Pulitzer Prize–winning images captured there during the May 4, 1970, shootings by John Filo.

Throughout my days at Kent State, and even the few years I spent as a photographer/reporter, I genuinely believed that my Quest for the Holy Grail was to seek out the right place at the right time, and capture an image that would make a difference. But the longer I plied my trade as a photojournalist, the more I realized that most of these famous and pivotal images relied heavily upon the photographers' ability to somehow distance themselves from their subject matter, and objectively document. And though a few dozen photographs in the 150-year history of photojournalism have inspired and initiated changes that saved thousands of lives, these freeze-frame moments rarely benefited the actual individuals whose anguish or embarrassment or grief or death or birth happened to be captured on film in that split second that the click of the shutter froze them in time.

Usually, the result was quite the opposite.

I don't think I was capable of verbalizing these thoughts at the time I got out of the biz. I relied upon much easier to swallow notions like "The pay sucks," "My editor is a jerk," or "I caught my live-in girlfriend in bed with another man and I need to quit my job and run away to my grandparents' farm in Kentucky to escape the human race" to justify my exit from a career that I had mistakenly believed to be my true calling.

I still do not think any less of the photojournalist with a video camera on his shoulder who, wraithlike, circles a bloodied Haitian (his sticklike arms reaching out as if to both plead "Why?" and "Help Me!") as the poor bastard lay in the middle of an earthquake-cracked street.

Does photojournalism sometimes put a human face to tragedy? Absolutely. And as hard as it is to see that kind of suffering pixilated (can't say "caught on film" anymore), I know it is still important work that sometimes needs to be done. We all still need morticians and sanitation workers and convenience store clerks. God bless 'em. I am just so relieved and thankful that I don't have to be that person doing that kind of work anymore, and I'm glad there are those out there who can.

Can't speak for others in the journalism biz, but it sometimes made me feel hollow. Like a charlatan. More akin to a pornographer of pain than a high-minded agent of truth or documentarian of the human experience.

So I thank God that my foray into photojournalism taught me at least one invaluable lesson: A single tear-filled hug of thanks from a mother who's had her lost son returned to her alive and well is worth more than ten thousand attaboys from a newspaper's city editor for snapping a decent front-page photo of a dying man walking around in flames.

Rustbelt Recollections: My Dad, the Devil, Ice Age Prophecies, and the Orange Bears

Family first. Religion second. Work third. Mountain rescue fourth. This was the mantra beat into my brain on my very first day as a mountain rescuer-in-training back in January of 1998. I have since learned that this mantra is more than just a way for the volunteer rescuer to keep his or her priorities straight. It's also an excellent mapping tool for charting the crooked path taken by a twentieth-century Rustbelt Refugee on his way to becoming a twenty-first-century Rocky Mountain Rescuer.

Family First

I was cursed with a perfect childhood, which made my growth into a dysfunctional adult especially difficult at times.

No one is born to be a mountain rescuer, and I am no exception. Seeing as how the first part of being a mountain rescuer requires the presence of mountains, I was disadvantaged from birth. I grew up in Niles, Ohio, and there were no mountains in Niles, Ohio, when I was a kid. Not surprisingly, that hasn't changed.

In fact, unless you happen to live in or be born within a 50-mile radius of it, you've likely never even heard of Niles, Ohio. Like too many of its neighboring communities, my hometown has been wasting away since the first cough that led inexorably to the steel industry's final death rattle in 1977. The catastrophic collapse of the American steel industry was an especially crippling blow to a town that, since its inception, relied on iron and steel for its lifeblood. Niles was built around the state's first iron forge back in 1809.

And just what the hell does the history of the first iron forge west of Virginia in the New World have to do with a child of twentieth-century Ohio who learns the craft of mountain rescue in the twenty-first-century Rockies?

Not a damned thing, for most people. But for me, a fair bit. It's history. More specifically, part of my history.

I've heard some liken history to a liquid. A river. A flowing river that eddies and whirls and swirls around and over and past us. I think of history as more of semi-solid. Similar to an adhesive. A glue that binds people to the past. People to each other. And people to place. I think history is a lot like Krazy Glue (not so much Elmer's Glue). Krazy Glue, like our own personal histories, sometimes unintentionally binds us to the places we touch. Although I have not lived there since 1985, that's how it is for Niles and I. It sticks with me to this very day.

And just like that inexplicably ecstatic construction worker in the Krazy Glue TV commercial from the '80s who finds himself in the surreal predicament of having his hardhat glued to a steel I-beam and lifted high in the sky while he giddily holds on to said hardhat with both hands for dear life, I also sometimes find my head stuck to a place while my flailing feet try to find purchase in thin air.

I suppose it's like that for all of us who willingly leave our hometowns and live out the rest of our lives as exiles, expatriates. Nowadays, Niles is woefully similar to so many other small, dwindling industrialized communities in the Midwest, in that its principal export is its young people. Niles was, and still is, the type of town that is just sort of there. There's not usually much going on in Niles. You grow up there, raise a family there, watch high school football on Friday nights, play softball, and maybe go bowling. Some folks long for that kind of life, and I totally respect that.

Which brings me back to my accursedly wonderful childhood. Memoirs are supposed to reveal that childhood was a terrible, scarring, and traumatic event for the author. That's apparently what folks expect in a memoir nowadays. No such luck, in my case.

Because, in the last few seconds of sanity before video games and home schooling took millions of children captive, I had neighborhood baseball games in the backyard. *Little Rascals* reruns on Channel 43. Before Kindles and eBooks made reading "convenient," I relished the intoxicating scent of the cheap newsprint that wafted from my Jonah Hex and Sgt. Rock comic books and thrilled to the exotically slick texture of the *Playboy* and *Penthouse* magazines stashed out in the woods behind Duane Hafely's house. Before Columbine taught us to fear our own children, we kids accepted bullies not as killers, but as simply mean and unpleasant ogres—an inescapable part of growing up. Timeouts were reserved for football and basketball, not child rearing.

Back in the days when Jimmy Carter was in the White House, the *Six-Million Dollar Man* was on television, England Dan and John Ford Coley were on the radio, and Boog Powell (looking like an enormous blood clot in those God-awful all-red polyester uniforms) played for my beloved losers, the Cleveland Indians, my family was pretty well untainted by the incidental tragedies that all families seem to accumulate as they mature.

The eldest of four, I had two parents who fiercely loved my siblings and me. And each other. My parents worked very hard to raise me and my two brothers and my sister as best as they knew how. Dad worked on the assembly line at Packard Electric (supplying the electric wiring harnesses for General Motors) and as a part-time barber. He dreamt of someday becoming a published science fiction writer. He taught us kids and just about every kid in the neighborhood the simple joys of playing baseball.

Mom worked her butt off as a physical therapy assistant at Glenn View Manor, a nursing home. She aspired to someday go to college and get her nursing degree. Speaking of glue, she was the adhesive that held both our immediate and extended families together.

If times were tough, my parents never let us in on that kind of stuff. They married young, and grew up right alongside of us. They insulated us from life's brutalities, and sacrificed a lot of their personal desires to keep a roof over our heads. We weren't sheltered, just *very* well cared for. Blissfully ignorant of much of the suffering that went on just outside our bubble.

We were allowed to be children. As children are wont to do, I completely took for granted all the wonderful and amazing things that made life at the Wood family home so unique. We lived at 219 Washington Avenue, in the kind of worry-free neighborhood that now exists only in the collective unconscious of Americans born in the middle of the previous century, near the middle of the country. There were enormous willows, sycamores, and elms lining the streets, and the roots from these behemoths often tilted the slate sidewalks at angles that made for great trip hazards (or ramps to jump if we were on our bikes) as we walked either to school or the Korner Dairy to buy milk, candy, or the aforementioned comic books (or pilfer the aforementioned dirty magazines).

In fact, the only time the Wood kids were ever exposed to the notion that the world wasn't all sunshine and rainbows was when we went to church. Our cross-town drive took us over the railroad tracks. There really was a wrong side of the tracks in Niles, and that's where we worshipped.

Religion Second

I was only five years old when Kentucky-born (Olive Hill) country western singer/songwriter Tom T. Hall immortalized this run-down part of Niles in his 1972 song "Pratt Street." Our church being on that very same dead-end street, I am intimately familiar with that neighborhood. The song wasn't one of his hits, and I'm probably the only person in America who still remembers it, but my respect for *real* country music songwriting rose immeasurably once I read these lyrics as an adult and realized that he had totally nailed it. Pratt Street had become the blue-collar home away from home for many of the Kentuckians who'd left the hills and hollers of their impoverished Depression-era childhoods in search of the prosperity that Big Steel promised. And everything from their lifestyle to the way they spoke served to alienate them enough that they were often treated with the same distrust and disapproval as all the other immigrants who worked at the mills.

Our church, the Niles Southern Free Will Baptist Church, was founded by another Olive Hill, Kentucky, native. He was a steel mill–working pastor, former moonshine runner, and Kentucky refugee known by most as Preacher Click. I knew him better as Grandpa.

Even as a kid, it was obvious to me that the building where we met to worship was not originally built to house the holy. It was a modest single-story home located in a run-down neighborhood built to house the relocated Appalachian workers of Republic Sheet and Tube. Sheet 'N' Tube, as it was called by those who toiled there, was one of the largest steel mills in the world for the first half of the twentieth century.

Sandwiched between two other run-down houses, our church was completely sided with those kitschy gray asphalt shingles that were supposed to look like bricks (they didn't). Only a small white sign with hand-painted black letters near the front steps hinted that there were Southern Free Will Baptists afoot.

For reasons unknown to me at the time, this part of town was the epicenter for many Appalachian expatriate families who hopped on the Hillbilly Highway that began in Olive Hill, Kentucky, in the 1930s. Most stopped for a couple of decades to work the coal mines of West Virginia, and then made one last push in the early 1950s to reach Niles and work in the nearby steel mills. I suppose you could go as far as characterizing the area as the Appalachian hillbilly bedroom community for the nearby booming steel mills. Other parts of Niles had similarly grouped neighborhoods dedicated to the

Italians (who made up more than a quarter of the city's total population), the Irish, African-Americans, Greeks, and Ukrainians who worked at the mill.

The church was God-awful hot in the summer, and devilishly cold in the winter. The dank and dungeon-like basement where Sunday school was held for "the older kids" smelled like old wet socks.

Sunday mornings on Pratt Street were typically pretty quiet. As a kid, I figured that everyone knew Sundays were holy, and therefore maintained an attitude of quiet reverence. But as I grew older, I learned to credit this sense of peace on Pratt Street not to a pious observance of the Sabbath, but to the harsh reality that the residents of Pratt Street were likely still in bed nursing hangovers. You see, I didn't have Tom T. Hall's world-wise narrative to go by in those days. I wasn't even allowed to listen to *that* kind of music. That's probably for the best. I feel fortunate that I was allowed—nay, encouraged—to cling to a sense of childhood naiveté for as long as I did.

Much of that untainted childhood was spent fidgeting in this and various other Southern Free Will Baptist churches and tent revivals throughout Ohio, West Virginia, and Kentucky. For in addition to my grandfather being an old school Baptist preacher (who refused to ever accept a nickel for his work as pastor of any of the gazillion churches he ministered for and to), my mom and my Aunt Opal were gospel singers. Although I was too young to remember, they toured many a church and tent revival in the early '70s, with Mom dragging me and my younger brother John along.

Her "group" (it sounds too hip to call three women singers with Mary Tyler Moore hairstyles wearing handmade dresses and two nervous-looking guys on guitar a band), the Faith Singers, wrote their own Bluegrass-style gospel songs, which they recorded and released as 45 rpm records. They sometimes appeared on local public access TV shows (once with my brother John balanced on Mom's hip as she sang, I'm told) and radio programs. The breakup of the Faith Singers years later didn't rock the music world like that of the Beatles, but nonetheless, I think it always remained a genuine source of disappointment to my mother.

Even after the breakup, we still attended church Wednesday night, Saturday evening, Sunday morning and Sunday evening. And sometimes on Monday night. We spent so much time in church that I once complained to my parents that there should be a summer vacation from church, like we had from school.

But back on Pratt Street, the Sunday morning neighborhood stillness would reign until about 10:30. Surprisingly, it was not the sound of the waking, bleary-eyed drunks loudly rehearsing the day's scheduled domestic dispute that disrupted the neighborhood's Sunday morning reverie. No, that weekly chore of reveille fell squarely upon the shoulders of the pastor slated to preach the Sunday sermon. And by preach, brothers and sisters, I mean *preach*.

At about 10:00 a.m., the deacons banished the little kids to Sunday school (in what was likely one of the converted bedrooms). The kids old enough to read would be cast into the smelly basement for Bible study.

Sometimes, I would stay and hang out with Grandma Click and the other adults instead of joining the army of kids that tromped dutifully off to their age-appropriate worship and educational sessions. To me, Grandma Click smelled just like a grandmother should smell as she sat there clutching a kerchief in her Sunday best. Like Aquanet hairspray. For her generation, how you smelled was a reflection of what hair treatment you applied that morning. I noticed my grandparents still smelled like grandparents, though, even when they were freshly laundered or wore scented hairspray or Brylcreem.

There was always lots of crying and nose-blowing going on as everyone testified. Between dainty dabs at the seemingly endless flow of tears from the corners of her eyes, Grandma doled out LifeSavers candy to me from her shiny black purse. But it wasn't just the lure of succulent LifeSavers that drew me to this portion of the church service.

Brothers and sisters, if you've never had the opportunity to attend a Southern Free Will Baptist sermon, you are missing out on some of the finest entertainment this side of the River Jordan, let me tell you. For it was not the subject matter, but rather the way it was delivered that amused, captivated … and sometimes even scared me.

Southern Free Will Baptists are more, shall I say, enthusiastic than their Southern Baptist or Primitive Baptist brethren when preaching their message of salvation. Usually, the preacher would start off slow and easy. Perhaps share an anecdote of something that happened to him sometime during the previous week in a conversational tone. These stories typically revolved around a situation where the pastor was ridiculed at work for not swearing, drinking, for-ni-cating, or gambling with his co-workers. Then, picking up steam, the preacher would move into the heart of the sermon. Shaking his head sadly, as if in pity for all the multitudes of sinners headed for the big afterlife barbecue, his voice would rise to match his increasing level of earnest intensity.

When the sermon rounded the corner on the way to the homestretch, the subjects of damnation and salvation were broached. By this time, the floorboards were shaking from the foot stomping, and the air was literally crackling with that unmistakable leathery gunshot sound that only a Bible thumped smartly for emphasis on a wooden pulpit could make. The preacher would be nearly yelling his message at this point, little flecks of spittle flying unnoticed from his mouth and landing on the first row of the faithful. The rafters rang with the cries of the congregation heartily encouraging the preacher (his shirtsleeves rolled up by now, his forehead covered in sweat) to "Tell it like it is!" and "Praise Jesus!"

If the preacher was really on a roll, he would lapse into a kind of frantic, rolling loop of speech that he coordinated with each inhalation and exhalation—like he was inhaling and exhaling the sermon in loud, rhythmic, hypnotic tones.

I often marveled that they could be up there, preaching non-stop, without ever consulting a scrap of paper or even referencing the Bible (though it was quoted extensively and accurately), for an hour at a time without pause. I once saw a young preacher so full of the spirit that he jumped over the altar and, to my complete amazement, cartwheeled Blues Brothers–style down the aisle between the wooden pews. It was both great fun and more than a little terrifying to watch otherwise staid and conservative adults act in this fashion.

So just what did Southern Free Will Baptists believe in? Dunno. As far as what it meant to be a Free Will Baptist, that's always been a bit fuzzy to me. I concluded that their mortal existence must have been universally miserable, because they were all practically overjoyed at the notion that someday death would swoop in, end all their suffering, and reward them for being so unhappy with life on earth by allowing them to join all their dearly departed in heaven.

From what I observed as a child, Free Will Baptist doctrine required all Free Will Baptist men to work at steel mills or make automobiles, drive 30-foot-long wood-paneled station wagons, have crew cuts, and wear thick black horn-rimmed glasses. Free Will Baptists were somewhat progressive for Baptists in that the menfolk were allowed to smoke or chew tobacco (which a great many of them did from early childhood, coming from long family histories of growing tobacco in the South).

Southern Free Will Baptist women had all apparently taken lifelong vows to always wear flower-print polyester dresses, have beehive hairdos, and cook amazingly delicious potato salad.

Hymns of devotion could be accompanied with musical instruments (but not electric ones—heaven forbid). Solos were, of course, strictly forbidden.

Although they did not believe in the Speaking of Tongues or the Handling of Rattlesnakes—Praise Jesus—as tests of faith, Free Will Baptists did believe strongly in the rites of baptism for salvation. This was usually accomplished by the pastor wading into a nearby muddy brown creek up to his waist and holding his hand over someone's forehead as they allowed him to lower them backwards under the water. Whether it was the exhilarating effect of the cold water, or the joy of salvation, the Born Again emerged from the water giddier than lottery winners and twice as ecstatic.

One of the more mystifying rites of the Southern Free Will Baptists revolved around—of all things—the washing of someone's feet. This wasn't done very often, I suspect because it couldn't have been all that pleasant to be the foot washer tasked with the odious chore of washing a deacon's toe-bejammed feet and then drying them off in front of the congregation.

I'm sure there were very serious, well-thought-out and important reasons based in scripture behind all these acts of devotion, but from the simple vantage point of a small boy, they made about as much sense as Olympic curling.

In other words, the Southern Free Will Baptist religion seemed to be just as well intentioned and no more or less silly than any other organized religion in the world.

Back in those simpler days, my fear of suddenly dying and going to hell scared … well, it scared the hell out of me. Pretty much anything that sounded remotely interesting or fun to a kid could land you in hell, from what I could tell. You have your eye on the neighbor's Big Wheel? That's coveting. Off to hell with you. You snatched a marker from your little sister's hand as she sat coloring a Scooby Doo coloring book? That's stealing. Off to hell with you. You feeling that sudden and powerful rush of hate that only children can feel after they have been unjustly accused of something by their parents? You aren't honoring thy Mother and Father. Off to hell with you.

Forget about performing sex—we weren't even allowed to say the word. Just ask my little brother Johnny, who at age five innocently attempted to ask my parents what S-E-X was as we were making our weekly drive to Grandma Wood's house. My mom spun around from the front seat of our 78-foot-long, puke green wood-paneled station wagon quicker than a Rock 'Em Sock 'Em Robot and smacked the letter X right out of his mouth before he could even finish spelling the word.

Heck, a kid could go to H E Double Hockey Sticks for doing things that they didn't even know were wrong in the eyes of God. Ignorance was no excuse. This worried me greatly. And as if all those fire-and-brimstone, pulpit-pounding sermons weren't enough to scare me into Godliness, there was my dad.

Now, I have been told that when I was a child, if something scared or really excited me, I would get a case of whole-body lockjaw. Virtually paralyzed, I became wide-eyed, speechless, and went stiff as a board. For a fair amount of time, apparently. This provided Dad with a great source of free entertainment. For though I have never once heard my dad tell a joke, he was an accomplished prankster.

So whether he once observed my horrified and stiffened reaction to a stinky latex devil mask (you know the one: red-faced, goatee, horns, pointy ears, widow's peak and all) in the Halloween aisle at Woolworth's, or he instinctually realized that I was pathologically frightened of ol' Lucifer, he saw his chance.

One night, when I was about four, just after lights-out at bedtime, my loving father popped up unannounced at the foot of my bed wearing that goddamn devil mask and a red Ghoulardi sweatshirt screaming "I'M COMING TO GET YOU!!!!!!!" thereby scaring the bejeezus, and the piss, out of me. I laid there for an eternity not moving, frozen and staring at the ceiling in a state of complete terror until either my mom came over to shake me out of it or I simply fell asleep.

Since birth, I had been told on a consistent basis by people I trusted at church that the devil was real, he was evil, he was after me and he was lurking around every corner, just waiting to drag me to the Lake of Fire. Was it any wonder that a personal appearance by the devil himself in my own home would inspire paralysis (and years of night-terrors)?

After a while, the devil made special appearances (like a cheap evil clown at a Chuck E. Cheese's birthday party) when and where I least expected him. Like outside my bedroom window, lit from below with a flashlight gripped in a hand that was shaking from his efforts to withhold his laughter. Or maybe he would pop out of my closet as I hung my clothes. Or casually stroll past me out of the bathroom.

He was everywhere, and each time he appeared, I would practically need to be strapped to a dolly like a refrigerator and wheeled away or have someone shake me out of it. I suppose if YouTube were around then and they accepted footage recorded on Super 8, my recorded paralysis would have made me famous.

I don't (completely) believe that my father intended to torture me with these pranks. He doesn't have a mean bone in his body. But as I outgrew my paralytic reactions to fear and excitement, I realized that he did have a mile-long mischievous streak that belied his conservative, proper nature. (And I've always loved him for that, perhaps because I have apparently inherited this trait. Much to the absolute terror of my own children. Blame it on your Grandpa, kiddos, not me.)

But to be fair to my Devil Dad (and the Southern Free Will Baptists), there was another agent hard at work trying to frighten me into being a good little Christian boy. His name was Jack Chick.

Jack Chick was the mastermind behind those ubiquitous little black-and-white religious pamphlets (manically—and some might argue mania-cally—authored, drawn, edited, published, and distributed by Jack Chick himself, at least in the early days). These little pieces of religious propaganda were often left on the table at the back of the church. Or you might find them on the countertop in a Laundromat. Or stacked on top of a bubblegum machine outside of Woolworth's. Or in a doctor's waiting room. Or next to the paper towel dispenser in a gas station's dingy bathroom. I never saw anyone put them in those places, they just seemed to appear with divine accuracy in places where sinners (or kids) congregated. I'm telling you, it was down-right creepy.

They positively terrified me with their very literal comic book represen-tations of God in heaven and the devil in hell. With titles like "This Was Your Life," "The Devil's Apprentice" and so on, they brilliantly played upon my fear of an eternity spent in hell, on fire and separated from my family. In my hor-rified Jack Chick–inspired imaginings, I was cast into the Lake of Fire alone, while the rest of my family looked down from heaven above, sadly shaking their heads as they sat upon their golden thrones (inside their golden homes located on—you guessed it—golden streets). Even then, I wondered dis-tractedly why just being in heaven at the right hand of God wasn't satisfying enough in and of itself. Why did our earthly visions of afterlife wealth seem to be so important to us? Did we really need to be surrounded by golden everything to be happy up there in heaven? Apparently so.

Anyway, one pamphlet—I do not recall the name of *that* particular little piece of horrifying genius—had an image that stalked me for years. Gave me nightmares. The simple image depicted a young, unrepentant mother clutch-ing her infant child in her arms. Not so scary in itself, except that they were both dead. In the previous panel, she and her baby had been turned away from the Pearly Gates. So there they were, in hell, standing on a wooden dock in the Lake of Fire (it also really bugged me that this wooden dock never caught fire after an eternity of exposure to flame—why didn't Chick just draw a dock made of stone?). Of course, the devil—goatee, horns, pitchfork and all—is there to welcome mother and child to the eternal and infernal barbecue.

Wait a minute, I thought, a baby can be sent to hell? What the heck (which at that time was as close as I dared to get to cursing)?!? What could a baby possibly have done to deserve banishment to that much-preached-about Lake of Fire? Apparently, the tract extolled the need for children to be baptized. Since all these tracts had scripture quoted throughout, I (naively) assumed that these were just pictures illustrating the Bible, which every card-carrying Baptist knew to be a literal, word-for-word interpretation of God's will.

Anyway, if a baby couldn't do much more evil than drool and poop in its diaper, and it could still end up spinning on a rotisserie in hell for all eternity just because its mom hadn't arranged for a man to sprinkle some water on its head and speak some magic words to save its eternal soul, what chance did I have of salvation? I was doomed.

The tracts didn't make me want to be a better Christian by performing good deeds and devoting my life to the service of Jesus. They just made me afraid to die before I had the chance to repent for sins that I didn't even know existed and being cast into hell. And while many might argue that a fear of damnation is what eventually drives a sinner to redemption, I beg to differ. That kind of Pavlovian response to the threat of damnation didn't sit well with me as a kid (though of course back then I couldn't say why), and it hasn't changed much since. In my opinion, having a rifle of righteousness pointed at your eternal soul, forcing you to do "what's right" in the course of your mortal existence just so you can be awarded a Get Out of Hell Free Card, is just not a valid reason to treat yourself and others with respect, compassion, and dignity.

I am nowhere near smart or wise enough to say with the remotest certainty that I know any more about God or his will—or what pleases or pisses him off—than the next shmuck. Or if he's even a he.

My parents quit going to church when I reached my early teens, and didn't rediscover their faith until we were all nearly full-grown adults. They never really explained why. We kids went to church for a couple years after that—more to be with my grandparents than to worship by that point.

The Southern Free Will Baptist occupation of Pratt Street ended in the late '80s when a drunk driver lost control of his car and plowed into the front of the Niles Southern Free Will Baptist Church. The building was beyond repair and demolished soon after. I visited the site in 2011, and was not too surprised to discover that it had never been rebuilt. All that remains now is an empty rectangular lot between houses. I wondered if the residents of Pratt Street were happy or sad to see the Baptists go.

By the time I entered high school, my grandfather, Preacher Click, had suffered a major heart attack and had to retire from Sheet 'N' Tube's massive mill in nearby Youngstown. By some miracle of fate (or divine providence if you are so inclined), he retired literally weeks before the crushing announcement by Republic Sheet and Tube in 1977 that they were shutting down the blast furnaces and closing their doors forever. He was one of the lucky ones that escaped with his pension relatively intact. He and my grandmother moved back to Kentucky, and our regular visits to church all but ended.

But that's not to say I didn't return to visit the wrong side of the tracks. The summer of my junior year in high school, I worked just a couple of blocks away from our old church at the prestigiously named Heaton Amalgamated.

Work Third

In 1997, I traded my Youngstown steel for Rocky Mountain stone. Having abandoned the flatlands of the Rustbelt, I now live in the far-off, mystical land of Colorado, where the mountains are tall and the grass is greener—literally. I am paid to get high at work, but probably not in the way that most folks would imagine most Coloradans accomplish that feat these days. I am employed to teach cell tower climbers, wind turbine technicians, and bridge inspectors how not to die and how to rescue each other. I also spend a lot of time volunteering with a mountain rescue team, searching for, rescuing, and sometimes recovering folks who've had a bad day in the mountains.

But whether I am 200 feet in the air on a cell tower teaching safe climbing techniques or volunteering my time alongside my fellow Colorado mountain rescuers to recover the body of a fallen hiker from the side of a mountain, I am still of Youngstown. Every now and then, something—like the smell of death—reminds me of that.

In the early '60s, instead of running *to* the mountains, my grandfather Preacher Click found himself fleeing them. The desperate pursuit of the American Dream drove he and his family (via Highways 64 and 77, which came to be known as the Hillbilly Highway) away from the greedy clutches of the coal barons and their company stores in a little-too-wild, not-so-wonderful West Virginia and Kentucky to the bustling streets of Youngstown,

Ohio. After relocating his family of seven, he devoted more than two decades of his life to the care and feeding of the spiritual needs of the other Kentucky refugees while simultaneously attending to the care and feeding of the blast furnaces. As reward for his dedicated service, the mill took three of the toes on his right foot. They were blown out the end of his boot like toothpaste shot out of a tube when a piece of steel was dropped onto his steel-toed boots from a malfunctioning overhead crane. A lifetime of hard work finally caught up with him in early 1977 when his black lungs and failing heart forced him into retirement.

Later that same year, when the blast furnace fires died on Black Monday, there was still a lot of metal to be had in the Mahoning Valley. It just had to be harvested from the businesses that died alongside the mills at Brier Hill, Struthers, and McDonald. The enormous steel carcass of Youngstown was ripe for the picking. In the mid-'80s, during the summer of my junior year in high school, I was one of the scores of human flies employed to help pick it clean. I worked my first summer job at Heaton Amalgamated.

Heaton Amalgamated occupied two or three city blocks. A bulging chain link fence ringed its perimeter and barely held the random scraps of rusty metal that threatened to spill over the top. Just walking by it made you want to get a tetanus shot.

Long before I became a mountain rescuer in Colorado, I performed my first body recovery while working there with my pal Will Pfeifer. Will would later go on to become an accomplished comic book writer, but on a particularly memorable, sweltering August day, he and I were just two scrawny kids hired as laborers tasked with moving piles of scrap metal to be sorted, sandblasted, painted, or recycled.

Normally, we were aided by Virgil, the yard's painter and heavy equipment operator. Virgil looked a lot like the white-trash version of the Wildman from Borneo. There was a space between his two front teeth wide enough to drive a Buick through. The bushy, jet-black hair on his head, heavily bearded face, and always-exposed chest was permanently frosted with over-sprayed orange paint from the high-powered spray rig he used to rustproof the metal (sprayed on liberally and without a respirator, thereby ensuring that the microscopic hairs lining his lungs matched the exposed hair on the rest of him). That paint was so toxic and noxious that it either killed or stoned every living thing within a 200-foot radius of his work area.

In fact, Virgil's affinity for paint fumes may have contributed to his spontaneous combustion a few weeks earlier during a Fourth of July barbecue when he unwisely tried to ignite his charcoal grill with a half-gallon of gasoline instead of lighter fluid. The resulting fireball landed him in the burn unit.

So we were without Virgil's heavy equipment expertise and his eau-de-Sherwin-Williams cologne on that particularly hot summer post-Fourth of July afternoon when yard boss Ralph approached us with an assignment.

Ralph was cool and endearingly odd. He sagely (and often) predicted that another Ice Age was nigh. He reminded us of his prognostic prowess most often over lunch each day. He was seriously worried that the next Ice Age would swoop in like an unannounced storm and wipe out humanity as we knew it.

"See if I'm not right," he would say to us, his mouth full of bologna sandwich and his eyes freakishly huge behind thick glasses. His wiry gray hair was streaked with a few remaining strands of black and stood at kinky attention—much like the abused wire brushes we used to scrape rust spots—as he sipped coffee from the red plastic cup that topped his plaid Thermos.

"You ever see the looks on the faces of those cavemen frozen in blocks of ice? They looked surprised!" he would say.

But on this particular day, Ralph had more mundane matters on his mind. "Why don't you boys clear up that big pile of scrap steel shelving back there in the corner of the yard?" Ralph asked us in his nasal voice as we finished our lunches. The aforementioned pile was as tall as the Great Pyramid at Giza, and seemed to be just as meticulously constructed.

But at least the pile was in the back of the yard, away from the eagle eyes of Rueben, the ass-kissing blowhard who went to Will's church. Rueben enjoyed ordering us around and then regaling Will's parents with tales of all the great life lessons we were learning by moving rusty pieces of metal from point A to point B and then back again.

Halfway through our task, Will and I found a body. It was the first time I experienced the smell of rotting flesh. The body was that of the missing Killer. Killer was the resident junkyard dog that disappeared in early June. Not much remained of that enormous German Shepherd (now renamed *Killed* by Will and I). There was a spiked collar and soupy pile of fur and bones—that was about it. After relaying the news of our find to Rueben (now not-so-jokingly renamed *Asshole* by Will and me), he charged us with scooping up the remains in a shovel and hurling them over the fence and into the Mahoning River on the other side—without hurling our lunch onto his boots as he stood watch over our efforts. Though it was difficult to choke back the bile, we were successful on both accounts, but only barely. The cloying, sweet-sick smell of death clung to the tiny hairs in my nostrils and the taste of rot hung in the back of my throat for days.

Who would have ever suspected that the only skill I salvaged from my time at Heaton Amalgamated would be my newly discovered aptitude for dealing with death and decay? A skill that would, two decades later, serve me so well as a non-paid professional mountain rescuer in Colorado. So although I wouldn't list having a cast-iron gag reflex as a marketable skill on my resume, it has come in handy more than a few dozen times on the body recoveries I've helped our Colorado-based mountain rescue team perform. To this very day, the earthy scent of death catapults me straight back to Killer, that dead junkyard dog. Straight back to my Rustbelt roots.

Heaton Amalgamated is still in business to this day, owing its success and longevity to both the boom in recycling and Ralph's failed Ice Age Redux prophesies.

Years later, I found myself out of college and out of work, looking for a way to pay off my student loans. The fading but still-seductive siren call of steel beckoned me back to the skeletal remains of the same mill, Sheet 'N' Tube, that had supported my grandfather's family. I was far from the first young man who had a tough time escaping the steel cage of the Mahoning Valley.

Another such young man, Kenneth Patchen, found himself in the same predicament half a century earlier. Patchen, son of a steelworker at Republic Sheet and Tube, eventually *did* escape, and went on to inspire and mentor such literary notables as Henry Miller, Jack Kerouac, and Allen Ginsburg through his poetry and paintings.

Young Patchen spent his post-Niles life in rebellion against the notion that a man's soul had to be sacrificed if he was to be a "company man." He had this to say about growing up in the looming shadow of Sheet 'N' Tube in his poem, "The Orange Bears" (the Orange Bears being the enormous, 500-ton pot-bellied blast furnaces whose flickering fires often lit the coal-black underbellies of the low clouds hovering over the town's night sky in the first half of the twentieth century):

> ... I remember you would put daisies
> On the windowsill at night and in
> The morning they'd be so covered with soot
> You couldn't tell what they were anymore.
> A hell of a fat chance my orange bears had!

Patchen's overworked father tended to these Orange Bears at the Youngstown Zoo—better known as Republic Sheet and Tube—thereby inspiring one of the poet's better-known (and most bleak) works, "May I Ask You a Question Mr. Sheet and Tube?"

Thirty years later, my grandfather, Preacher Click, would give twenty-five years of his life in service to those same Orange Bears.

And nearly two decades after my grandfather retired, my kid brother Danny and I devoted one hot and dirty summer to the care of the Orange Bears, though by then the zoo formerly known as Sheet 'N' Tube was but a fraction of its original size and now went by the name of Texas Steel Association.

We worked in the exact same buildings that Patchen's father and my grandfather sacrificed so much of their lives in. I have little doubt the enormous rats populating every dark corner of that place had a long and storied family history there as well. We swiftly learned why my grandfather—and everyone else in the mill—carried his lunch to work in a steel pail (thermos of Maxwell House coffee and bologna sandwich topped with Miracle Whip wrapped in wax paper nestled inside) instead of a brown paper bag. The rats ate through a brown-bagged lunch within minutes if it was left unattended.

But at least the rats stuck around. The bears' former caretaker—the Steel Workers Union—was nowhere to be found. Worker safety and decent wages had long since taken a back seat to production by the time we clocked in. The work was loud, dirty, and dangerous. Smashed hands and feet were daily occurrences, due in large part to the fact that many of the guys we worked with were either drunk or high on crack. The drunks had it tougher than the crackheads. The crackheads could hide their paraphernalia in their pockets and light up without much effort, while the poor drunks had to clock in fifteen minutes early each day, just so they could stash their forty-ounce bottles of malt liquor in various dark corners of the mill without being caught during the shift change. They returned from each break smelling to high heaven of Schlitz.

Fights were semi-regular occurrences as well. I once witnessed a welder tackle his foreman, hold him down, and then spray-paint the foreman's entire face neon orange because the foreman had called the welder a "stupid nigger." Even though the foreman had to be admitted to the hospital to get the paint out of his eyes, the welder was able to keep his job because everyone (including upper management) thought the foreman was an irredeemable asshole. Besides, the Suits running the mill didn't want the incident turned into a discrimination case.

My brother was nearly decapitated as he slung an enormous metal

grinder onto his shoulder and the trigger was accidentally depressed. Unbeknownst to him, the secondary safety switch that was supposed to keep this
exact problem from occurring had been disabled (to allow the user to work
faster), and the grinding wheel jumped to life at 2,500 rpm's. It raced across
his neck, leaving behind an enormous gash that missed his jugular vein by
mere centimeters. My brother took a whole day off to recover.

Also during my watch, the men who kept the bears orange were forced
to piss in their own flame-resistant suits. The restrooms were on the far end
of the mill, and they were not permitted enough breaks during their twelve-
hour shifts to abandon the blast furnace long enough to both eat lunch and
urinate. Good times, good times.

Anyway, the Orange Bears are all extinct now. The last of them, the Jean-
nette Blast Furnace (immortalized as "Sweet Jenny" in the Springsteen bal-
lad "Youngstown"), was finally claimed by the wrecking ball the year after I
traded Ohio steel for Rocky Mountain stone in 1997.

Ironically, though Preacher Click's generation flocked to Youngstown
hoping to escape the crippling rural poverty so prevalent in West Virginia
and Kentucky, the Appalachian Regional Council recently listed the city of
Youngstown as a part of Appalachia. Instead of escaping Appalachia, the hill-
billies brought it with them.

Youngstown's only (dubious) source of pride these days is its consistent
ranking as a city with one of the highest murder rates in the country. As for
Niles, it has gone from being a prosperous bedroom community for the Italian, Irish, African-American, Greek, Ukrainian, and displaced Appalachians
who owned their homes and worked at either the steel mills or General Motors, to being a tired, shrinking, high-crime town full of houses rented out to
employees of the nearby Eastwood Mall.

And as if the kick in the nuts represented by the disintegration of the
iron and steel industries weren't bad enough, Mother Nature took her own
cheap shot at Niles. On May 31, 1985, just a few days before my high school
graduation, one of the most destructive tornadoes ever recorded east of the
Mississippi mowed a half-mile-wide, 47-mile-long path through Ohio and
Pennsylvania. It was classified as an F5, with top wind speeds of more than
300 miles per hour.

Our twister was the most powerful of the dozens that formed first in
Ontario, then tore through Ohio and Pennsylvania, finally petering out in
New York State that day. In all, 250 people were killed (nine in Niles alone),
and thousands were injured.

The swath of destruction carved by this twister on steroids missed our house by a little over half a mile. Power and phones were knocked out for almost a week. We all spent the first two nights after the twister sleeping in the basement, huddled around a small AM transistor radio—hungry for the smallest scraps of information. We heard that my junior high school had been turned into a temporary morgue, and that martial law had been declared.

The passing of time ground to a halt. There was nowhere we could go (unless it was on foot) and not much to do (school was out, work was canceled, stores were closed). No TV to watch.

I was anxious, because all the roads were closed and I was due to leave for Marine Corps Boot Camp the day after our now-canceled graduation ceremony. Immediately after that, I was supposed to report to Kent State University for my first semester of college.

God, how I wish at the time I had recognized the priceless opportunity afforded us by that deadly funnel cloud. Those two days and two nights, spent playing catch in the yard by day and Monopoly by candlelight at night, were the last we ever spent as a complete, happy, innocent family. We were still as yet untouched by the everyday tragedies and melodramas that befall all families as children grow up and parents grow old.

After that second night, there would always be one of us kids out of town. Or the ghost of some old, unresolved conflict lurking in a corner. After that second night, I would be the first to leave home. Johnny, Cathie, and Danny would soon follow suit. After that second night, we would all come back home occasionally, sometimes with our tails between our legs, sometimes with a new girlfriend or boyfriend proudly in tow, the scent of the world upon us.

But for those two nights, it was just us. I'm sure at the time all we could think about was how bored we were. It was as if we were under house arrest. God, if we even had an inkling of what we were about to lose, I think we would've wept instead of cheered when the power finally came back on and the roads opened back up. There aren't many moments in my life that I wish I could go back and re-experience, but I'd say that one tops the list.

In my mind, the twister that tore Niles in half on May 31, 1985, didn't do me the favor of plucking me up from the mundane, black-and-white world of the Midwest and plopping me down in the colorful, mythical land of Oz. It did something much more interesting. It alerted me to a truth that I was blind to at the time. I had been living in the magically Technicolored land of Oz all along.

Indeed, there's no place like home. And there never would be, ever again.

Falling Down and Getting Dirty

"**Stupid** people don't deserve to be rescued."

"Charge the hell out of the incompetent bastards."

I've often heard these statements uttered by an indignant member of the tax-paying general public when a hiker or climber or skier is rescued after doing something that (in the tax-paying general public's expert opinion) was foolish enough to warrant them being left to die. So, to recap popular sentiment: Let them die, or make them pay for the privilege of living.

As a mountain rescuer, the very idea of leaving someone to die in the backcountry is an anathema to me, and the notion of charging folks once they've been found or rescued is similarly inconceivable. And besides, being a former card-carrying member of the Stupid Club, you'll never hear *me* say such a thing. Because for me, only simple dumb luck—or perhaps divine intervention from the Southern Free Will Baptist God of my youth that I had lost track of—has kept me from becoming a victim needing rescue. Or a body in a bag.

You see, in my mid-twenties, I walked away from the Rustbelt and a career in journalism and hid myself away on my grandparents' hundred-acre farm in rural Kentucky. I used every excuse I could concoct to keep me on the farm and focused on my two secret projects. I was going to become a big-time sponsored rock climber. And I was also going to write the Great American Novel.

But my Thoreau-inspired isolation from society did not produce a masterpiece like *Walden* or *Civil Disobedience.* No, my masterpieces of that era included three angst-filled and self-absorbed journals, two heavy-handed Lovecraftian science fiction tales that no one wanted to publish, and a hairy-palmed handful of erotica that I sold to *Penthouse.* That's right, I said *Penthouse* (and a couple of lesser-known but equally depraved digests, that is). I had gotten the idea years earlier from a college roommate who had earned a year's worth of rent from just a few single-spaced pages of silly and formulaic sex yarns sold to *Playboy.*

So guys, you ever wondered if those letters that read something like, "Dear Penthouse Forum, I never thought I'd be writing to tell you this, but last week at the comic book convention, I was approached by a trio of smoking hot Princess Leia's who said they really wanted to see what kind of firepower I was packing under my Chewbacca costume. Well, one thing led to another, and before you could say Lando Calrissian, there I was—being smothered by their ample, heaving breasts that were bursting with desire as they pawed at each other in a valiant attempt to reach my throbbing light saber …"?

… *Those* kind of stories? Well, hate to break the news to you true believers, but they are *all* fake—likely crafted by ex-English majors and former journalists like yours truly attempting to cash in on both their wordsmithing prowess and (predominantly male) adolescent fantasies. Sorry.

Laugh at me or condemn me, at least I was earning a living once again with my writing. God knows it beat the living hell out of my day job as a delivery boy supplying greasy pizza to the trailers and shacks that dotted the hills and hollows of Olive Hill. Selling just two of these ridiculously salacious stories to "Penthouse Forum" (produced on a computer powered by a small generator that I had acquired by trading a Homelite chainsaw and a beat up old '66 Jeep CJ) earned me more than a month's worth of wages from Giovanni's. And to be perfectly honest here, producing the pornography didn't make me feel cheap, but delivering pizzas sure did.

In a vain attempt to retain some semblance of privacy while corresponding with these publications (this was in the days just before the Internet made email the preferred means of communication), I established a post office box in the nearby town of Grahn. (Interesting piece of trivia about Grahn: It was the occasional summer home away from home for one of Kentucky's more famous long-haired sons, little Charlie Manson. His maternal grandparents lived there.) It was from my Grahn post office box that I mailed my manuscripts and received my checks. After all, it just wouldn't do for the mailman to deliver envelopes postmarked from *Penthouse* magazine to Preacher Click's mailbox.

But the day I checked my clandestine P.O. box and discovered that a large manila envelope containing my T-shirt (reading "My Letter Was Published in Penthouse!!"), along with a check for my work, had already been opened and rifled through, I knew my secret was out. As I slammed the small P.O. box door shut in frustration, relocked it and walked out, the knowing-but-toothless-grin and conspiring wink from the clerk at the post office counter confirmed my suspicions. Before I completed the twenty-minute drive back to the farm, I knew that a goodly portion of eastern Kentucky's telephone lines would be abuzz with the hot gossip that the long-haired hippy grandson of Preacher Click was one of them preeverts who wrote for dirty magazines.

In the days and weeks that followed, my Aunt Deloris, who practically ran the switchboard for this gossip hotline, made certain that I was aware that she was aware of my less-than-lofty literary efforts by her incessant and smugly phrased inquiries as to the success of my "second job." But if she or anyone else ever clued in my grandparents about my secondary source of income, they never let on, bless their hearts.

This live-and-let-live philosophy was also a kind of unspoken and unsigned contract between all of the residents at Preacher Click's Hillbilly Home for Wayward Humans. We had all fallen from grace, and we knew we were there because there was nowhere else to go at the time. So although we may have had our differences, we kept the peace.

And as far as my fantasies of becoming a world-class sponsored rock climber, only a smattering of natural talent, absolutely no connections in the close-knit climbing community, and no money to travel to rock-climbing Meccas like Yosemite were the only things that stood in my way.

Since I was staying at my grandparents' farm in Kentucky after leaving my West Virginia newspaper job (and civilization in general), I naively assumed that the ample free time from society and any female companionship afforded me by my Appalachian hideaway would allow me plenty of opportunities to improve my climbing. Never mind that I didn't have enough money for a decent pair of tight-fitting, rubber covered rock climbing shoes. It was bare feet or combat boots for me back then.

I had very little rock climbing gear. I owned two black oval non-locking carabiners I bought from the nearby Army Surplus Store. I had a chalk bag given to me by a friend in West Virginia the previous Christmas. A helmet? Fuhgeddaboudit.

I also had a cheap harness and a rope. The rope was the only thing of any worth that I salvaged from my last relationship, and I was very proud of it. I believe it was a red BlueWater (apologies to my present employer) 10.2 mm dynamic 50 meter rope, for those of you out there who care about such things (as I did and still do, obviously, since I now work for PMI, a rope manufacturer). The only knot or hitch I knew was the one I used to tie my shoes. Back in those days, I was a big proponent of the "If you can't tie the knot, tie a lot" school of thought.

Mike, my fellow redneck refugee from West Virginia, and I did our best to respect each other's society-hating and anti-social ways. He was living in the trailer that was parked beside my grandparents' house, and I was holed up out in the little cabin at the edge of the woods. We would often go a couple of days without really interacting with each other, except maybe to say *pass the lard* over breakfast. Though we did sometimes climb together (Mike always with a cheap cigarette dangling out the side of his mouth), I still enjoyed being out on the rock alone the best.

So, it followed that when my mind was cluttered with my first attempts at writing the Great American Novel and the indignity that I then associated with using my degree in journalism to deliver pizzas in Appalachia, I would just disappear into the poplars and pines in search of new rocks to scale. Never a word to anyone where I was going, what I was doing, or when I planned to return. Nowadays, my inner mountain rescuer cringes at the very thought.

The property owned by my grandparents numbered about a hundred acres, but it was surrounded by hundreds more that were too rocky and hilly for homebuilding—but perfect for exploring. For me, the gritty sandstone and white limestone cliff faces that ringed the heavily forested, dark ravines and valleys were like my own personal playground. With my favorite mutt Blondie by my side, I would scour the densely wooded cliff bottoms in search of either a new route to climb or a new cave to explore.

Climbing the rocks without a partner or even a rope to catch you if you fall is known as free soloing. It is a style of climbing that requires the concentration of a Zen master, the agility and balance of an Olympic gymnast, and a Superman-like sense of invulnerability. I had at least a little of the first two traits and a lot of the last, and so it went that I would routinely hurl myself at nearly every rock face I could find. The resulting sense of euphoria I felt after successfully scaling a cliff, alone and without a safety net, was all-encompassing. And addictive. I found myself pushing my limits more and more often.

One chilly January night in 1993, after downing a goodly portion of a twelve-pack of Milwaukee's Best by the campfire, I decided I would take the most direct route back to my cabin. This meant climbing straight up and over the 80-foot cliff that stood between my smoldering campfire and my cabin up above. It was near midnight, and the trees around me were spiked with the hoarfrost that formed when the humid Kentucky air mingled with the frigid temps of a suddenly clear night.

I had no headlamp, the rock was icy, and I was drunk. Spelled out in that way, one might draw the conclusion that maybe I had some sort of death wish. Or that maybe I was terminally stupid and therefore deserved to die. I liked to say that I was just bored and hungry for some adventure.

You say toh-mah-toe, I say tomato.

Either way, I am hard-pressed at present to come up with a rational explanation as to why I did what I did back then. I guess the best I can do is say that I craved that rare and elusive sense of truly being *alive* that one only feels when faced with death. So instead of labeling this a *death wish*, it might be more accurate to describe it as a *life wish*.

You say poh-tah-toe, I say potato.

I had climbed this particular route dozens of times in the daylight, and had committed the moves to memory. Although I had a tough time walking a straight line to the base of the climb, my senses cleared the second my bare hands grasped the frigid rock. Everything suddenly came into focus. The climb was not particularly difficult—except for the final few moves near the top. There was only one perfectly executed sequence of moves that would keep me from peeling off and going splat. If I put my left hand where my right should be, or if I relied on the wrong nub for a foothold, game over.

When at last I scrambled up and over the top, I rolled onto my back with my feet still dangling over the edge in space. It was very still, and I could see every single star in the universe twinkling overhead, winking at me as if to say, "Nice job kid." My sense of invulnerability increased tenfold.

And so it was, later that year on one warm and hazy fall afternoon that I set out from the small one-room cottonwood and clay-chinked cabin that I called home to climb and explore. After making the half hour trek to a huge amphitheater of 100-foot-tall rock walls that ringed the rhododendron-covered slopes below, I scrambled up the steep embankment to the base of the climb and set my machete and Little Debbie snack cakes on a small rock ledge. There was a dark cleft in the sandstone about 25 feet up a 45-foot-tall section of cliff that looked promising as a potential cave entrance. At least to me, anyway.

The waterfall that roared over the edge of the cliff in the center of the amphitheater in the spring was now reduced to just a trickle in the fall, and the pitter-patter of its impact with the rocks below lent a soothing, almost tropical, atmosphere to the setting.

Blondie, obviously in possession of a hell of a lot more common sense than I, worried herself with burrowing into the leaves to find a cool spot to sleep while her master sized up the climb.

I knew that the dark hole in the cliff face wouldn't likely pan out. Sandstone, at least in those parts, doesn't typically lend itself to the formation of caves of any real substance. But this was really more about having an excuse—not a reason—to climb that rock wall.

So there I was, stripped to the waist, wearing my trusty red bandanna and rolled-up blue jeans, chalk bag clipped to one of my rear belt loops with one of the two carabiners I owned, ready to free solo the tall vertical face.

My plan, if you could even call it that, was to crawl up the sandpaper-like, slightly less than completely vertical wall to the potential cave, rest there, then follow a six-inch-wide crack that led up and out of the right of the "cave" ceiling to an easy finish to the climb. Sizing up the route's difficulty, I didn't see anything that gave me pause.

Rock climbers often use a rating system designed to grade a climb's difficulty. Although this scale is largely subjective, it does help a climber to decide if a route is above (or below) his or her ability. In the U.S., the Yosemite Decimal System (not to be confused with the Dewey Decimal System) is most widely used by climbers. Since my subscription to *Rock and Ice* magazine was my only real connection to the goings-on in the rock-climbing world, I measured my abilities (using that Yosemite rating system) against those of the superhuman freaks featured in the magazine. It was akin to a lonely, obese housewife obsessing over and yearning to be one of the supermodels featured on the cover of a grocery store tabloid.

And like that poor lonely housewife, I judged my worth as a person on a scale. Not the scale that measured my weight, but the Yosemite scale that was supposed to serve as a yardstick of my climbing capabilities. Since I seemed to have little control over my financial worth at that time, I figured I at least had some modicum of control over my worth as a climber. And I was completely unaware at the time how utterly self-absorbed and shallow all this was. Measuring up against that Yosemite scale became all I cared about. Outside of getting laid sometime in the next century, of course.

As I said, the Yosemite scale is highly subjective (a factor I used in my favor at every opportunity), and was very familiar to most climbers.

Class 1 would be considered walking, with a low possibility of injury and little chance of death should you trip and fall. Steeper scrambling with a greater chance of serious injury would be considered Class 2 or 3, depending on the amount of exposure. A rope is recommended, but not required, for a Class 4 climb. An un-roped fall could result in death or serious injury. A Class 5 climb would be considered vertical rock climbing in the classic sense. A rope is a must (unless you were planning to free solo the climb, as I was that day). To further assess the difficulty of a Class 5 climb, it can be broken down to a decimal rating.

Class 5.1–5.5 climbs require the use of hands and feet, some upper body strength. A beginner walking off the street and attempting an "easy" roped climb is usually at this level.

Class 5.6–5.9 climbs are typically attempted by climbers who have pretty good strength, practiced technique, and good balance.

Class 5.10–5.15 climbs can only be completed by climbers with superb strength, balance, route finding skills and, often, bow legs to make room for their enormous balls. Only a handful of people in the world climb at that lofty 5.15 level.

I pegged the climb I was about to attempt in the 5.6 to 5.7 range—well within my abilities to attempt it un-roped at that time.

But just as your eyes can often be bigger than your belly when selecting a meal from the menu, so it goes for one's ability to judge a climbing route's difficulty while standing safe and sound on good ol' Mother Earth. I started the climb without giving much thought to the sequence of moves I would have to make two or three moves into the future. You can see where this is going.

I never reached the cave. Before I knew what had happened, I had run out of handholds. What at first looked like a relatively simple crawl (remember 5.6–5.7?) up a steep but climbable wall of sandstone, full of ample handholds and pock-marked with enormous foot placements, quickly morphed into a sheer wall of sandpaper (probably 5.11–5.12 for a stretch of about 8 or so feet).

I couldn't climb up. And I couldn't climb down. Cliffed out. Stuck. I estimated that I was about 25 feet off the deck now. In spite of myself, I began to panic. The primordial parts of my brain that warned me not to climb the rock in the first place began to take over. I was doused by an ice-cold bucket of doubt that drenched me from the top of my sweat-covered head to my quivering legs (the quivering legs are so common among climbers that they are universally referred to as Elvis legs).

My breathing became shallow and rapid. My heart rate doubled. In fear, my widened eyes frantically scanned the rockscape overhead as my fingers trembled with the effort it took to support my weight. I daren't move, lest I peel off the rock from my precarious perch. As crazy as it sounds, I'd never been in a situation like this before.

In retrospect, I probably only spent a couple minutes desperately clinging spider-like to the gritty rock. But Jesus, it felt like an hour. I didn't even have the luxury of being able to look down between my legs and pick a landing zone. The tip of my nose was a scant inch from the rock, and to avert my gaze from that square foot of rock directly in front of my face to look down meant possibly shifting my balance and losing my tentative grip. And since it was not a clear, unobstructed line of fall below me, if I simply let go, it would be like falling down a 25-foot-tall cheese grater before hitting the ground.

Like a cat stuck up a tree, I held on as long as I could, my panicked mind racing. If I've ever had a "Fuck It!" moment in my life, that was it. I shoved off the rock with all my might, both arms and both legs straight out, in the hopes that if I pushed out off the rock far and hard enough, I would have only my crushing impact with the ground to contend with. For the first time that day, I had an actual plan.

For those of you out there that don't think a 25-foot fall is cause for alarm, I suggest you take the 24-foot-tall extension ladder out of your garage. You know, the one that you use once a year to clean the leaves (or maybe your kids' tennis balls) out of your gutters. Now, lean it up against your house, climb up to the second story, and then scramble up onto the roof. Now once you are on the roof, walk backward (feel free to Moonwalk if you are so inclined) to the edge till only your toes are on the edge of the shingles and your heels are out in space. Now jump.

On the way down, feel free to exercise your right to religious freedom and pray that the impact won't drive both of your femurs up into your chest cavity.

In that brief airborne moment, whizzing through the thick Kentucky air, a single thought (other than *OH SHIT*, that is) raced across my brain. No one had any idea where I was, and wouldn't even think to come looking for me until after the sun went down. If—*if*—I survived the fall, I was likely going to lie at the base of the rock in agony. For hours. Maybe till morning. Or even longer.

Then I hit the deck, a tangle of arms and legs and leaves, rolling and cartwheeling down the steep hillside that angled down and away from the base of the cliff. When I finally came to rest, I found myself flat on my back looking up at the sky through the canopy of trees that loomed almost mockingly above me.

First thought: *I'm alive.* Second thought: *I'm conscious?* Third thought: *I don't think anything is broken!* And finally: *Holy shit, thankyouJesusthankyou JesusthankyouJesus!!*

Blondie scrambled down the steep, soft, leafy slope that had obviously helped break my fall and began licking my face as a fit of relief-inspired, uncontrollable laughter wracked my scratched, scraped, very sore—but relatively intact—frame. I probably laughed for a good five minutes, tears welling up in my eyes, rolling around in the damp leaves, hugging the smelly dog who'd been my boon companion since childhood.

That fall pretty much shattered my illusions of ever becoming a big-time sponsored rock climber. My desire to someday become a big-time mountaineer remained intact. But now I needed to find some mountains. I promised myself right then and there that somehow, some way, that's exactly what I'd do.

I'd find me some mountains, and maybe in the process, I'd at long last find myself or at the very least, find a version of myself that I could live with.

Dynamite and Two Motorcycle Helmets

Misery loves company. Whoever coined that phrase obviously wintered in Appalachia at some point in their life. While I plotted and schemed ways to escape Appalachia and seek my fortunes in the western mountains, I was joined by one of my friends from Parkersburg, Mike Reece. The farm had picked up yet another stray. (Now, Reece is not Mike's real last name, but because of his current job as a miner with a blasting license, I have changed his name so he can keep his job.)

Although I was maniacally protective of my privacy at that time, I was relieved to have a kindred spirit take up residence in the mobile home that my Aunt Deloris just vacated. She had met a really nice old gent named Bill, gotten hitched and moved in with him. I was happy for her. Another lost soul from Preacher Click's Hillbilly Home for Wayward Humans had found their way again.

Mike was several years younger than I, and was probably the skinniest man in Carter County. If he stood sideways, his paper-thin profile would nearly render him invisible unless he had a cigarette hanging out of his mouth—which was most of the time.

Like me, Mike had a fondness for Kurt Vonnegut's work, rock climbing, cheap beer, and all things redneck (except bigotry and racism of course— zero tolerance for *any* of that crap). And especially for things that exploded.

Kids, you'd do well *not* to try *any* of the things I'm about to describe at home.

Mike and I would often pool our tips from delivering pizza (I was able to get Mike a job at Giovanni's with me) and place extensive mail orders for exotic shotgun ammunition. How it was legal to manufacture, sell, and ship commercially produced shells that turned your shotgun into a flamethrower for three seconds, or contained two slugs connected by piano wire (bolas), or were packed with small nails (flechettes), amazes me to this day. That stuff *had* to be illegal in some way, or at the very least, its use in direct violation of the Geneva Convention.

No discarded TV, washing machine, can, or bottle in the dump over the hill was safe. (There was no trash service in this part of Appalachia, so most people just tossed all their trash over the side of the nearest hill or burned it in fifty-gallon drums.) I have no idea how many bales of hay we incinerated with those flamethrower shells, but I'm sure that I remain on half a dozen government watch lists after all the crazy shit we ordered.

But Mike was always pushing the envelope, and when he started making his own shotgun shells like some mad scientist, I knew we were headed for trouble. After the second of my grandfather's old shotguns blew up in his face, we decided to stick to commercially manufactured ammunition and turned our attention to safer endeavors—like bomb making.

With the infamous *Poor Man's James Bond* handbook as our guide, we set out making bombs that mostly relied on ingredients like black powder and other easily obtainable household items. I can't really say why we became so fixated on making bombs, other than we did so because we could. Or maybe we did it just because it was really fun to blow shit up.

I hate to wax too nostalgic, but these were the days before the Unabomber was caught (forever casting doubt on the sanity of every poor soul who lived in a cabin and enjoyed their own company, like, say, ummm—yours truly) … before Columbine and 9/11. The days when you could still have that kind of redneck fun without fear of being labeled some kind of *ist*. An extrem*ist*, a fundamenta*list*, or a terror*ist*.

Since there were no close neighbors to speak of, and as long as we didn't blow anything up too close to the house, no one seemed too awfully concerned about our explosive antics. Like I said, everyone down there viewed our activities as good clean redneck fun.

I did have one scare, though. I should have listened to that teeny-tiny voice in the back of my head that warned me not to proceed when we tried to make a bomb from a can of calcium carbide. The dry calcium carbide pellets are stable, but once you add just a few drops of water, the resulting chemical reaction produces a flammable gas.

Calcium carbide had been used in the headlamps of miners and cavers for decades. When the calcium carbide pellets are mixed with water in a very small mounted canister and then lit with a small flint, the flame is very bright. When a polished metal disc is mounted just behind the flame on a helmet, it casts a very even and bright light. But with the recent widespread use of battery-powered headlamps, calcium carbide headlamps were quickly falling out of favor with all but a few die-hard cavers. Hence the surplus of calcium carbide pellets that made it so easy for us to procure a big tin of the stuff.

We figured that if just a little water and a few pellets made for a very bright little flame, then a *lot* of water added to a *lot* of pellets would make for a really *big* flame. And where was a large supply of water available? Why, down at the cow pond in the middle of the pasture of course. So after perforating the large can of calcium carbide pellets with a dozen or so holes and duct-taping the lid down tight, we went through the cattle gate and into the pasture to the small pond. Our plan was to tape a kerosene-soaked rag to the can, light it, and then chuck it into the pond. We theorized that when the water infiltrated the can and produced the gas, the flaming rag would ignite the rush of gas and we would be treated to a huge fireball.

We performed our traditional countdown under the watchful eyes of the two cows and the horse that stood nearby, lit the rag, and tossed the can into the pond. But instead of a massive ball of flame, all we got was a weak sizzle and some smoke on the water as the rag fizzled out and the can sank to the bottom, leaving a trail of milky roiling bubbles behind it. Lots of milky roiling bubbles. Fifteen minutes worth of them.

We were disappointed, but accustomed to occasional failures. But when we turned from the pond, and ended up face to face with the livestock that was patiently waiting for us to leave their water supply so they could get a drink, I realized in horror what we had just done. Our failed bomb had just poisoned their only supply of water.

Absurdly, my first impulse was to scoop up a cupful of the murky brown water and taste it myself to see if it had indeed been fouled by the can of calcium carbide that now sat dissolving at the pond's mucky bottom.

In a panic, we led the cows and the horse back up to the barn and locked them in their stalls after filling a few buckets of water for them from the hose. How could I explain *this* one to my grandparents???

I spent the next two nerve-wracking days standing guard over the water supply and doing everything in my power to keep the animals away from the befouled pond. I knew that the pond was spring fed, so I reasoned that if I waited long enough, maybe the toxic waste dump we created might be flushed clean by the influx of the spring's untainted water.

On the third day, I cautiously allowed the two cows to approach the pond and slake their thirst. I spent the rest of that day dreading the moment when I would come out to the field after using the bathroom at the house and find the poor creatures on their backs, all four legs pointed up in the air, swollen tongues hanging out of the sides of their mouths, and dead as dead could be.

When this did not happen, I thanked the Patron Saint of Failed Bomb Makers (there had to be one, I reasoned, since they had saints named for just about everything else), and promised him or her to be more careful when planning our next pyrotechnic folly. It wasn't long in coming.

The morning when I was awakened by Mike knocking insistently on my cabin door, I knew something was up. Mike rarely stirred before 11:00 a.m. When I groggily opened the door, he had a big smile on his face and a greasy paper bag in his hand. Like a kid who had convinced his mom to pack his favorite lunch and couldn't wait to show it to his classmates, Mike proudly held the bag out and opened it for me. The only thing in the bag was a foot-long, tightly rolled cardboard tube, dotted with beads of water. *Dynamite.*

I gingerly reached into the bag with the intention of grabbing the stick to examine it closer. But as I quickly discovered upon touching the stick with my bare hands, that wasn't water beading up on the surface. It was nitroglycerin, and the instant I touched it, I was greeted with a twanging headache, right behind my eyeballs. Think about the worst brain freeze you've ever had—and then quadruple it. It hurt that much. I decided to leave it in the bag until I could find some gloves.

As we crossed the field on the way back to the house to find said gloves, I nearly asked Mike where he had found the dynamite. But I quickly realized that the less I knew, the better. This little piece of ignorance might afford me a clearer conscious when I later addressed the judge. If it came to that, of course.

Admittedly, I didn't know all that much about dynamite, and relied on Mike's expertise on the subject. This was back in the last few days before the Internet made knowledge about such things so easily accessible. The sum total of my knowledge about dynamite had been gleaned from a few cheap spy novels, Burt Reynolds movies, and television shows like *The A Team* and *The Dukes of Hazzard*. But Bo and Luke Duke never had to wear gloves when shooting their dynamite-tipped arrows! What the hell? I'd been misinformed! So what to do?

This was to be a special occasion, and blowing up another television or washing machine just wouldn't do. So we decided that whatever we blew up, it needed to be at least somewhat productive. Maybe a stubborn stump, or a road-blocking rock. And we also came to the conclusion that a whole stick of dynamite would likely be overkill for these tasks. And provide only *one* explosion. In a stroke of genius that would have made ol' King Solomon proud, we sagely proclaimed that we would cut the stick of dynamite in half and get *two* big explosions. Brilliant!

And no, I'm not making this up. How do you cut a stick of dynamite in half, you ask? Why, with a really sharp knife, of course. A quick trip back to my grandparents' kitchen, and we were in business. After donning the leather gloves, I gingerly removed the dynamite from the paper sack and carefully placed it on the oil-soaked workbench in the barn, next to the vise.

Earlier, Mike and I had flipped a coin to determine who would be the idiot who tried to cut a stick of dynamite in half with a kitchen knife. Guess who lost *that* toss? I picked up the knife (my palms, like the dynamite, perspiring furiously), and like a reluctant surgeon, readied myself to saw through the 1½-inch-thick explosive cardboard cylinder.

As I ever-so-gently touched the edge of the blade to the cylinder, knife held at an arm's length, sweat dripping down my forehead and into my slitted eyes, an uncertain grimace covering my clenched jaw, I recalled my little promise to that Patron Saint of Failed Bomb Makers. My promise to exercise at least a modicum of common sense the next time I played with fire.

Cautiously eyeing the explosive, I again noticed the little beads of moisture on the exterior, and suddenly recalled a piece of trivia I had once read about dynamite and then filed away in the *Why the hell do I need to know THAT?* department of my brain. I remembered reading that the first outward sign that a stick of dynamite is aging and therefore becoming unstable is that it begins to "sweat" out the pure nitroglycerin from the cardboard and sawdust that kept it stable. In this state, just about any sudden movement could trigger an unplanned explosion.

That stick of dynamite on the bench was indeed sweating more than the proverbial whore in church. I lifted the blade, backed away, and whistled out a huge sigh from between my teeth, which were still grinding against each other. I felt like I'd been holding my breath for an hour.

We wisely decided that maybe a bigger blast from a whole stick of dynamite, observed from a farther distance, might be a safer option than blowing ourselves in half. And besides, if we tried to halve the dynamite and the ensuing blast didn't kill us, then my grandmother *would* when she realized we had blown up the sharpest knife in her kitchen drawer.

Another myth about dynamite (perhaps perpetuated by the animated Wile E. Coyote in his never-ending quest to obliterate the Roadrunner in the Looney Tunes cartoons) is that you simply light a fuse sticking out of the end of the stick of dynamite, then throw it and run. In the *real* world, dynamite is typically detonated by a small explosive charge inserted into the end of the stick. Known as a blasting cap, it erupts when a small charge of electricity is passed through it, thereby triggering the larger explosion of the nitroglycerin in the dynamite.

Mike had already procured a blasting cap from the same place he "found" the dynamite, and scrounged all the speaker wire he could scavenge from my Jeep, his truck, and my uncle's trailer. All we needed to complete our project was the car battery we borrowed from the old '58 Willys Jeep farm truck that sat rusting away in the waist-high thistle in the middle of the field.

We flipped the coin again to determine which one of us would be the lucky idiot who carried the backpack containing the dynamite down the steep, heavily wooded hill to the rock we had chosen to destroy. This time, Mike lost, and he ever-so-carefully slung the dynamite-laden backpack over his shoulder while I hefted the car battery in one hand and the speaker wire in the other.

As we made our way through the pasture and over the hill down into the woods, Mike walked along like a man—well, like a man with dynamite strapped to his back. We reached the rock after about twenty minutes of very careful hiking. This rock, right in the middle of the new road we were cutting from the pasture above to our favorite swimming hole in Big Sinking Creek (simply called Sankin' by everyone but the cartographer who had named it on the USGS map), had stymied our road-building efforts.

We had no rock drill to make a hole in the rock that would allow the blast to fracture the enormous rock, but we were hoping that by simply setting the explosive in a crack near the surface of the rock and detonating it that we'd get lucky and the blast would fracture it enough for us to break up the remaining pieces with a sledgehammer. We could then cart away the rubble, thereby eliminating the last real obstacle to the completion of our "road," which wound its way around the edge of the limestone cliff, down through the rhododendrons, ending up at the sandy bottom where Sankin' snaked its way through the bottom of the half-mile-wide ravine.

This time around, we made safety our number one concern (well, at least as much as one could make safety a priority when playing with unstable dynamite). To this end, we were both sporting dusty old red, white, and blue Evel Knievel–style motorcycle helmets that we had discovered in the barn loft, and added an extra 20 feet of speaker wire to buy us some more distance from the blast.

Mike unslung his pack, put on some gloves, fished the dynamite out of the paper sack, and set it down inside a small crack in the rock. He fished the blasting cap out of his pocket. It was the size of a very skinny AAA battery, with two small-diameter wires sticking out of one end. In a useless and comical attempt to protect himself, Mike flipped the scratched plastic visor down on the helmet as he delicately inserted one end of the blasting cap into the end of the dynamite stick.

We then hurriedly spliced the sections of speaker wire together until they reached a safe area around the corner of a rock face, some 100 feet away. This was where we planned to connect the speaker wires to the positive and negative Jeep battery terminals, thereby sending a charge back to the small blasting cap stuck in the end of the stick and destroying the offending rock. After making the final connection to the two wires on the blasting cap, we ducked around the corner of the rock and readied ourselves.

After chugging and then crushing our last two cans of Milwaukee's Best beer, we commenced the countdown (which we now thought of as being almost as exciting as the explosions that usually followed).

10 ... 9 ... 8 ... 7 ... 6 ... 5 ... 4 ... 3 ... 2 ... 1 ... Mike touched the one wire to the negative post on the Jeep battery, I touched the other wire to the positive.

1 ... 1 ... 1 ... Nothing.

Two more tense minutes of kneeling there in the leaves, and still nothing. After five minutes, we mustered the courage to peek around the corner of our hiding spot to see what the hell had happened. Or hadn't happened, in this case.

Upon closer inspection of the wire, we discovered that one of our twisted splice connections had been pulled apart during our hasty retreat to the safe zone. After first checking to make sure the wires were not still attached to the battery terminals on the other end (hey—we may have been dumb, but we weren't stupid. Well ... not *totally* stupid, anyway), we re-twisted the wires together and hurriedly retook our places at the battery.

We skipped the countdown this time and instead opted for a simpler— but less dramatic—"Ready, set ... GO!!" The resulting blast was so forceful it knocked us both to the ground from our squatting positions behind the rock. I felt as if someone had delivered a heavily booted flying kick to my chest with both feet. Our ears were ringing too loud for us to hear our own loudly shouted "YEEEEE-HAW!!!" yells as we regained our feet and once again peeked around the corner of the rock face.

The buried rock was still in the middle of the road, but had been denuded of all the moss that covered it and the dirt at its edges had been blown away. Small tendrils of smoke curled up from the rock, and the smell of burned leaves permeated the air. There was not a leaf, blade of grass, or small branch left on a tree within a 150-foot radius of the rock. As we explored the devastation, we discovered short sections of speaker wire hanging from the tops of trees hundreds of feet away.

The rock had won, but we were as giddy as schoolboys with our successful (and relatively safe) detonation. It was a hell of a kick in the pants.

We trudged back up the hill, carrying the heavy battery between us, still wearing our trusty motorcycle helmets (we had forgotten they were still on, such was our sense of wonderment) and stupid lopsided grins.

I can't begin to imagine how ridiculous we looked to my grandparents, who were both seated on the wood porch swing and eating ice cream sandwiches as we approached the house.

"What in tarnation were you boys up to down there?" my grandmother asked.

My grandfather, who knew exactly what in tarnation we'd been up to down there, simply asked, "You boys shoot some dynamite down there?" as he licked some ice cream off the back of his liver-spotted hand. He asked the question in the same conversationally innocent tone as if he had asked us, "So how was the fishing down at the creek?"

Now, Preacher Click's first job at the ripe ol' age of thirteen was running the wires to the explosive charges that were set to blast out coal deposits in the mines of West Virginia. He knew the sound of dynamite exploding, and I knew that there was no sense in denying anything. Especially since Mike and I were both still sporting our Evel Knievel helmets and smelled to high heaven of smoke and explosives. So we sheepishly removed our helmets and admitted that yes, we had indeed shot off a stick of dynamite. I suddenly felt very, very foolish.

"Okay, thought so. Y'all pert-near knocked the house here off its foundation," he said.

And that was all he had to say on the matter as he returned his attention to the business of rocking on the swing with my grandmother and finishing up his ice cream sandwich. That was it.

Life for me in Kentucky at that time was often lonely and difficult, but it was punctuated and made bearable by surreal moments of sublimely pleasurable idiocy such as this.

The Initial Call-Out

Often, when we are called out to respond to a search or a rescue, we throw every means of transport available to accomplish our mission: To help those who are having a bad day in the mountains. On this search in 2014 for a missing father and son from Minnesota, we employed two helicopters, a snowcat, snowmobiles, skis and snowshoes on the first full day of the search. This particular search turned tragic when they were found deceased nearly 100 days after they were reported missing. Photo by Tom Wood.

Broken Hearts, Shattered Glass, and Second Chances

I'm often asked how I ended up here in Colorado. Short version: I moved back to Ohio from Kentucky, became a roofer, met a girl, married her, and less than a year later pulled up stakes and abandoned Ohio.

But why Colorado? My answer is pretty simple. I moved to Colorado because it wasn't Ohio. The truth of the matter is, I'd never even been to the state of Colorado before moving here. I knew one person in the whole damned state. But I needed a change, and it needed to be a drastic one. I figured that if I just closed my eyes and took a huge leap of faith, I'd somehow land on my feet. Folk singer John Denver, and authors Stephen King and Ayn Rand seemed to think pretty highly of Colorado, and that was good enough for me.

So we left the Rustbelt and lit out for the Rocky Mountains. But after driving cross-country and crossing the Colorado state line back in 1997 ("You Are Now Entering Colorful Colorado!"), let's just say I was overwhelmingly under-impressed with what I saw at that eastern border. Obviously, someone had made a dreadful mistake by placing that sign where it was, because the terrain surrounding our packed-to-the-ceiling Chevy Blazer looked no different than the rolling wastelands of Nebraska that we had just spent an entire *day* crossing. I guess you could call the landscape colorful, if you counted the three differing shades of *brown* that we glimpsed through our bug-splattered windshield as being colorful.

And worse, try as I might, I couldn't see any mountains. Wasn't the entire state supposed to be made up of thousands of mountains? This landscape was more boring and bleak than the one we just left back in Ohio.

Where were the snow-capped peaks? Where were the quaint mountain villages? Where were the goddamn *trees*? The people? Where were all those buffalo roaming? Where were the all fucking deer and the antelope playing? Two-and-a-half hours after crossing the state line, all we'd seen were some

64

tumbleweeds blowing across the highway, one gas station, and a handful of rusty grain bins.

Out of the corner of my eye, I saw my wife struggling to choke back a disappointed sob. *I've made a HUGE mistake,* I inwardly moaned to myself. But after another solid hour of driving across the empty plains, I caught sight of what *looked* to be a mountain range off in the very distant distance, and breathed a cautious sigh of relief.

Over an hour after I spotted that first hint of a mountain range, we entered the bustling, disappointingly urban metropolis that was Boulder, Colorado. Lots of things instantly captured my attention.

For someone coming from the crumbling industrial backdrop of Ohio and the balmy hardwood-covered hills of Appalachia, I quickly realized that Colorado had the feel of a foreign country—and not just because we were now in sight of snow-capped mountains that towered two-and-a-half miles above the state of my birth.

First of all, the cars were not pockmarked or ravaged by rust. (If I didn't know better, I would swear that for every single snowflake that falls in Ohio, there are three grains of salt dispatched to the roads in a (vain) attempt to keep them drivable through the long, gray winters.) In northeast Ohio, if you stared long enough at your car's fender, you could watch the rust bloom right before your eyes. It was practically the state pastime.

Secondly, hardly anyone smoked. This was especially true in the People's Republic of Boulder, where my wife and I spent our first Colorado night. I quickly learned that in Boulder, smokers were routinely captured for lighting up in public, even back then. We passed several of them that had been crucified upside-down from the solar-powered traffic lights on Broadway as we made our way into town.

Thirdly, almost no one who lived in Colorado was born there. Everyone we talked to was either from California, Texas, Missouri, or Ohio. Colorado natives (as they like to call themselves) are so rare, in fact, that I'd heard up until 1992, each child born in the state was issued its own license plate bracket and bumper sticker denoting their status as Colorado Natives (which must have *royally* pissed off the Apaches, Arapahos, Bannocks, Cheyenne, Comanche, Jicarillas, Kiowas, Navajos, Pueblos, and Utes who had been calling Colorado home for a millennia.

Everyone in Boulder seemed to be ridiculously fit and in shape. And white. And drove Subaru Outbacks.

Two days after our arrival, I had a job in Golden as a foreman for Western

Roofing, a company that installed the same system of roofing that I had worked with in Ohio. The day after that, we found a lovely 700-square-foot cabin to rent from a wonderfully tough old Dutch woman named Betty in the hills above Evergreen. I'm (kind of) sad to report that I would keep both that job and that house *much* longer than I kept my wife.

In my heart of hearts, I knew that our marriage had been in trouble from the start (words of wisdom: no matter how cool it sounds at the time—never, ever marry a Goth chick who once believed she might be a vampire). But that did little to assuage the crushing guilt and sense of loss I felt when less than a year after moving to Colorado, she moved out to live with some friends.

The increasing frequency and vehemence of our arguments and fights had twisted us both into something barely recognizable to either of us. We allowed those dark and ugly and nasty parts of our personalities that we most despised to govern our interactions with each other.

I hated the man I'd become. And as much as I wanted to blame my partner for the failure of our union, I knew damned well that I was just as much—or probably even more—to blame than she. My temper was off the charts. I sure wish I could explain away (or simply cover up) my volatile behavior at that point in my life. But I can't, so I won't.

Just before she moved out, I'd become so enraged after one of our arguments that I put my right fist through a window, severing all of the tendons across the back of my right hand. The instant and overwhelming shame I felt was much more difficult to bear than the pain of the wound I had inflicted upon myself.

I later told friends (and the ER staff who knew I was full of shit but didn't press the issue) that I had fallen down some stairs and put my hand through a window at the bottom or some such nonsense. It took a lot of surgery to reconnect the tendons that had snapped like rubber bands and retracted when they were cut. The damage was profound enough that I had to resubmit my handwritten signature to my bank because it had changed so much that none of the tellers would cash my checks. It was nearly two years before I could tie my own shoes without difficulty. But, like a masochist, every time I did try to tie them, I made sure to figuratively punch myself in the face as I struggled, using that humbling situation to once again remind myself that even a momentary loss of control could scar you (and those near you), literally and figuratively, for the rest of your life. Since then, I've seen this happen many, many times in the mountains. One momentary lapse in control or caution, and then *Blammo*—the mountains win again.

My marriage, and perhaps no small part of my sanity, was slipping away.

Now, I am not one of those pathetic people who go through life bemoaning all of their past decisions and blaming others for their life's failures. I wouldn't say I'm terribly proud of some of the things I've done and said, but I come by most of my mistakes pretty honestly. I take ownership of my fuck-ups, not out of a sense of pride, but because I somehow feel it's my duty. No one else wants them anyway. Besides, regret accomplishes so little, and changes nothing.

I have learned a lot from my mistakes, and although I sometimes wish I could learn some of life's lessons in a less-painful fashion, mistakes seem to be the way that really works for me. So therefore, I do not regret most of them.

Surprisingly, I felt few regrets in regards to my marriage's epic failure. As painful as it all was, I felt I was at least learning something about myself. Not to say that I felt blameless when it came to our struggling marriage. I just felt as if both my behavior around my wife, and the fate of our marriage, were completely beyond my control at that point. The whole world seemed to be made of shit and I kept stepping in it.

One lonely October evening in 1997, I paged through *The Canyon Courier*'s classified ads. *The Courier* was the weekly newspaper for the Evergreen area, and in it I noticed an ad announcing that someone from the Alpine Rescue Team was giving a free seminar on avalanche awareness the following week at the local library. For more information, the little public service announcement advised me to call Alpine member Ron Bookman, and listed his number. I knew as much about avalanches as I felt I knew about ways to save a marriage at that point.

"What the hell, why not?" I asked myself aloud. (In those days, I talked aloud to myself *a lot*, and rarely had nice things to say to myself.)

When I called and spoke to Ron, he spoke briefly about the avalanche seminar, and then encouraged me to call a fellow Alpine Rescue member by the name of Roy Wyatt. Roy was in the process of gathering up potential members for Alpine's upcoming Prospective Member Class of 1998.

"What the hell, why not? I asked myself aloud. Again.

I called the number Ron provided and ended up speaking with Roy, who was serving as the rescue team's Prospective Member Director. When I explained to Roy that I knew less than nothing about mountain rescue, he assured me that I would be taught whatever skills I'd need. What they were looking for in new members, he informed me, was dedication, a willingness to learn, and a good attitude. I reckoned I possessed at least a couple of those traits, and told Roy that I would love to sit in on their new member orientation, which, as fate would have it, was taking place the following day at the Alpine Rescue Team Headquarters.

Although I didn't know it at the time, Roy was a fellow Rustbelt Refugee. My senior by twenty years, he had grown up in Youngstown, Ohio, where he had gone to the same high school as my mom. His family used to live down the road from my grandfather, Preacher Click's old house (when he briefly lived across the street from the steel mill). Like my grandfather and I, Roy had also worked at Republic Sheet and Tube. Roy was a former marine who went to Kent State, and originally, his family hailed from Dubois, Pennsylvania (which was also my father's hometown). Like me, he was a big fan of the Cleveland Indians. Weird. Just weird.

How and why I picked up the newspaper on that particular day and took the initiative to call Ron and then Roy, I can't explain. I suppose I was looking for a diversion. Something, *anything*, to take my mind off of the mess that was my life at that moment in time.

I went to the meeting the next day, which was attended by about forty other people who also had an interest in learning more about joining the Alpine Rescue Team. I was surprised to discover that the entire team was comprised of volunteers, and that the building, all the vehicles, and gear were purchased through donations.

The first thing they told me to do was to check with my spouse and/or family to see if they'd be okay with me devoting so much time (especially during that crucial first year on the team). Then they told me to check with my employer to see if they'd take issue with me suddenly leaving work to go on a mission. And lastly, they reminded us to check with our churches to see if they'd be alright with the Sunday field trainings we'd be required to attend.

Family first, work second, religion third.

After explaining a little bit about the team, we received a tour of their amazing headquarters (which they called The Shack for reasons I'll explain later).

I took the application they handed me, filled it out, and quickly mailed it in the next day. I was excited by the possibility of being selected to the Prospective Member Program. I had been kept plenty busy by my duties as a foreman for Western Roofing, and hadn't had much time to make new friends or even get out into the mountains. What little free time I had, I wasted watching my marriage implode and feeling sorry for myself.

When my estranged wife called me the next day, I explained my interest in joining the Alpine Rescue Team. Her response would have been comical had I been capable of laughter at that point in my life.

"The Alpine Rescue Team?" she asked suspiciously. "Isn't that like *Baywatch*, but on skis?" To be fair, my own notions of mountain rescue were ill-formed at best back then as well. Like most Americans, what I knew of mountaineering and mountain rescue came from movies like *Cliffhanger*, *K2*, *The Eiger Sanction*, and Spencer Tracy's *The Mountain*.

And the more I thought about the possibility of being selected to join the Alpine Rescue Team's new member class, the more I realized that this just might be the puzzle piece I had been looking for since my teens—a way to combine a deep love for the outdoors, a desire to help others, and a need to belong to an organization that stood for something worth believing in.

A couple months after the orientation, I was notified that my interview date was to be January 7, 1998. Of the more than forty people who turned in applications to join the team, an interview panel was going to interview everyone and then select fourteen people for the 1998 Alpine Rescue Team Prospective Member Class.

The fateful day of that interview was one of the worst—and best—days of my life.

When the day arrived, I rushed home from work to the small cabin that I alone now rented. I intended to hurriedly shower, change into some clean clothes, and then head to The Shack in the hopes of convincing the interview panel that I would be a good fit for the rescue team. I didn't know why I felt that to be the case, I just did.

My wife and I hadn't spoken to each other in person for weeks. In fact, she refused to tell me where she was staying and would not give me a phone number where she could be reached. *She* had to call *me*, and our last few phone conversations had degenerated into useless contests of, "Who Can Get In The Last Word And Then Hang Up First." But the moment I walked in the door that day, her mother (who was working as our unofficial mediator) called from Pennsylvania to inform me that my wife was officially throwing in the towel and wanted a divorce. Immediately.

I opened my mouth to protest—and then closed it. Right up until that very second, I still clung to the improbable notion that we might somehow still be able to salvage our marriage. But hearing her mother speak those words brought me to the grim realization that there was nothing left to save. In a robotic, emotionless voice that I scarcely recognized as my own, I agreed with her mother that it was for the best and promised that I would try to locate a local attorney to broker our divorce. I then told her mother that I would call her back to pass on the information that she could in turn relay to her daughter about a time and a place to meet with the attorney.

I held myself together long enough to say goodbye to my mother-in-law, hung up the phone, and then the dam broke. A torturous moan escaped my lips as I sunk to the floor next to the phone. I felt pretty confident that that was probably the worst moment of my life to that point. I felt like everyone near and dear to me could see right through me. I felt like the world's most miserable failure. I had let my wife down. I had let my family down. I had let her family down.

I had let myself down. I lay there on the floor sobbing for an hour or so, lost in misery and wallowing in a sea of self-pity. Pa-thetic. Literally picking myself up off the floor, I stumbled from the house and got into my truck. I was already twenty minutes late for my interview when I pulled into The Shack parking lot.

Red-eyed, stinking of sweat, tar, and misery and still wearing my filthy roofing clothes, I looked down in dismay at my hands that were still covered in black caulking from work. I was in such a pitifully preoccupied state of mind after receiving the phone call that served as the death knell for my marriage that I'd completely forgotten to clean up as I had originally intended.

I blew my nose for the fiftieth time in the last hour, took a quick look at my red-rimmed eyes in the rearview mirror, and stepped out of my truck without being fully conscious of what I planned to say or do during the interview.

I took a deep breath, walked into the building, and hoped that I didn't externally appear as messed up as I internally felt. It felt like I was walking into an intervention. Which, unbeknownst to me, I was.

I don't really remember much about the interview itself. It was a blur. I *do* remember thinking on my way out the door after the interview that I really didn't have much to offer the team other than a strong back. I hadn't found the time yet to become a big-time rock climber or mountaineer in the short time I'd spent in Colorado. I had no medical training. I didn't know how to ski, and years earlier, I'd broken my ankle the one and only time I'd tried snowboarding. My time with the marines had taught me how to follow orders, and to respect authority when it was necessary to do so. I possessed a blue-collar, midwestern work ethic. But that was about it.

Apparently, that was enough. What the five folks on the committee saw in me that day, I'll never know. But I'm sure glad they did.

Though I didn't know it at the time, being accepted as a new member of the Alpine Rescue Team saved my life. It gave me a rock to cling to throughout the divorce, which was finalized a few months later. It gave me some of the best friends I've ever had. It led me away from the brink of self-destruction, gave me purpose, and taught me to truly value the lives of the people I share this earth with.

It's hard for me to imagine what my life would be like right now if I hadn't picked up that copy of the local newspaper and responded to that small classified advertisement announcing the Alpine Rescue Team's upcoming avalanche awareness class.

But there's one thing I *do* know. Back in my college days at Kent State University, I had a know-it-all journalism professor who once pulled me aside and sanctimoniously predicted that I'd never find a career in newspapers. It took twenty-five years and several career changes, but it gladdens my heart and lifts my spirits to look back at the moment he told me that and gloat about just how wrong that asshole was. I *did* find a career in newspapers, just not as a journalist. Instead, I found a career as a non-paid professional mountain rescuer by answering a classified ad in a newspaper. And I'm good with that.

The Alpine Rescue Team—It's Like *Baywatch* On Skis, Right?

"**The** Alpine Rescue Team—it's like *Baywatch* on skis, right?" As I said earlier, this was my soon-to-be-ex-wife's response when I shared my desire to join the local mountain rescue team waaay back in 1997.

I can't recall my response to this somewhat comical assessment, but I can say with a fair bit of certainty that neither David Hasselhoff nor Pamela Anderson (or whatever her last name is this week) has ever flexed or bounced their way across an avalanche path as members of our organization. Or any other mountain rescue team, for that matter.

But all joking aside, my ex-wife's misinformed estimation of the Alpine Rescue Team was really not all that uncommon. Popular film and reality TV re-enactments often portray mountain rescuers as the beautiful people. Larger-than-life backcountry experts who risk their lives as casually as most people cross the street. Gore-Tex–clad superheroes who rappel out of helicopters all the time. And often singlehandedly save the day. But in *real* reality (not what passes for reality on TV these days), this perception is so far from the truth as to be laughable.

Though we've had our share of members who do look fetching in their Gore-Tex, and some who are exceptionally selfless and others who are very proficient in the art *and* science of backcountry rescue, most of us are really just regular folks trying to help out other regular folks who are having a bad day in the mountains.

By the time I was selected to join the ranks of the Alpine Rescue Team, I was but one of the hundreds of volunteer mountain rescuers who had staffed the team during its nearly forty years of existence. Hell, I wasn't even the first person with the last name of Wood to join the team. There were several men of Wood before me.

Of course, nobody knows when and where the first mountain rescue took place. But likely (according to the research of mountain rescuer Dr. Christopher Van Tilburg and mountain rescue historian Dee Molenaar), the first organized volunteer mountain rescuers were the Augustine Monks of Aosta, Italy. In about 1050, they lived and worked high in the Italian Alps at a monastery that staffed two hospices founded by Archdeacon Bernard of Menthon. When wayward travelers coming through the Alps from Switzerland needed rescue, it was these selfless Monks who came to their aid. Amazingly, this remote monastery, located at 8,110 feet elevation, is still in operation. The work begun by Bernard of Menthon and the Augustine monks there was held in such high regard that in 1923, Pope Pius XI named Bernard the patron saint of mountain climbers. And yes, the famous St. Bernard breed of mountain rescue dogs (originally descended from a line of dogs known as Roman Molossus and then Hospice dogs) were indeed named after Bernard of Menthon in the 1700s.

Mountain rescue as we know it today is relatively new to the United States. Evolving from the many proud traditions of European mountaineers who emigrated here in the last half of the nineteenth century, it's come a long way from the days when mountain rescue was typically a function of local climbing and mountaineering clubs. The first of these clubs in the U.S. was the Appalachian Mountain Club, founded in 1876. It was soon followed by similar organizations all over the country, and especially in the Pacific Northwest.

But up until the late 1930s, there were still only a handful of such clubs and organizations scattered throughout the country, and I would hazard to guess that they probably spent more time rescuing their own members than anyone else. Back then, the whole notion of the average person going into the mountains for *fun* was still a hard concept for most people to swallow.

But as America's economy flourished, more and more Americans found themselves with a surplus of time and income at their disposal. And in the West, more roads were being cut farther and farther into the backcountry, thereby making the mountains more accessible.

In these western United States, the need for organized search and rescue became apparent as more and more people started to live and recreate in the shadows of those purple mountains and all their majesty. Arguably, five states felt this need most, based on their terrain and exploding population: California, Washington, Oregon, Utah, and Colorado.

Then came World War II. I've heard it said that in modern history, war paradoxically facilitates giant leaps in medical technology. Some even go as far as arguing that in this way, war has helped medicine to progress more rapidly than it does during the peaceful interludes between wars. Whether these statements are accurate or not remains a source of debate, but it is hard to underestimate the influence that World War II had on organized mountain rescue in America.

In November 1939, roughly two years before the U.S. declared war on Germany, a highly publicized battle caught the attention of Charles Minot Dole, then president of the National Ski Patrol. During the Soviet Union's invasion of Finland, two Russian armored divisions were destroyed by Finnish soldiers. On skis. Although the Finnish soldiers were outmatched by the firepower and superior numbers of the Russians, the well-trained Finnish soldiers used their familiarity with the difficult local terrain to their advantage and cleverly stalled and thereby embarrassed the Soviet military. This inspired Dole, and he lobbied the War Department to create a similar unit within the United States Army. He argued that a specialized unit trained to fight in the harsh winter conditions of the mountains might someday be needed to combat the Germans (who already had divisions of trained mountain warriors) if we ever were forced into a war with them.

Soon after, the National Ski Patrol began recruiting for this newly formed division. It remains the only civilian recruiting agency in U.S. military history.

In December of 1941, the 87th Mountain Infantry Battalion (which later became known as the 10th Mountain Division) was formed at Fort Lewis in Washington State. At first, these skiing soldiers trained on the flanks of 14,411-foot Mount Rainier. They soon moved to Camp Hale, Colorado, and trained in the snow and mountains at an elevation of 9,000 feet. By the time the Army Mountain Warfare School was built at nearby Camp Carson in 1942, thousands of newly recruited soldiers were learning how to ski, survive, and fight in the mountains. It was a brutal and unforgiving environment, and many soldiers succumbed to hypothermia and frostbite as cold weather training methods and gear evolved alongside their training.

Once these soldiers were trained, they were shipped off to fight in the mountains of Italy. I'm not sure what ol' peace-loving St. Bernard would have had to say about his beloved mountains becoming the bloody proving grounds for America's mountain warriors, but that's what they were. In the course of their Italian Campaign in WWII, the 10th Mountain Division suffered 992 fatalities and 4,154 wounded over the course of 114 days of combat.

After World War II, something very interesting happened when these mountain warriors came home. Many of them discovered that they had fallen in love with the mountains.

These army-trained mountaineers played a major role in the development of skiing as a major sport and as a vacation activity, and reportedly some two thousand 10th Mountain Division veterans found post-war work in skiing-related jobs (like filmmaking, outdoor gear manufacturing and sales, ski magazine publishing, and ski coaching). They built more than fifty ski resorts, and their contagious passion for the hills led to an explosion of people recreating in the high and remote corners of our country.

But it wasn't just the commercialization of skiing that was being driven by the 10th Mountain Division vets. Many of the volunteer mountain rescue teams formed in the years after the war listed 10th Mountain Division veterans as their founding members.

In 1959, at the Timberline Lodge on Mount Hood, the Mountain Rescue Association (MRA) was formed by several mountain rescue teams from California, Idaho, Washington, and Oregon, whose ranks were peppered with 10th Mountain Division–trained veterans. This was to be the country's first national organization dedicated exclusively to mountain search and rescue safety and education. Serving as a kind of parent organization to all of the local teams now popping up throughout the mountainous areas of the United States, the MRA was founded on the premise that there should never be a charge for SAR work performed in the mountains. "No charge for rescue!" is still our battle cry to this day.

Here in Colorado, the first two organized mountain rescue teams were the Rocky Mountain Rescue Group (RMRG), formed in 1947 in Boulder, and the Arapahoe Rescue Patrol (ARP), formed in the mid-'50s near Denver. A short time later in 1959, the Alpine Rescue Team—the rescue team that I now think of as family—was formed. Sadly, it was created in response to a specific tragedy.

Lover's Leap, a 400-foot-tall rock face within shouting distance of Highway 285 in Jefferson County's Turkey Creek Canyon, was quickly becoming a popular place to climb back in the late 1950s.

On June 27, 1959, a group of four young men set out to climb the prominent crag. Most of the climb was—and still is—relatively straightforward, with the hardest (crux) move being just a dozen feet from the top. I would imagine that it was a much more serene climb back then. Nowadays, the dull roar associated with the increased levels of highway noise from the now-busy four-lane Highway 285 ruin what was likely, back then, a pleasant wilderness experience only occasionally tainted by the sound of a few passing cars headed up the narrow canyon.

After successfully completing the climb, the group safely rappelled down the first and second pitches (a pitch is typically between 80 to 160 feet, depending on convenient stopping points like ledges, or the length of the climber's rope). On the third and final rappel, they hammered a piton in a crack that would serve as their rappel anchor. The first climber completed the long rappel without incident.

The second climber wasn't so lucky. After he began his rappel, the piton anchoring his rappel rope bent, then worked loose and finally popped out of its crack. The climber fell to his death, taking the group's only rope with him. The remaining two climbers were suddenly stuck mid-wall. They needed rescue.

The technical rope rescue on Lover's Leap was carried out by three volunteer fire departments: Idledale, Evergreen, and Indian Hills. With the help of some local climbers who happened to be in the area, they accomplished the complex technical rope rescue of the two stranded climbers, as well as completing the body recovery of the fallen climber.

The accident served as a wake-up call to the members of the three departments. Recognizing that each of the departments was ill-equipped and not well trained for technical rope rescues of this magnitude, they decided to pool their resources and personnel to form a single team whose sole purpose was dedicated to backcountry search and rescue in the mountains and canyons that are the eastern gateway to the Rockies. (Alpine Rescue is unique in Colorado since all other SAR teams cover only a single county. We are the primary search and rescue team for three Colorado counties: Jefferson, Clear Creek, and Gilpin.)

And as was the case with many of the other SAR teams forming around the nation at roughly the same time, two of the men (Gordon Stucker and Dave Pratt) responsible for the formation of this new squad of mountain rescue specialists were World War II mountain warfare veterans. They used their military-honed mountaineering skills to train the other seven original members. (These nine charter members and mountain rescue visionaries included David A. Pratt, A.R. Clark Jr., Albert G. Lambert, William H. Pickett, Richard G. Perkins, Ralph L. O'Neal, John Eugene Lines, Wayne Drake, and Gordon Stucker.) The Alpine Rescue Team was born.

More than fifty years and thousands of missions later, the Alpine Rescue Team has not only survived, but flourished. And that bent piton that started it all? It was later recovered by then-Indian Hills Fire Chief Dick Perkins from the base of the climb, and is now on display at the Alpine Rescue Team's headquarters in Evergreen. Each year, in honor of the tragedy that spawned a mountain rescue team, the Bent Piton Award is given to the team member who demonstrates outstanding performance on a mission. (Winning this award in 2006, with fellow Alpine member Jerome Stiller, for helping to safely execute a difficult technical rope body recovery from a remote peak in southern Colorado was one of the proudest moments in my career as a rescuer.)

From then on, thanks in large part to a relatively high call volume for the time, the team grew. In 1962, Alpine was the second rescue team in Colorado to become a fully accredited member of the recently formed Mountain Rescue Association. Since then, three current Alpine members, and one former Alpine member, have served as president of the MRA. No other team in the MRA has spawned as many presidents. Given my mixed feelings on all things political, I'm still not sure if this is a good thing or not.

In the early days, Alpine was rather homeless. The Evergreen Library and the Elk's Lodge served as early meeting places for the team. It was during this formative period, when all the team's rescue gear was stored at the Elk's Lodge, that the rescue team's headquarters was (only somewhat jokingly) nicknamed The Shack.

As the team grew in size and scope, it became apparent that it would take some sort of miracle for the team to ever be able to afford a real base of operations. That miracle came along in 1973 when Alpine's original patron saints, Byron and Ruth Angevine, donated the land, a fair bit of money, and a lot of inspiration to the fledgling team so that they could build the headquarters they needed on Independence Mountain in Evergreen. Although it was a far cry from a shack now, the name stuck, and remains to this day.

But the team still wasn't finished growing, and The Shack's location on Independence Mountain eventually became too small and was too far from the major roads and highways that connected Evergreen to the high mountains in the team's jurisdiction.

In 1988, construction began on a new high-tech Shack out near Interstate 70 at the El Rancho area of Evergreen. By the time the "new" Shack opened its doors in November of 1990 on land donated by the Foothills Fire Protection District, its construction had already been completely paid for by the generous donations of both other volunteer organizations and the general public. Equipped with a climbing wall, three large garage bays, a state-of-the-art communications room, full kitchen, and a large meeting room, this was to be the team's permanent home.

As Colorado's population boomed, the number of missions the team was called upon to perform rose accordingly. Although the number of people on

The Alpine Rescue Team Headquarters, aka The Shack, is located in Evergreen, Colorado, and its construction was entirely funded by donations. Photo courtesy of the Alpine Rescue Team.

the team fluctuated wildly from a couple dozen in the early days to over a hundred by the time the team settled into the "new" Shack, we now remain steady at fifty to seventy field-active members. The efforts of these field-active members are now supported by our associate members, who do not participate on trainings or rescues, but rather donate their time and services to help with our fundraising, mountain safety education, communication, and operational needs. We couldn't run the team without them.

The team still relies completely on donations to purchase and maintain all our gear and keep the lights on. We do apply for a couple grants each year to purchase equipment, but everything else is either purchased through donations, or is sometimes "loaned" to us by the sheriff's departments we serve.

Each member's personal gear is completely paid for out of their own pockets. This, along with the fuel consumed by the thousands of miles an active member drives each year, can easily add up to hundreds or thousands of dollars. Each member drives around with, at a minimum, enough gear to perform SAR work and survive for forty-eight hours below treeline in three seasons. Those of us who have been around awhile carry enough gear to ply our trade and survive above treeline in all four seasons for three days. This can take up a lot of space, and is the reason why most of us here in Rescue-World rarely share a ride with our spouses.

We have no paid staff on the Alpine Rescue Team. Now, we do have a core group of senior members known as Mission Leaders (ML), who are on call for twenty-four-hour periods. They are the only members duty-bound to respond once we get a call, because they are the individuals charged with co-ordinating Alpine's response with the sheriff, or Flight For Life, or whatever organizations are responding to a particular call. This mission coordination is now accomplished via two-way radios and both texts and emails sent to our cell phones. Although we are dispatched by the three county sheriff's departments that we have a Memorandum of Understanding with, we remain fiercely independent of them. This saves our sheriffs a lot of paperwork and money, and allows us the freedom to run our organization as we see fit.

We are fortunate enough to have fantastic working relationships with all three of the sheriffs who rely on us to perform search and rescue in their counties, and we are on a first-name basis with many members of their staff.

The Alpine Rescue Team's response area is roughly the size of Rhode Island at 1,300 square miles. Within all that space are three national forests (Arapahoe, Roosevelt, and Pike), four fourteeners (peaks whose height meets or exceeds 14,000 feet above sea level), two ski and/or snowboarding resorts (Loveland and Echo Mountain), untold numbers of thirteeners, and four popular ice climbing areas. It's some of the busiest backcountry in the U.S.

It takes a lot of vehicles and gear to cover such a large and geographically diverse area. Our two primary response vehicles (Rescue 1 and Rescue 2) were custom-built to our specifications, and cost more than many people's homes (especially mine). Our communications van (Comm4) is a converted over-sized 4WD passenger van. We have six ATVs and six snowmobiles. Again, all donated or purchased through donations.

Up until the late '90s, most of our calls were for searches. Now, searches and rescues are usually about dead even in frequency.

But we do a lot more than just "play in the dirt," as we like to call our rescue efforts. Alpine trains every Wednesday at The Shack, and every other weekend we train out in the field. That is six trainings a month *at a minimum.* Then there are the hours we pour into maintaining our vehicles and equipment. We also do a lot of Preventative Search and Rescue education (PSAR—I warned you we *do* love our acronyms). These events range from presentations on avalanche awareness given to snowmobilers (our fastest-growing demographic for backcountry rescues), to Hug A Tree classes given to Cub Scout packs and Girl Scout troops. Fundraising is another necessary evil that requires a lot of our resources.

One of the things that, in my humble opinion, makes life on Alpine so interesting is the variety of the types of calls we get each year. Given the varying nature of terrain in our response area, we get calls for searches above and below treeline, winter technical rescues, avalanche rescues, high-altitude rescues (many near 14,000 feet in elevation), high-angle technical rock rescues, low-angle scree rescues, swift water rescue support, and helicopter evacuations.

And speaking of helicopters, we are very conservative when it comes to their use in the backcountry. Privately owned and operated helicopters are expensive—like hundreds or thousands of dollars per hour kind of expensive. Sometimes this cost is taken care of by the county sheriff's office that requests the choppers, sometimes the air ambulance service donates their services for SAR. The only time that a hiker or climber or snowmobiler will see a charge from the helicopter service is when they are transported by that helicopter to a hospital for their injuries. In those cases, they will receive a bill, just as they would if they were transported by a ground ambulance. Military helicopters are an (often invaluable) option for us, but one that typically takes more time to get all the required clearances to use them. And besides, helicopters—even under the best of circumstances—are a resource that should be used judiciously when working at altitude. The risks associated with the helicopter transport of a tired hiker who twisted an ankle almost always outweigh any benefits that could come from the wasteful use of such a valuable resource.

One of our senior members, Charley Shimanski, jokingly likes to say that just as the Buddhists believe that each and every person is allotted so many breaths in their lifetime before they die, so it goes that each of us is only allotted so many helicopter rides before we are on one that crashes. That number might be only one, or it might be five thousand, but it *is* a finite number, and we have no way of ever knowing when that number is up. And it is a sense of humor like Charley's that is so essential to the sanity of the mountain rescuer.

We all know that mountain rescue is serious business. As rescuers, we work very hard to project the image of ourselves as dedicated, non-paid professionals. And while we always tackle the mission at hand with complete seriousness, I feel that we desperately need to avoid taking *ourselves* too seriously.

If you look closely at the walls of our headquarters, tucked in between the official proclamations of thanks from politicians, yellowed newspaper clippings tacked to the wall, and next to photos of our ice-rimed members waving summit flags atop the world's high peaks—you'll find a framed photo from the '80s of eight of our members (male and female) mooning the camera at the base of an ice climb. Can you imagine the look on your boss's face in Corporate America USA if you put a photo of eight pairs of (blindingly white) cheeks on the wall of your cubicle for all the world to see? Probably not.

And look! Next to all the fancy brass and glass plaques from the local Chamber of Commerce, the Rotary Club, and the Red Cross—it's a gnarled bristlecone pine tree trunk adorned with various trinkets and artifacts including, but not limited to: a chunk of melted aluminum (from a torched snowmobile), broken toy helicopters, busted toy snowmobiles, a cracked aircraft altimeter, a sticker that reads "emergency helicopter exit only," and the tag cut from one of our Mission Leader's Fruit of the Loom white bikini brief underwear. This is our team's inglorious monument to our failures and embarrassing moments as mountain rescuers. It is lovingly known to Alpine members as the Windy Peak Airplane Magnet Aw-Shit Award, and the trinkets hanging from it are the contributions of past recipients.

This award symbolizes so many of the things that I truly love about mountain rescue. First and foremost, it is a recognition of our humanity. Our fallibility. It also symbolizes that cherished spirit of true irreverence that runs crookedly through the heart of mountain rescue. I feel that the Aw-Shit Award, bestowed each year upon the team member who had the year's biggest fuck-up, is our most important award.

And yes, I am a previous winner. Twice over. The first time was for an embarrassing incident with fellow teammate Mark Nelson that involved a funeral and two brand new snowmobiles left out overnight stuck in the snow. The second time, I was awarded the Aw-Shit Award for getting into someone else's car (while they were still in it) after an all-night search.

The Aw-Shit Award serves as our yearly reminder to both

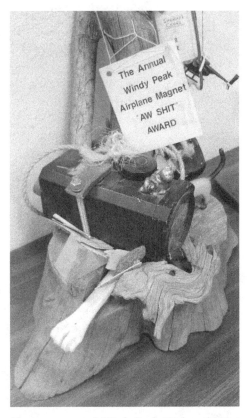

The not-so-coveted Windy Peak Airplane Magnet Aw-Shit Award is bestowed each year on the team member who makes the biggest goof during a mission or training. The author has twice been a recipient of this award that pays homage to the irreverent spirit of mountain rescue. Photo by Tom Wood.

honor that irreverent spirit of mountain rescue's independent nature, and to lighten the hell up. For in mountain rescue, sometimes our sense of humor is the only weapon we have at our disposal when we are faced with tragedy in the backcountry. The temptation to take things too seriously is sometimes a strong one, and one that we must avoid if we hope to remain happy and sane while doing our important work in the place I like to call RescueWorld.

Ernest Hemingway is famous for saying, "There are only three sports: bullfighting, motor racing, and mountaineering; all the rest are merely games." And although mountaineering *could* be thought of as a sport, it is most certainly not a *team* sport. It's a solo endeavor performed by individuals. And so it goes that mountain rescue teams can be thought of as extensions of these free-spirited mountaineering individuals.

Hell, given the fiercely independent nature of most mountain rescue teams in the U.S., it's a wonder to me that a national organization like the MRA exists at all sometimes.

For just as the mountains attract many hikers, climbers, and mountaineers who march to the beat of a different drummer, so it goes for many of the men and women who sign on to help those having a bad day while enjoying the freedom of the hills.

The very dynamic and eclectic nature of non-paid professional mountain rescue itself often cries out for an eccentric and unconventional approach. It follows that those who are drawn to this type of service for lost or injured hikers, climbers, and skiers in the mountains might be a little ... off as well.

In fact, the more time you spend around almost any volunteer mountain rescue team in the world, you'll find that most of us possess (and sometimes flaunt) a strong sense of independent irreverence that you won't likely find in EMS organizations that are dependent on mill levies or those that are forced to march to the PC beat of a Human Resource (HR) Department. And God help mountain rescue the day that we have an HR Department.

(Hold on for a moment here while I step up onto my soapbox.) The way I see it, if you can't go to the mountains or the backcountry and let your hair down once in a while (whether to recreate or to rescue), where else is left? In our politically correct society's quest to never offend *anyone*, we've taken a lot of fun away from *everyone*. (Okay, sorry about that, I'm stepping back down now.)

In non-paid professional mountain rescue, this kind of financial and institutional independence is essential to the survival of each and every volunteer organization. As the Langdale-Ambleside Mountain Rescue Team (from the Lake District in Britain) says on its website, "Self-funding means freedom—to experiment, to acquire the best equipment for the job, freedom from bureaucratic interference and cost-cutting to which so many public services have fallen victim, and freedom to enjoy the team spirit which rewards and respects initiative and competence in a way which binds and disciplines a team to the ultimate benefit of all."

So just who are these people who dedicate and donate so much of their time and effort "that others might live"? And what motivates them? I've noticed two distinct personality traits that seem to be present in the folks who dedicate years of their life in service to mountain rescue.

First of all, those who give that much of their lives to mountain rescue simply love helping people. Although a love of the backcountry and a deep respect for the awesome might of nature are important traits found in the mountain rescuer, it is their obsessive desire to help their fellow human beings that keeps the career mountain rescuer going year after year after year. After all, it is not unusual for most mountain rescue teams to go a couple of months with absolutely no calls, and if you joined mountain rescue strictly for the thrills, this is when you are likely to discover that you'd rather be climbing or skiing than sitting through yet another classroom presentation on line search techniques. From what I've seen, this is why adrenaline junkies make for terrible rescuers. These folks eventually discover that there's a lot of standing around going on in mountain rescue, and that they'd rather be out recreating than being stuck back at Operations shuffling around in a parking lot inhaling diesel fumes from the rescue truck while waiting for a field assignment.

Secondly, career mountain rescuers have a screw loose—and I say that with the utmost respect. Professional mountain rescue has come a long way since its humble beginnings across the pond. But even with all the modernization of mountain rescue techniques and tools—and the equally modern concept of risk management—it is still a dangerous undertaking at times. It follows that those willing to put themselves at risk for total strangers, year after year, with no financial reward or loaded gun to their head, are cut from a different cloth. Like the bumper sticker says, "You don't have to be crazy to work here, but it helps." Or, as Joseph Conrad once said, "There is nothing more enticing, disenchanting, and enslaving than the life at sea." And so it goes for the life in the mountains, dedicated to mountain rescue.

So I say to my fellow mountain rescuers, remember to lighten the hell up—and may you always be a little ... off.

Irritable Bowels, a Big Mountain, and By the Way, Have You Met My Nephew?

When I began my mountain rescue career with Alpine, I had several years' worth of backcountry sins to atone for.

And walking onto the team as a guy who didn't know Gore-Tex from Tex-Mex, I looked back and saw that just about every fun thing I ever did when I lived east of the Mississippi broke every single one of the rules for backcountry survival that mountain rescuers swear by. For just as Moses came down from the mountain with two stone tablets engraved with ten rules to live by, mountain rescuers preach that anyone who ventures into the wild should *always* follow these Ten Commandments for survival:

1. Thou shalt always carry a <u>map</u>.
2. Thou shalt always bear with thee thy <u>compass</u>.
3. Thou shalt ever bear upon one's person a <u>flashlight/headlamp</u>, forgetting not the <u>extra batteries</u>.
4. Woe is he who brings not the <u>extra food.</u>
5. A coat of a thousand colors benefits thee not at all, lest it be one constructed of <u>Gore-Tex.</u>
6. I say unto thee, wear thy garments in <u>layers,</u> lest thee suffer the untold agony of the damned and chilly.
7. For all manner of afflictions, carry whither thou goest a <u>first-aid kit,</u> and take comfort in thy <u>moleskin</u> for that bane of all of those who wander—the heel blister.
8. Whether thou endeavors to cut the Gordian Knot, cleave the loaves and fishes, trim a hangnail, or cut off an arm trapped under a pesky boulder, a good sharp <u>pocketknife</u> is of the highest priority.
9. When thou seekest warmth, not Divine Inspiration, from a burning bush, <u>waterproof matches</u> must first kindle that flame.

10. Rather than curse your own darkness, light thyself a <u>candle</u> (or any other type of <u>fire starter</u>).

Known collectively as the Ten Essentials in the mountain rescue community, they are the things that no one should ever leave home without.

But while spending every summer of my childhood and a goodly number of years as an adult in Kentucky, I rarely reached a number as high as ten as far as survival essentials when leaving the safety of my grandparents' home in search of adventure. In fact, the few essentials I did carry bore little resemblance to the real Ten Essentials. The Appalachian version of the Ten Essentials looked a little different.

For food, forget about Clif Bars or protein-packed gels. For the price of a single PowerBar, you could buy an entire box of Little Debbie Oatmeal Cream Pies. We rarely carried water. As a child, I carried plastic bottles of Dr. Pepper. As a young adult, I carried water's closest relative, Milwaukee's Best beer, to slake our thirst.

We did make sure to always carry a knife. Usually a big one. My 16-inch-long machete (made from a single lawnmower blade stuck into a homemade handle made of hickory) worked well to hack trails through the dense underbrush, dispatch the occasional copperhead, open cans of baked beans, gig frogs, and left lifelong reminders on my shins of how *not* to swing one.

For a fire starter, we carried plastic soda bottles full of gasoline. Which goes a long way toward explaining why I spent a good deal of my childhood sans eyebrows.

Given the damp, humid climate and relatively warm temps, cotton was always the fabric of choice. Usually worn in the form of butt-hugging Daisy Duke blue jean cutoff shorts worn in conjunction with knee-high tube sox during the '70s and anything in camouflage by the time the '80s rolled around.

Forget about a compass (the Yankees were north, Virginia was east, the South was south, and west was where some young man had once been commanded to go), a map (you needed a compass to make this item worth carrying), or a first-aid kit (who needed a first-aid kit when the opening of a Band-Aid package constituted the extent of your medical knowledge?). And besides, a trusty shotgun would do more to get you out of a jam than any of those things. Given the large numbers of venomous snakes, wild dogs, and wild people (there are more than a few well-protected pot-growing operations going on down in them thar hollers), a single 12-gauge easily equaled three of the Ten Essentials, and ensured we would always be home in time for Grandma's delicious (and lard-laden) home-cooked dinners.

While I was learning to appreciate the importance of the *real* Ten Essentials as part of my mountain rescue training, my divorce was finalized. Thankfully, I had little free time available to mourn the death of our marriage. RescueWorld was quickly becoming the place where I spent most of my free time. I was learning lots about mountain rescue and I was learning it fast.

One of the first things I figured out (after how lucky I was to still be alive) was that mountaineers usually made the best mountain rescuers—and not simply because they knew how to move and survive in treacherous mountain terrain. No, it was because mountaineers were privy to a hard-earned nugget of information that can't be learned from a book. Can't be gleaned from a self-help video. Can't be picked up from a motivational speaker who charges tens of thousands of dollars on the lecture circuit to share his tale of tragedy turned profitable business venture.

"Alpinism is the art of suffering," said Polish mountaineering legend Voytek Kurtyka. In other words, you won't find too many impatient mountaineers with low tolerances for pain.

You're also not likely to ever see mountaineering become an Olympic event, either, because mountaineering often consists of several long hours or days worth of slogging through absolute, mind-numbing boredom that are punctuated by a few seconds of sheer, piss-in-your-pants terror. Mountaineering is all about single-minded perseverance and the will to succeed.

Or at least, these were the things that everyone told me about mountaineering. I had yet to climb much more than a ladder in the course of my first year spent in Colorado. But as a Prospective Member (PM) of the Alpine Rescue Team, I was hoping to find other neophytes/suckers to venture into the backcountry with me and learn the ways of the Force.

One of my first forays into the mountains was with a fellow Alpine classmate by the name of Jerome Stiller. Jerome was a dark-haired, blue-eyed, former New Yorker with a ton of rock climbing experience. Being a former New Yorker, Jerome had no qualms whatsoever with sharing his first impression of me after our first Alpine Prospective Member class.

"What a kiss-ass!" he told me over a beer the week following the class. I had to admit that I could see where he was coming from, and why. Because at the end of that first class, Roy (the PM Director from Youngstown that I had already spoken with on the phone) put a name up on the blackboard in front of the class and said he'd award extra credit on our next quiz if we could identify the significance of the name he had just scrawled in big white letters. The name? Louis Sockalexis.

Now, Roy is a very serious, taciturn, and soft-spoken man who (in front of our class) we'd yet to see crack a smile. So obviously, this *had* to be an important person that everyone in mountain rescue needed to know about. Everyone in the class was certain that Louis Sockalexis *must* have been some great mountain rescuer, or world-famous climber. Perhaps a founding member of the Alpine Rescue Team. Or maybe a great Greek thinker who waxed philosophic on the subject of mountains.

I knew very well who Louis Sockalexis was. I saw his likeness on a daily basis, but I held my tongue as long as I could stand it. After a few minutes of guesses that were getting more and more outlandish, I raised my hand.

"It's Tom, right? Roy asked. I nodded. "Who is Louis Sockalexis?"

"It's *this* guy," I said as I rolled up my right sleeve to show the caricatured face that was tattooed on my right bicep. You see, Louis Sockalexis was a very popular, late nineteenth-century Native American baseball player. In fact, by most accounts, he was the *first* Native American baseball player, and he played for Cleveland. As in Indians (though back in those days they were known as the Cleveland Spiders). It was his highly caricatured (and many activists cry *too* caricatured) likeness that has been the logo for the Indians for the last fifty or so years. Chief Wahoo.

Roy finally cracked a smile, and I was labeled a kiss-ass. But when I explained to Jerome why I had that tattoo, and what it actually meant to me (that the Indians were the token team of Rustbelt losers and the only safe topic of conversation for male members of my family), he eased up on the kiss-ass label. A little.

So in concert with the lessons I was learning in RescueWorld, I took to learning the art of mountaineering. Given my meager income and experience, I did my best to learn as much as I could on the trips I could afford.

A few months after beginning our mountain rescue training, Jerome and I decided to tackle Dead Dog Couloir, a local mountaineering classic. Along with Jerome's friend, Jake, we would strap crampons to our feet, rope up, and use our ice axes to climb this narrow and steep (a 40–50 degree slope) permanent snowfield that led up to the saddle between Grays and Torreys Peaks (two of the four fourteeners in our response area). It was an impressive alpine climb with almost 3,000 feet of elevation gain. I have no idea why it is called Dead Dog Couloir.

Setting out at 2:00 a.m., we hiked the 7 miles to the base of the climb.

Known to mountaineers as an *alpine start*, this early, early morning launch for a long climb is the best way to cram a lot of climbing into a single day. On the way in, Jerome and I were feeling a little less than fresh, as we had stayed up much too late drinking beer and planning the next day's adventure. We were plagued that morning by something mountaineers call a *hangover*.

Jake, whom Jerome knew through a mutual friend, had wisely opted not to join us the night before for our pre-climb celebration. Jerome informed me that previous evening that he had rock climbed with Jake a few times, but had never done any mountaineering with him. And that Jake seemed to be a pretty good guy, as he had recently given Jerome a pair of insulated pants that had shrunk too much when Jake washed them after his last mountaineering trip. Jerome was wearing them that day.

After the long hike in, we roped up, fastened our crampons to our double plastic insulated boots, and started the steep climb. The rope was to be used in the event that if one of us took a fall, the other climbers could fall forward and dig in their axes and arrest that climber's fall when the rope got taut. For me, it was one of the first times I had the chance to use all of the expensive gear I had just spent most of my last paycheck to purchase. Wearing the crampons, I couldn't help but feel like a drunken duck walking around on razor blades, which, I suppose, was pretty much what I was.

Initially, Jake was our lead climber, with Jerome second and me third. Shortly after the stunning sunrise, I couldn't help but notice some peculiar smells wafting through the air, being carried by the downdraft from above. Wrinkling my nose in distaste, I wondered if there was a sewage treatment plant located at the 13,400-foot finish to the climb.

"Jesus Jake, what the hell?" Jerome shouted to Jake, who was tied to the rope about 30 feet above him. Jerome was tied in about the same distance above me. Obviously Jerome had caught a whiff as well.

"Guys, you might want to climb past me and take the lead, this always happens," he said breathlessly. "I have Irritable Bowel Syndrome, and every time I climb at altitude, it gets pretty foul."

"Well *that* little piece of information would have been nice to know before I was forced to climb for two hours with your smelly ass in my face," Jerome muttered as he climbed up and past Jake. I followed, holding my breath as I climbed through the noxious cloud of gas that hung around Jake like Pigpen's cloud of dirt in the Charlie Brown comics. I then ascended past Jerome to take the lead spot. Climbing lead on a steep snow climb like this one is grueling work, because you have to route-find *and* break trail through snow that gets softer and stickier as the day heats up.

It was a beautiful June morning, and an hour after the sun came up, I looked down between my legs and realized that we had climbed several hundred feet already. When I finished climbing a particularly steep spot that topped out at a small bench, I stopped, dug in my ice axe, and began belaying Jerome by running the rope around the head of my buried ice axe and pulling up slack as I held the axe into the snow by standing on it. This way, if Jerome took a fall, the rope would be tight and only allow him to fall a short distance. I had seen the technique (known as a boot-axe belay) illustrated in books, but this was my first chance to practice it in the field.

The rising sun, now reflecting off the blinding snow, was really starting to heat up the air around us. As I dutifully pulled up rope, Jerome and Jake climbed up toward the little bench where I was perched above and to the left of them. I caught a slight movement out of the corner of my eye—little snowballs were forming above and beside me, then rolling down the steep slope.

I was giddy by the indescribable beauty and thin air of the place where I sat. The sky was cloudless and so blue it hurt, and I couldn't help but feel like I was finally climbing out of the funk that had dogged me in the months leading up to the finalization of the divorce. This was one of those Kodak moments that so completely validated my move to Colorado.

Then the avalanche hit. Like a massive, undulating albino snake, it flowed past me, to my left, down the center of the narrow chute toward Jerome and Jake, who were only about 20 and 50 feet below me. I was on a slightly elevated bench off to the side of the chute, and it completely missed me, hissing as it went past.

"Avalanche! Avalanche!"

Jerome looked up, then dove to his left and fell face first onto the snow, burying the pick of his ice axe as he did so in the classic self-arrest stance.

Up above, I clamped down on the rope in preparation of what was to come as the torrent of snow narrowly missed Jerome but caught Jake with its full force.

Jake disappeared under the snow for just a moment, then popped back up as the rope between he and Jerome suddenly pulled taut. Jerome, in spite of having his ice axe and the front points of his crampons dug into the snow, was pulled down the slope as Jake was carried downhill by the snow.

And then suddenly the rope between Jerome and I was taut and slipping unchecked from around my axe and through my gloved hands. It was like trying to hold back an accelerating freight train, the force was so great. As the two climbers below were being pulled down the mountain, I looked to my right and realized with dismay that in another 10 feet, I'd be out of rope, and since the end of the rope was tied to my harness, I would soon be joining Jerome and Jake as they were unwillingly dragged down the 1,000-plus feet we had just climbed.

Nine feet, eight feet, seven feet, six feet …

Now back in Kentucky, Mike and I had always relished our redneck countdowns that typically ended with a glorious explosion. But in that fleeting moment of absolute terror, I knew that when I reached zero this time, there would be no cause for celebration. I would be yanked off my feet and pulled down the mountain like a hapless fisherman who's hooked a diving whale.

Five feet, four feet, three feet … and then the rope simply stopped moving. I looked down the slope, and Jerome was hanging below me, still dug in, attempting to arrest Jake's fall. Jake, hanging on the rope below Jerome, was buried chest deep in the snow that had suddenly stopped flowing and set up around him like concrete. His arms were free, thank God. He cried out with a grunt that both of his legs were bent painfully back behind him, but he didn't think they were broken.

As he hastily began to dig himself out, Jerome and I kept him on belay. If we went down to help him, we would have been exposed to any other subsequent slides that came barreling down the center of the chute. Even though we had on avalanche beacons and were armed with avalanche probes and shovels, we didn't want to push our luck. I kept a wary eye on the chute above in the event that if a second avalanche occurred while Jake worked frantically to free himself from the entombing snow, I could at least shout a warning.

"Oh God, Oh God," he said, as he dug frantically to free himself with his ice axe.

"What's wrong?" Jerome and I asked simultaneously.

"I just shit myself," Jake moaned.

"What?" we asked, again in unison.

"I SAID I JUST SHIT MY PANTS! AGAIN."

And indeed, as he freed himself from the snow and crawled out of the hole he'd been in, we were greeted by what had to be the foulest smell to ever come from a live human being's body.

And then *another* avalanche hit. But this one was smaller, and Jake was able to avoid it by climbing a few steps up and to his left.

Although we were within sight of the top of the nearly 3,000-foot climb, we decided that discretion was indeed the better part of valor and began our nerve-wracking down-climb. I was positively shaking from the effects of the adrenaline that had flooded my body, and kept a watchful eye on the slope above as we made our hasty retreat.

Once we were off the slope and out of danger, Jake immediately began shedding his harness and be-shitted Gore-Tex pants, thereby unleashing the full force of the biohazard that his innards had rejected and then ejected. His bowels weren't irritable, they were positively *furious*.

"Jesus man, we're still roped to you, couldn't you have waited?" Jerome choked, as we both hastily untied ourselves and backed away from Jake.

"Dammit, this always happens," Jake said, as he struggled to remove the rest of the ruined clothing from his lower half.

"Wait a minute, so you knew you would get sick from the altitude and didn't think to TELL US?" Jerome said. "What the fuck? Jesus God that is the worst thing I've ever smelled in my entire life!" Jerome is nothing if not outspoken.

Jake said nothing as Jerome and I walked to what we assumed was a safe distance away and readied ourselves for the long hike out. Fifteen minutes later, we looked up in time to see Jake walking at a fast clip away from us. When we shouted out to him, his one-finger reply made it clear that he had had enough of our company and wanted to walk out alone.

When Jerome and I got back to my truck, Jake was there waiting, his soiled clothing wrapped into a ball and tossed into the bed of my truck. We said little as the three of us piled into my truck and sat crammed together on the bench seat. We rode with the windows down. Jerome sat fuming about Jake's bowels *and* the fact that Jake had broken one of the rules of the back-country by taking off and hiking back solo. And when Jerome suddenly realized that those shrunken insulated pants he received as a gift from Jake (and was now wearing) had been disrespected in exactly the same manner as the pants that were now rolled up into a ball in the bed of the truck, he let Jake have it with both barrels.

It was a tense hour-long ride back to the parking lot where Jake had parked his car. He got out without a word, grabbed his gear, tossed it in his trunk, and drove away. I never saw him again.

I learned three very important lessons that day. One: Even in June, avalanches can happen in Colorado. Two: Never attempt a serious climb with someone you've never met before. Three: Do not climb with someone who shits himself.

After that thrilling experience, I continued my RescueWorld education by attending as many trainings and then missions as I could.

Just shy of a year after our odiferous mini-epic on Dead Dog Couloir, Jerome and I were sharing an ice-cold pitcher of beer with some fellow PM Alpine members at a pizza joint in downtown Golden after a nice mellow Friday afternoon of rock climbing at nearby North Table Mountain. It had become somewhat of a weekly ritual to meet and climb at the end of each week. We called our informal group the Friday Afternoon Rock Team, or FART. Yeah, real funny, I know. We cracked ourselves up, we did.

As we sat in the booth, we were joined by a dark-haired woman in her early twenties. Jerome introduced her as his friend, Maren. She couldn't stay long, she explained, because she was on her way to play Dungeons and Dragons with her brother and was running late. I'd never heard of a grown woman playing Dungeons and Dragons before. I was intrigued.

And when I next saw her a month later, I was a lot more than intrigued. Once again, I fell head over heels in love. But unlike the last time I fell, this time I landed on my feet, not my face. We were married that December, outside in the snow at 10,000 feet. We were wearing our mountaineering boots. Our reception was held at The Shack.

Life was good, and Jerome and I made big plans to climb a big mountain. The biggest one in North America, in fact.

When Jerome and I attempted to climb Denali (back then this mountain was still named Mount McKinley, so named for the rotund president born in my hometown of Niles, Ohio) in Alaska that next April, Maren was six months pregnant.

We didn't summit North America's highest peak on that attempt in 2000, but I was grateful to have a wife who was so supportive of my desire to climb and my addiction to mountain rescue.

Our daughter, Sarah, was born in July.

The following summer, I climbed Mount Rainier in Washington with a group of eight other Alpine members. And yet again, Maren was pregnant, this time with our son, Seth, who, like his older sister, was born at home in our little 900 square foot cabin. The only place in Colorado that I'd ever known as home was getting smaller by the minute.

My passion for climbing and rescue was putting a strain on my roofing job, so I moved into homebuilding and general contracting. I first worked with fellow Alpine member, Scott Amdur, then later with fellow home-birthing father, Jason Scott. Scott and Jason were both great partners and even better friends. I felt fortunate to escape eleven years of roofing with no drug addictions or surgically installed pins or rods holding me together. I count myself as one of the lucky few.

When my wife discovered that she was again pregnant (I've since come to believe that the birth control device known as the IUD stands for It's Utterly Defective), we were surprised but far from upset. We had always wanted three children, and always wanted them to be close in age. And besides, we had purchased our first home in nearby Conifer, and now had a whopping 300 more square feet of space.

When I explained to Maren in early 2004 that I wanted to attempt to climb Denali *again*, she was, once again, eerily supportive for a woman who would have to care for three children under four years of age, continue working her part-time job as a surveyor's assistant, and begin her internship as a homebirth midwife in my potentially month-long absence. I felt like a selfish jerk. Maybe I was.

This time, Jerome and I would be accompanied by fellow Alpine member, Angie Lucht. I felt much better about our chances of conquering the 20,320-foot peak than I did on our initial attempt. I was now in much better shape and more familiar with the art of suffering. Or so I thought.

Our spirits were high that early morning when we set out from the 17,200-foot camp for the summit. It was day twelve of our climb, and we were happy with the speed of our progress. We had the benefit of nearly twenty-four hours of daylight, but our proximity to the Arctic Circle meant that the oxygen content of the air at 20,000 feet was more like the oxygen content of the air on the more equatorial Mount Everest at 22,000 feet. Even the simplest of physical acts, like blinking, left us winded.

But as summit day wore on, the weather took an unexpected turn for the worse. At one point, I realized that we had been stumbling through the snow in a whiteout for over an hour. I could barely see the orange-flagged wands that marked the route. I estimated the winds were blowing at 25–40 miles per hour, and that the windchill had dropped the temps to the minus 50-degree Fahrenheit range.

All the other climbers attempting the summit that day had either summited and passed by us on their way back down, or turned around because of the worsening weather conditions. It was just us.

As we gained the summit ridge, our progress was painfully slow. For every step I took, I had to stop and take several breaths. This was the moment I had been working toward all of my adult life. The moment when I climbed a big mountain, stood on top, looked around, and considered my life a success and worth living.

I was leading the three of us, and we were all roped together. But with every step, the visibility worsened. When I lifted my foot and prepared to set it back down, I couldn't tell if I would be setting it down on snow, or out in space. The light was *that* flat. When I stopped at one point to rest and look around, I realized in horror that I couldn't see anything. I was enveloped in a hazy whitish-gray void. I couldn't even see Angie, the person tied to me 20 feet back. I turned and, hand over hand, followed the rope back to her. Jerome joined us from the back.

"What do you think we should do?" Angie yelled into the howling wind. We had been climbing for ten straight hours without a real break. We estimated, based on the topography and the shape of the ridge we were climbing, that we were at about 20,100 feet.

We decided to keep going up for another five or so minutes, and that if we couldn't see the next wand, we would turn around and head back. After all, we still had several hours of arduous hiking and route-finding to get back down to our tent at 17,200 feet. We would be hard pressed to make it back safely as it was. We were only about 120 vertical feet from the summit.

After ten minutes of hiking and seeing only gray and then more gray, I stopped. For that one brief moment, I was the highest person on the North American continent. I had only one reason to press on, and it was a selfish one—I wanted to summit. But I now had four compelling reasons to turn around: Maren. Sarah. Seth. Hannah. At that moment I realized, in my heart as well as in my head, that the summit was just a hunk of rock. The only importance it had was the importance I attributed to it. I had four living and breathing people back in the Rockies who loved me. And depended on me. That's what made my life a success and therefore worth living. Nothing meant more to me than that, and so I turned around.

As a man who spent the first half of his life making a lot of questionable decisions, I can say with pride that this was one of the smartest decisions I'd ever made.

Seventeen hours after we set out for the summit, we stumbled back into camp and collapsed into our tent. The next day, we broke camp and began our descent. When we reached the 14,000-foot camp, we knew we were only a day's hike from the landing strip where we would be picked up and flown back to the world of steaks and beer. We lightened our packs by handing out what extra food and fuel we had with us to the climbers who were camped out and acclimatizing.

But at 11,000 feet, we were hit with another storm. The storm was so bad that we spent the next four days stuck in our tent. We had to set an alarm to go off every two hours so we could go outside and dig out the tent to keep it from collapsing under the weight of the falling snow.

Since we had foolishly given away most of our food, we had to ration what little we had left. We were allotted one single packet of instant oatmeal per day. For four days. And if that quote about alpinism being the art of suffering was accurate, I felt like I was an accomplished master at that point.

When the weather *finally* broke, we quickly packed up and literally *ran* down the mountain to the airstrip. The next day we were back in civilization. I had lost a dozen pounds, and could not wait to get back home and hug my wife and kids.

After that trip, I backed off on my mountaineering and climbing and focused more on my duties in RescueWorld. Climbing suddenly seemed a very selfish endeavor to me, and business had picked up in RescueWorld to the point that I was getting my mountaineering fix from the increased number of searches and rescues we did.

So when Jerome asked me to participate with him in a joint mock mission with Boulder County's Rocky Mountain Rescue Group on May 17 in 2007 at Eldorado Canyon State Park, I was inclined to do so until I learned that it was to be an evening training. Jerome and I were to play the part of two climbers stranded mid-wall, and RMRG would respond to the late evening call to get in some practice carrying out this sort of rescue in the dark. But since I had already made plans to do something with the kids, I declined. My family was more important.

When my pager blew up with the news that RMRG was requesting mutual aid for a rescue in Eldorado Canyon that same afternoon, I was first under the impression that they had decided to move the joint training to the afternoon instead of the evening, and I paid little heed.

But soon after, my phone announced that it had an incoming call from Paul "Woody" Woodward (one of Alpine's Mission Leaders). I couldn't fight off the feeling that something was wrong.

"You need to get ahold of Jerome's next of kin, he's taken a fall in Eldo and RMRG is loading him onto Flight For Life as we speak," Woody informed me in a hurried and clipped tone. "He's headed to St. Anthony's Central, and unconscious. Can you get there to meet the chopper when they land and act as his advocate if you can't get ahold of any family?"

I said I could, and jumped into my truck and tried not to wreck as I dialed 411 on my phone. I knew that most of Jerome's family lived back East, but he did have a sister and two nephews in Pueblo. I was pretty certain her name was Susan, but did not know if she had kept her maiden name of Stiller or not. Thank God, she had.

I called the number that information provided, and she answered. I informed her of what I knew at that point, which wasn't much. By chance, her son, Jerome's twenty-something nephew, Ari, was in Denver at that time. She relayed his number, and I called him as well. He agreed to meet me at the hospital.

By the time I reached the hospital, I knew more about the accident from the phone call I received from Alpine Mission Leader Ric Ondrusek. He had made it to the rescue just as they loaded Jerome onto the helicopter.

When I declined Jerome's offer to act as a victim for the mock rescue, he instead enlisted Brian Stuebe, a veteran rock climber and Alpine member. The exercise wasn't scheduled till the evening, so they decided to get in a climb before the training. The route they chose, named Rewritten, is a Colorado Classic.

But as Jerome, who was leading, reached the top, Brian later reported that he heard Jerome yell "ROCK!" and two seconds later, he saw Jerome falling straight toward the location where he was belaying him, bouncing off the rock wall as he fell.

Apparently, Jerome was climbing on a section of rock where he could not place any protection (called a run-out), and had somehow fallen or been hit by falling rock. The pieces of protection that he had installed below pulled out when the force of his fall broke the rock flakes that held his protection in place. He had fallen between 60 and 80 feet before his last piece of protection held and Brian was able to arrest his fall.

He hung from the end of the rope above Brian, bloody and unconscious. Since they were a couple hundred feet up the climb, they needed to be rescued. For real. Luckily, it was a busy Saturday, and several climbers had heard Jerome's yell and watched him fall from across the canyon. One of the climbers said the fall was so horrific that he gave up climbing after witnessing it.

After 911 was called, RMRG was on-scene in no time, and carried out the technical rescue like the rock stars they are. In fact, Jerome could not have picked a better place to have an accident requiring a well-run technical rescue. RMRG is one of the best.

I didn't think about this much at the time, but I was experiencing the flip side of mountain rescue. Instead of being the rescuer, I was now the concerned friend, the distraught family member clinging to the hope that everything would turn out okay, and grasping for any information about what was going on.

I'd rarely, if ever, seen this aspect of the work we performed in Rescue-World. It was humbling, and gave me invaluable insight into just what goes through the minds of the folks I'd kept at an emotional arm's length back at Mission Base.

When I arrived at St. Anthony's Hospital, I rushed to the emergency room and spied a young man who looked like a younger and more blonde version of Jerome. This was indeed his nephew Ari, and I introduced myself to him as a nurse took us back to where Jerome had just been taken after being unloaded from the chopper up on the helipad.

Jerome was a mess. In addition to all the blood, his eyes were swelling shut. He had taken some serious hits to the head, and his doctor later said that his helmet had undoubtedly saved his life. As soon as Jerome recognized us, he made an attempt to sit up, but was held down gently by the doctor attending to him. As the doctor turned to face us, I was relieved to see that it was Dr. Brian Rolfson, one of our Physician Advisors for Alpine. Dr. Rolfson was also a climber—both Jerome and I had ice climbed with him in the past. He was in the process of assessing Jerome, who was (mostly) regaining consciousness.

"By the way Tom, have you met my nephew Ari?" Jerome asked weakly after noticing that he was standing next to me.

"I have, we just met out in the lobby," I informed him.

Since Dr. Rolfson knew me, and Ari was family, we were allowed to stay in the room.

My friend's injuries were significant. Dr. Rolfson informed us that he had shattered the left orbital below his eye, his right scapula was broken, the fourth lumbar in his spine was broken, his right tibial plateau was broken, he was concussed, and covered from the top of his head to the tips of his toes with contusions and lacerations that required dozens of stitches.

"Tom, by the way, have you met my nephew Ari?" Jerome asked again.

"I have, we just met in the lobby," I said. Again.

I shot a quizzical look at the doctor, who informed me that repetitive speech was a common side effect for someone suffering a serious blow to the head. And since they hadn't yet run any tests on Jerome, it was too early to determine if any permanent brain damage had occurred.

"What's your level of pain right now, buddy?" Dr. Rolfson asked Jerome, who was trying to see what part of his leg was presently being stitched up. "Give me a number between one and ten."

"Six," Jerome said in an almost dreamy tone.

The doctor seemed satisfied with this answer, and turned his suturing efforts to a large cut on Jerome's face.

"Tom, by the way, have you met my nephew Ari yet?"

"Doc, is there any way to make this son of a bitch any less ugly while you're fixing him up?" I asked with a smile.

Although Jerome was lying still, with his eyes closed as the doctor and the attending nurse sutured a huge facial laceration, he weakly lifted his left arm and flipped me off.

Jerome was going to be fine. Mostly.

After twelve days in the hospital and two months in a wheelchair, Jerome still had very little idea what caused him to fall, and this gnawed at his very core. Indeed, Jerome was one of the most cautious and safest climbers I'd ever met. That was why I climbed with him in the first place. The fact that someone as careful as Jerome could suffer such a fate really shook me up.

At first, Jerome seemed to power through his recovery with very few physical or emotional scars. Hell, two hours after the cast was removed from his leg, he was out on the rocks, climbing like nothing had ever happened.

But in the weeks and months that followed, it became obvious that Rewritten was more than just the name of the climb where Jerome had fallen. It was also what the accident had done to Jerome's love of climbing. It had somehow rewritten a part of Jerome's DNA, his very essence. He eventually lost all interest in climbing and sold every piece of gear he had accumulated in the thirty-odd years he'd identified himself, first and foremost, as a climber.

Soon after that, he lost interest in RescueWorld as well, and left the Alpine Rescue Team. His absence left only myself and Rich Solosky from our original PM class of fourteen members.

"I didn't even realize that I had lost interest in rock climbing until the day I looked at the latest issue of *Climbing* magazine that lay on my coffee table, untouched and unread since I had received it in the mail days earlier. I used to devour those things the second I got my hands on them," he later confessed. "That's when I realized it was time to move on."

It was hard to think of my friend as being anything other than a climber and a rescuer. But I guess redefining the way you think of someone is a hell of a lot easier to do than giving their eulogy. RescueWorld may have lost a rescuer, but at least my kids have managed to keep hold of a man they've come to think of as their Uncle Jerome. And for that, I am truly grateful.

It was hard to press on in RescueWorld without my pal by my side. I was beginning to realize that although it's relatively easy to join a mountain rescue team, *staying* on a mountain rescue team is another matter entirely.

Search

Map, compass, and GPS skills are a must when we are carrying out searches. Photo by Tom Wood.

Search and rescue missions often happen when Mother Nature is having a bad day, as was the case here. In early 2015, we spent two days searching for a missing hiker in whiteout conditions near St Mary's Glacier in Clear Creek County. Once conditions cleared and the avalanche danger lessened, the hiker was found buried in an avalanche by a search dog from Summit County. Photo by Tom Wood.

A Tale of Two Marines:
The Thin Line Between Pity and Disgust

If you ever want to piss off a Colorado Front Range mountain rescuer, bring up the name Lance Hering. Just don't expect them to actually *admit* that they are pissed.

As non-paid professional rescuers, we typically shy away from publicly passing judgment on those who need our services. (We don't like to say *un-paid professional rescuers, that makes it sound as if we receive no compensa-tion at all for our efforts in RescueWorld. We receive plenty of compensation, it's just not in the form of dollars and cents.) We do this because once we start passing judgment of this sort, we're climbing out onto a slippery slope.

As I mentioned earlier, I have done (much) more than my fair share of stupid things in my day, and to look down my nose at the actions of one of our subjects would smack of hypocrisy in my book.

Ninety-nine percent of the time, when someone needs to be rescued or searched for in the backcountry, they have made a mistake of one sort or another. These mistakes range in seriousness from the simple honest ones (tripped and broke a leg or didn't bring extra batteries for a headlamp or GPS), to the more blatant and borderline stupid ones (took acid and attempted to climb a 700-foot-high technical rock climb or brought one day's worth of food and water for a seven-day hike in order to lose weight—both true stories).

Once, we even responded to the same place for the same person three times in the same day (a troubled teenager who kept escaping from a group home and scaling a nearby cliff and threatening to jump off if his counselors didn't promise to let him go home).

Very rarely are we asked to locate or rescue a completely blameless per-son in the backcountry. Lightning strikes come to mind.

But just because we aren't supposed to pass judgment on the motives or actions of our subjects, that's not to say we don't from time to time. We are only human, after all. And as human beings, it can be difficult at times to keep our personal feelings locked up. Which brings me—somewhat hesitantly—back to the case of Lance Hering.

It was a beautiful summer evening on August 29, 2006, when Lance Hering, twenty-one, and his pal Steve Powers, twenty, met up with the intention of spending some quality time together in the great Colorado outdoors. Powers later told authorities that their informal plan was to spend a couple hours bouldering in Eldorado Canyon State Park, a world-renowned rock climbing Mecca located between Boulder and Golden in Boulder County.

Trad climbing (short for traditional climbing, which involves the climbers installing their protection as they climb, clipping in the rope to each piece of protection as they ascend) in the cool evening at Eldo (as the park is commonly called) is not all that uncommon a practice.

Many of the south-facing routes in Eldo get blasted with direct summer sunlight for most of the day, which makes them too hot to comfortably climb during the afternoon in the summer months until the sun dips below the mountains to the west.

Bouldering in Eldo, on the other hand, *is* an uncommon practice. A completely different type of rock climbing, bouldering involves free climbing around on the rocks with no ropes, and never climbing more than 10–15 feet off the ground. Bouldering only requires two pieces of gear: a pair of rock climbing shoes and (most of the time) a crash pad situated below the boulderer to cushion the fall of a climber who "peels off" the rock. It's a good workout and a great way to improve technique, but not a type of rock climbing that is very popular in a place famed for the dizzying heights and aesthetic beauty of its climbs.

According to Powers, shortly after the sun set, Hering peeled of the rock from about a height of about a dozen feet, struck his head (he wore no helmet and they had no crash pad with them) and rolled down to the trail. Horror-struck, Powers rushed down to where his friend lay. Blood poured from a gash on Hering's head. According to Powers.

Powers yelled several times for help, but none came, since most climbers had left the park once darkness set in. Afraid to leave his friend, who drifted in and out of consciousness, he stayed by his friend's side all night. Again, according to Powers.

Just before the sun came up, Powers decided to risk leaving his friend alone while he made the long hike out of the park to find a pay phone to make the call for help. At 5:13 a.m. on August 30, 2006, Steve Powers reached a phone and reported his climbing partner Lance Hering had taken a fall and hit his head late in the previous afternoon while bouldering in Eldorado Canyon.

When Powers returned with Boulder County Sheriff's Office deputies and members of the Rocky Mountain Rescue Group (RMRG) a short time later, they found some blood on a rock, a water bottle, and nothing else. Hering was nowhere to be found.

The search for Hering, who was a lance corporal in the United States Marine Corps home on leave from the war in Iraq, was on. The following timeline is pieced together from reports made public by the Boulder County Sheriff's Office and the *Boulder Daily Camera.*

Day One: No trace of Lance Corporal Lance Hering is discovered, despite the efforts of twenty-five searchers from RMRG, a helicopter flyover by the KCNC TV news helicopter, and three dog teams from Front Range Rescue Dogs. Hering's Marine Corps photo and description is circulated to several area hospitals in the event that the dazed and wandering Hering might be suffering from amnesia, picked up by someone and brought in for treatment. Hering's family is notified of his disappearance. Powers assists searchers as they expand their search out from Hering's last seen point.

Day Two: Eldorado Canyon State Park effectively closes to the public as searchers comb the park for clues to Hering's whereabouts. No sign of Hering is discovered.

Day Three: The search area widens, and searchers from across the state join authorities and Hering's family in the search effort. No additional clues to Hering's location are discovered.

Day Four: More than a hundred professional rescuers from a dozen Colorado SAR teams, now under the direction of the Boulder County Emergency Services staff, are augmented by more than a hundred additional citizen and military volunteers as they search Eldorado Canyon and nearby trails. The search effort is complicated by uncharacteristically cool, wet weather and heavy fog, which makes for treacherous footing (so treacherous that a searcher with the Arapaho Rescue Patrol slips, injures his ankle, and has to be evacuated via a litter trail-carry to a waiting ambulance). A Denver Police Department helicopter takes advantage of an afternoon break in the weather and makes use of their Forward-Looking Infrared equipment, hoping to locate any significant heat sources (like the heat generated by a still-living but unconscious lance corporal) inside the park. All search efforts once again prove to be unsuccessful.

Day Five: Once again, Boulder County Emergency Services supervisors field approximately two hundred professional and civilian ground searchers, targeting the original area where Hering was last seen four days earlier. A large group of retired and active duty marines from across the country joins in the massive search effort. The Hering family makes a public appeal for private citizens to join in the search of the peripheral areas around Eldorado Canyon State Park. The busy command post for the search is relocated to a larger area just outside the park to minimize its environmental impact.

Day Six: More of the same.

Day Seven: Even more of the same.

Day Eight: Emergency Services officials scale back the search based on the lack of success to that point.

Day Nine: Steve Powers is arrested and jailed by the Boulder County Sheriff's Department on misdemeanor charges that he falsely reported the disappearance of Lance Hering. An arrest warrant is also issued for Lance Hering on similar charges.

Investigators had become suspicious of Powers almost immediately, since there were several holes and discrepancies in his story. They cited the improbability of his timeline of events, and the fact that his narrative of the event begged more questions than it answered. The complete lack of clues and evidence gathered by the hundreds of searchers over the course of eight days also led authorities to believe that something was amiss. When Powers was at last confronted by detectives, he reluctantly admitted that he had helped Hering stage the disappearance in the hopes that the faked death and/or disappearance would give Hering a head start on his escape from the marines. Powers claimed that Hering desperately wanted to avoid returning to active duty in Iraq.

The sheriff's department also announces that it plans to seek restitution for the tens of thousands of dollars expended in the search effort. (Most of the expenses incurred were for the overtime of the sheriff's department personnel and for the use of several private helicopters involved in the search. Not one cent of expense was incurred from the use of professional volunteer SAR members who searched.)

The official search effort in Eldorado Canyon State Park is called off. It is the largest and most expensive search ever conducted in Boulder County.

Day 18: The Marine Corps officially declares Hering "away without leave" when he does not return to his unit.

Day 22: The Boulder County Sheriff's Department makes public the surveillance tape that shows Hering boarding a Greyhound bus in Denver at about the same time that Powers led searchers back into Eldorado Canyon State Park to search for him. The bus is headed toward Iowa.

Day 35: Powers tells the *Boulder Daily Camera* that Hering feared returning to his unit because they would be re-deployed to Iraq, and that Hering could be suffering from a Post-Traumatic Stress Disorder as a result of the combat he had previously witnessed in Iraq on his first tour of duty there.

Day 808: On November 16, 2008, a now long-haired and gaunt-looking Lance Hering and his father, Lloyd Hering, are arrested by authorities in Port Angeles, Washington, as they attempt to board a private plane piloted by the senior Hering. Lance's father, a Vietnam vet himself and a commercial pilot, says he only recently learned of his son's whereabouts. Further, he says that he was preparing to fly his son to Virginia to see a psychiatrist, then to Texas to meet with an attorney, and finally on to Camp Pendleton so that his son could turn himself in. But when police examine the digital camera belonging to the father, authorities find photos of Lance Hering and his father hanging out together at the Burning Man Festival in Nevada earlier that year.

That's the very abbreviated, very objective recounting of Lance Corporal Lance Hering's staged disappearance and subsequent arrest. Here's a more subjective look.

As a member of the Alpine Rescue Team, I participated in days four and five of the search for Hering. Being a former marine myself, I felt it my duty to look for the young soldier. In the course of those two days, we found a lot of things that were never reported by the sheriff's department or the media. We found a very disgruntled mother bear with her cubs. A hole full of rattlesnakes was discovered by a searcher when she inadvertently stepped into it (barely avoiding getting bitten by the dozen or so angry reptiles).

We found a pile of human vomit (yes, vomit) near the point on the trail where Hering was last seen. I was more than a little thankful that I was not the rescuer asked to scrape the chunky pile of barf into a plastic bag and carry it back to the command post so it could later be analyzed in the hopes that it contained traces of Hering's DNA.

I heard rumors that more than a few secretly grown marijuana plants were discovered in the more remote corners of the park.

But my biggest discovery was this: I really hoped that someone would find Lance alive. I was genuinely moved by the other former marines searching for Hering. At the end of both frustratingly fruitless days that I spent searching, I saw several former marines hug each other like the long lost brothers that they were as they openly wept over their failed efforts to find a fellow Jarhead. Many had come from out of state to participate in a search that obviously brought up a lot of past issues for them. I felt that many of these former marines were searching for something other than a lost and injured fellow marine. They seemed to be searching for a way to make peace with something they had lost in the course of their service. It was indeed hard not to feel a fierce sense of kinship with these total strangers. And for the missing lance corporal as well. As the saying goes, "Once a marine, always a marine."

When I personally witnessed Hering's mother collapse, overcome with grief, dehydration, and exhaustion as she walked out of the canyon at the end of another day of searching in vain for her son, my sense of resolve to find a fellow marine strengthened.

When I later discovered that the young marine's disappearance was a sham, I first felt a powerful wave of anger at being duped. Then disgust with the young man for his desertion, swiftly followed by a dizzying sense of déjà vu. The last time I'd seen a disillusioned marine take such extreme measures to evade the clutches of the USMC was twenty-one years earlier, when I was in the midst of my own training to become a Leatherneck.

My decision to join the marines was not one based on altruism alone (though that did play a role). I needed money for college.

The summer before a tornado ripped through Niles, Ohio, and forced the cancellation of my high school graduation ceremony, my parents called me into a meeting around the old roll-top desk in their bedroom. This cluttered old desk (refinished as a joint effort between my mother and I) served as the family office. My parents explained to me that if I had my heart set on college, I had two options. I could work for a year after graduation, live at home, and save my money for tuition. Or, I could join the Marine Corps Reserves in the hopes that the government would help pay tuition.

My father's salary at Packard Electric and my mother's wages at the nursing home just weren't enough to support my other three siblings still at home, pay the bills, and put me through college.

I've always been so very grateful to my parents for that brief but honest assessment of their financial status. I felt like it was the first time that they treated me as an adult (which of course is a moment so many teenagers yearn for but sadly never get to experience).

After this State of the Family Address, I signed the next eight years of my life over to the Marine Corps Reserves. This allowed me to get tuition money for my first semester at Kent State University without falling a year behind my peers. I'd still have to work two part-time jobs to get through college, and still have to rely on my folks to help pay what I couldn't cover—but at least my enlistment made college a possibility. No one on either side of my family had ever graduated from college, and I had high hopes to be the first.

So at the tender age of seventeen, I pledged my life to my country. I entered the three-month-long torture and brainwashing (and believe it or not, I don't mean that in a bad way) program known as Marine Corps Boot Camp on Parris Island, South Carolina, in June of 1985.

Back in 1985, when I was a seventeen-year-old recruit at Parris Island.

Say what you want about the military, but when it comes to the marines, what you see is what you get. There are no illusions about using your experience as a marine to find a career when you re-enter the civilian world. The Marine Corps trains you to be a warrior. Period.

You don't leave the corps with aspirations for a career in anything (unless you want to grow up and be a civilian contractor for Blackwater in Iraq, that is). If you get out with a pulse and an intact sense of self, that's reward enough. I liked that. So I guess you could say the brainwashing worked.

I began my training at Parris Island with my pal Joe Hendry, with whom I had attended Niles McKinley High School. Joe would also be my roommate at Kent State University when we finished boot camp. If we finished boot camp.

My training went along without event until late one morning, about midway through that sweltering summer (the South Carolina heat was so withering, in fact, that I went in weighing 178 pounds, and left at 155) when our drill instructor, Staff Sergeant Tucker, called us all to attention at the foot of our racks.

"Private Lowe, front and center," he said.

We all stood locked at attention, our eyes tracking down the alphabetically ordered row of recruits to Private Lowe's vacant spot. Momentarily, the sullen form of Private Lowe emerged from the drill instructor's glassed-in cubicle/office at the end of the barracks.

Private Lowe stopped in front of the drill instructor, facing him, his back to his seventy-plus fellow recruits of Platoon 2063 who lined either side of the walkway that separated the two perfectly spaced rows of beds.

"Private Lowe, about face!"

As Lowe pivoted and turned to face us, none of us had a clue what this was all about. But it was obvious that we were looking upon the tear-streaked face and slumped form of a defeated man.

I remembered that Lowe was absent from morning chow that day, but that was not surprising. Private Lowe was on weight control (in typical sensitive marine parlance, the slightly overweight Lowe was considered a "fat-body") and had some dietary restrictions that frequently limited his trips to the Mess Hall.

"Lowe, go get your foot locker, bring it up here, and start packing your shit," Tucker commanded.

As Lowe dragged his footlocker (the footlocker eliciting a nerve-jangling screech as it scraped across the spotless concrete floor) back to center stage under the watchful eye of the drill instructor and began loading its contents into two large green duffel bags, the room was completely devoid of any sound other than the soft sobs that escaped Lowe as he packed.

"I want you all to look at this fat piece of shit," Staff Sergeant Tucker said, as he began to pace up and down our ranks. "Last night, Private Lowe here thought he could escape the clutches of my beloved corps by trying to kill himself."

Tucker, his barrel chest puffed out to its fullest, paused for effect as Private Lowe continued to "pack his shit." An impossibly long stream of snot hung off the end of his pimpled nose, unwiped.

(Attempted suicide is not an uncommon side-effect of serving in the corps. Although it is the smallest of all branches in the military—aside from the U.S. Coast Guard—marines consistently lead all other branches in suicide attempts according to both the U.S. Military and the Centers for Disease Control and Prevention.)

"Private Lowe is a FUCKUP!" Tucker yelled, making us all jump. "But he's not a fuckup because he tried to kill himself. He's a fuckup because he failed," Tucker continued. "And the corps doesn't need failures. Private Lowe is such a fuckup, he couldn't even kill himself properly!

"Anybody here want to know the funny part?" Tucker asked. No, none of us wanted to hear the funny part, because we all strongly suspected that it wouldn't be funny at all, not one little bit. But of course he told us anyway.

"The funny part here is that this retard tried to kill himself by swallowing a bottle of Tylenol. That's like ASPIRIN!!" he screamed, as he bent down over Private Lowe, hands on his hips. (Lowe had been given some mild painkillers by one of the camp dentists after having a tooth removed a few days earlier.) Private Lowe simply knelt there in front of his empty footlocker with a blank look on his face.

"I think this is some seriously funny shit. In fact, I want this entire platoon to join me in laughing at this seriously funny shit," he said. When he was greeted by silence, the drill instructor set his jaw and growled, "Laugh! That. Is. An. Order!"

Now, I am embarrassed to say that I participated in this disgusting farce for about the first ten seconds of the minute/eternity we were commanded to laugh. Those ten seconds made me feel dirtier than all the toilets I scrubbed earlier that day. *Do they make disinfectants for your soul?* I wondered silently. I quit laughing.

I knew why Staff Sergeant Tucker was staging this pathetic melodrama in front of us. As Tucker knew, perhaps the only thing many of us fear worse than death is embarrassment or ridicule. In the Spartan, twisted (but discomfortingly effective) psychology of the Marine Corps Drill Instructor, Tucker was trying to dissuade anyone else in the platoon from contemplating suicide as an escape option at the expense of Private Lowe (who was now beyond his help anyway and would soon be beyond his reach).

But although I understood his reasons for making an example of Lowe, it didn't mean that I had to continue playing along in what was likely the worst, lowest moment of that man's life.

When the echoes of the forced laughter subsided, Lowe finished packing his bags and Staff Sergeant Tucker commanded him to turn and face his soon-to-be former comrades one last time. It was the highly polished floor that held Lowe's gaze.

"Are there any pussies in this room who feel sorry for this piece of shit?" Tucker asked, as he eyeballed the ranks of recruits still standing at attention, daring us to challenge his methods. The silence in the room was now as heavy as the moisture-laden July air. Seconds ticked by. Sweat trickled down the faces of the cast-in-stone recruits lining each side of the barracks.

My body may have been standing still and rigid, but my mind was racing as my eyeballs darted around the room to see if anyone would dare pick up the gauntlet that Tucker threw down. I felt horribly ashamed for Private Lowe, who had admittedly been somewhat of a sad sack, but undeserving of this kind of ridicule. I also felt a small amount of kinship for the man since, like me, he hailed from northeast Ohio. A town called Stow, actually. Private Lowe from Stow. A few months and a lifetime earlier, I had probably sat in the bleachers across the football field from him as our teams played each other.

At that point, I had something of an epiphany. If being a marine meant being fearless and standing up for what you believed in, I reasoned, then I wasn't being true to either myself or the corps by being a sheep and not voicing my true feelings about this situation. To my mind, standing there in silence and saying nothing was akin to being an accessory to spiritual murder. High-minded lessons in group psychology aside, I realized that these next few hours experienced by Private Lowe might well be some of the most important in his life.

Staff Sergeant Tucker had made his point, now someone needed to step in and help a wounded soldier. My heart in my throat, I decided to err on the side of my conscience, even though it likely meant a beating. (Drill instructors were not supposed to physically strike you anymore, but they did anyway. They were just more selective about when and where they did it.) All these thoughts raced through my mind in a matter of seconds. *Oh fuck it,* I thought, and startled myself by actually speaking up.

"Senior Drill Instructor Staff Sergeant Tucker, this recruit feels sorry for Private Lowe," I said in a cracked and uneven voice as I pried my feet off the spotless floor and took a step forward.

Tucker comically jumped up into the air as if someone had rammed a hot poker up his ass and raced over to me in disbelief.

Now, Tucker was at least a foot shorter than my six-foot, four-inch frame. It was usually hard to keep my mouth from involuntarily twisting into a one-sided smile as the diminutive (but muscular) man had to push a footlocker up next to me and jump on top of it in order to get his ebony face as close to mine as possible. (I strongly suspected that Tucker suffered from a classic case of Short Guy Syndrome, since his ire seemed disproportionately focused on the taller recruits in the platoon. In fact, in his office earlier that week, he had cracked me over the head with his telephone three times because I responded to one of his height-challenged fits of anger with an involuntary smirk.)

But at that moment, I could find nothing amusing about the situation, and simply stood at attention with my mouth set and my eyes fixed straight ahead.

"Are you a pussy, Private Wood?" he bellowed, as he kicked Private Lowe's empty footlocker across the floor toward me and jumped on top of it, pointing his rigid left index finger at my left eyeball and waving his right palm (all five fingers splayed wide) an eighth of an inch from the tip of my nose.

"No sir!"

"Then what do you have to say for yourself?"

"Sir, this recruit feels sorry for Private Lowe, and this recruit is not a pussy. That is all, sir."

Although I realized I had singled myself out (something you strive very hard to avoid in Marine Corps Boot Camp) by speaking out, this was the very first time in my young life that I can honestly say that I stuck my neck out and took a hard stance on something I believed in, and was willing to pay the price for it. Consequences be damned. I also felt like I wanted to throw up.

If you've ever seen films like *Full Metal Jacket* or *An Officer and a Gentleman* or *Jarhead,* you can imagine the expletives and dressing-down by Staff Sergeant Tucker that followed, so I don't think I need to go into detail about that.

At the end of his rant, I was instructed to pick up and carry both of Private Lowe's heavy duffel bags and escort him past the other recruits, down the exterior concrete stairs, and across the manicured lawns to Sick Bay. This was where the Other Than Honorable Discharge would be initiated that would likely follow Private Lowe around for the rest of his life.

Our trip to the Sick Bay was, for the most part, a quiet one. What do you say to someone who feels so trapped by a decision he's made that he's willing to end his life to escape the responsibility for such a decision? Never mind that Lowe attempted to kill himself by overdosing on aspirin. I had no doubts that if other more potent means had been available to him, he would have used them (the marines keep a close count on all ammunition issued to recruits during boot camp for this very reason).

What can you say but, "Sorry, man." I could think of no other comforting words. It was as if the whole of my efforts at communicating my compassion went into providing fuel for my initial admission of pity to the drill instructor. That was all she wrote, the tank was empty, the well was dry, and I could not think of a single helpful word to say to Private Lowe. I simply set his duffle bags down beside him at the Sick Bay admissions desk, said "Sorry, man," did an about face, and marched briskly out into the South Carolina sun.

Surprisingly, there really was no backlash for my admission of pity for Private Lowe from Staff Sergeant Tucker. Was this because I had begrudgingly earned the drill instructor's respect by voicing my honest opinion? Probably not. In the sometimes twisted logic of soldiering, he did exactly what was expected of him. Tucker was actually a hell of a good drill instructor, and I still respected him despite the Lowe incident. I think (or maybe hope) that he knew my prolonged punishment and ridicule would have only served as an unpleasant reminder of the incident for *all* of us in Platoon 2063.

There were no words of encouragement or congratulations from my fellow recruits for the stand I took on behalf of Private Lowe. In fact, a couple of my fellow recruits took to calling me a pussy whenever they had the chance, and shoved elbows into my side as they walked past me in the chow line. That was all good and fine with me. My conscience was clean (disinfected even!), and I slept like a baby in my rack from then on.

After that day, I never heard the incident mentioned again, and it was almost as if the whole thing had been created completely within the confines of my own stubbly shaved head. I went on to serve the next several years as a combat photographer (which is a *lot* less cool than it sounds) while I completed my journalism degree at Kent State University.

I had mostly forgotten the incident until more than two decades (and a full head of hair) later, when I was confronted with the story of yet another young marine who was desperately in search of an escape hatch from the corps.

As I discovered in the days after Powers was arrested for faking Hering's disappearance, the *real* Lance Hering story had begun in 2004, when Hering and his pal Steve Powers first became partners in crime. For real.

According to their cover story, they explained to the court that they were "urban explorers," not burglars, when the police discovered them trying to gain entrance to a Boulder department store through a roof hatch after tripping an alarm. The fact that they fled the scene, briefly eluded police, and were clad in black and wearing ski masks did little to help their case.

They were each charged with felony attempted burglary and given a two-year deferred sentence on the condition that they stayed out of trouble. Hering's enlistment in the Marine Corps was indeed viewed by the courts as a step in the right direction. Hering and Powers kept their word and stayed out of trouble. For a whole eighteen months, anyway. When both Powers and Hering were charged with the falsified missing report charge while Hering was home on leave, it was a misdemeanor and a violation of their deferred sentence agreement.

Powers, who apparently did not have as good an attorney as Hering, was convicted. He would now carry the stigma associated with being a convicted felon for the rest of his life. Until Hering was found and arrested, Powers was made to pay more than $30,000 in restitution to Boulder County. Hering, on the other hand, received what amounted to a slap on the wrist from both the marines and Boulder County once he resurfaced.

Although desertion during a time of war is still listed in the military law books as a crime punishable by death, Hering served only thirty-three days in the brig, did not receive a reduction in rank, and was simply discharged from the military.

Hering struck a deal with Boulder County prosecutors and pleaded guilty to a misdemeanor charge of false reporting for his faked disappearance from Eldorado Canyon State Park. In exchange for the guilty plea, he avoided going to trial and received a continued deferred sentence on his original felony attempted burglary case from 2004. Hering was also required to complete two hundred hours of community service and attend therapy sessions for treatment of the stress and trauma that stemmed from his tour in Iraq. His family paid restitution to Boulder County. On April 5, 2011, all charges were wiped from his record when he successfully completed the terms of his agreement with the Boulder District Attorney.

So while the whole disappearance hoax in Eldorado Canyon was Hering's idea, and it was Hering that deserted the military, he walked away with a clean record and his friend Steve Powers is now a convicted felon.

In the years since then, Hering had more run-ins with the legal system, and became somewhat of a celebrity within the Boulder climbing community.

Although both Private Lowe and Lance Corporal Hering sought the same end (a way out of their obligations to the Marine Corps), their methods differed wildly. As did my own personal feelings for each of the two young men. One marine's escape attempt filled me with pity and sympathy, the other with incredulous disgust and even anger.

At first blush, my pity for Private Lowe and my disgust for Lance Corporal Hering (even to me) seemed utterly out of whack and without merit. Lowe never even made it through boot camp, while Hering not only made it through boot camp with high marks, but served in a combat zone in a time of war before deciding to renege on his sworn oath to serve.

Upon closer inspection, I came to realize that it was the circumstances surrounding Hering's desertion (for that's what it was, no matter what his attorneys later tried to call it) that really left a sour taste in my mouth and pushed my buttons. And since I've never actually met Lance Hering and looked him in the eye, I can only draw my own conclusions from the information I have gathered since those two frustrating days I spent beating the bushes in 2006.

So this brings me back to my original conundrum. Why the pity for Private Lowe and the disgust for Lance Corporal Hering's actions? Maybe because I felt that Hering bought his way out of trouble. I sincerely doubt that Private Lowe's father picked him up in a private plane and flew him all over the country to meet with specialists and attorneys after his failed suicide attempt. Hell, I'll bet he was lucky if the marines even paid for his Greyhound bus ticket back home.

Maybe because I felt angry with Hering because he and Powers duped the entire SAR community into looking for Hering. Nobody likes being lied to, especially when that lie leads to *hundreds* of people putting themselves at risk for someone who didn't even care enough at the time to tell his own mother not to worry. There were a dozen different ways Lance Hering could have staged his disappearance that wouldn't have put hundreds of caring, concerned searchers at risk. After all, it wasn't like he disappeared from a wheat field in Kansas or even from downtown Boulder. Eldorado Canyon State Park is *not* a safe area to unleash a couple hundred civilians (many with the best of intentions but absolutely no SAR or backcountry experience). There are cliff faces hundreds of feet tall, loose rocks everywhere, and all the dangerous wildlife you could hope to find in Colorado.

Maybe I was angry because it is such a tall order for us in the SAR community to convince the public that there should never be a charge for search and rescue when we have the Lance Herings and the "Balloon Boys" of the world hoaxing us into believing them and then taking advantage of our willingness to help our fellow man.

When I scrutinize my personal feelings about Private Lowe and Lance Corporal Hering, I realize that it is indeed a very fine line between pity and disgust. I look at both marines as wounded warriors. But as I see it, what separates them is that Lowe's actions hurt no one but himself. Hering's deceptions put others at risk on his behalf—some in the rugged terrain of Eldorado Canyon, some in the legal system. And while Lowe stood face to face with all the repercussions of his decisions, in Hering's case it was the people who tried to help and protect him who paid the highest price for his actions.

Being Found is Not the Same Thing as Being Saved

ALPINE MISSION LEADER CALL DISPATCH

REF OVERDUE HIKERS,

49 YO MALE AND 9 YO FEMALE AT ECHO LAKE

This message on my pager (which jolted me from the twin pleasures of a perfectly cooked cheeseburger and a sunny, lazy Saturday afternoon) was unique among the hundreds I had received in my then thirteen years as a volunteer mountain rescuer. This seemingly innocuous page from the Clear Creek County Sheriff's Office on April 22, 2010, filled me with a heretofore unknown sense of terror and inescapable creeping dread.

My world had changed, my circumstances had become inverted. I was no longer the naive offspring of a backwoods boy from the wilds of central Pennsylvania and a teenage bluegrass gospel singer from West Virginia. My ass didn't belong to Uncle Sam. My days as a neophyte journalist—observing but rarely interceding—were long past. Shit, I couldn't even play the mountain rescue rookie card anymore.

I was now a Mission Leader (notice the caps here) for the Alpine Rescue Team. And since I was the designated on-call Mission Leader, the responsibility for organizing the search and rescue of these two (poor unfortunate) human beings rested solely in my lap. *God help them.*

How could this have happened? Surely there must have been a mistake. I had spent more than a decade trying to evade the cloak of responsibility that eventually weighs so heavily upon the shoulders of those on our rescue team who are blessed/cursed with longevity in mountain rescue and a burdensome sense of ... duty.

Even though I was now forty-three years old, I still enjoyed carrying heavy shit on my back up the mountain to assist with rescues, and then carrying (an amazingly disproportionate number of) heavy people back down off the mountain. Nothing filled my pounding heart with more joy than looking at the sweaty, headlamp-illuminated smiles of my fellow rescuers from the other side of a litter as we were being lowered down a scree field. I liked being a grunt.

I was always the first to ridicule those long-in-the-tooth (and often heavy-in-the-ass) members of mountain rescue teams who no longer went into the field, and contented themselves with working exclusively behind the scenes. With no small amount of condescension in my voice, I referred to them as "Rescue Politicians," while I thought of myself as a "Rescue Technician."

But with my recent promotion, I was now seen by others (and maybe even more so by myself) as having gone over to the Dark Side. Management. I feared that my new responsibilities as Mission Leader were just the first step toward the abandonment of my status as Rescue Technician, followed by the inevitable downward spiral to a career as a Rescue Politician.

I felt (and still do, actually) that this kind of responsibility could only lead to maturity. Maturity is the harbinger of old age. Death follows soon thereafter. So it was with mixed feelings that I accepted the job of Mission Leader.

There are roughly a dozen Mission Leaders on Alpine. Each serves between two and five twenty-four-hour shifts each month. During that twenty-four-hour on-call period, you have to live your life differently from the rest of the volunteers on the team. If the pager goes off, you have to respond.

Forget about rolling over and stuffing your pager under the pillow if it goes off in the middle of the night, you have to get up and respond. Forget about going for a run or hike, because you have to always be within cell or pager range and respond. Forget about having a few drinks (or partaking in any other consciousness-altering medicines like Nyquil or Theraflu, for that matter), you have to always maintain a clear head as you might suddenly find yourself talking with the sheriff, a distraught parent, a helicopter pilot, or maybe even the National Guard as you respond.

And don't even think of going to dinner in the same car as your family unless they don't mind leaving their meal unfinished, rushing out of the restaurant with you, listening to an hour and a half's worth of static-sprinkled, acronym-laced radio traffic in the car on the way to a mission, and then sitting there patiently for hours while you spend the night in the mountains searching for someone.

On our rescue team, the Mission Leader is like the general who commands his army. There is no such thing as rescue by committee on Alpine.

Though I wouldn't go as far as calling the job of Mission Leader a dictator-ship, it is pretty close.

Having been selected for that position only a month or so before that page, this was the very first time I was not only required to respond, but also charged with the coordination of our response to that 911 call to search for two overdue hikers.

While searches may not be as glamorous, or provide the same instant visceral thrill as a rescue, they are a big part of what we do nonetheless. It is called SEARCH and Rescue, after all. Searches tend to get more attention from the media these days because they last longer than most rescues and therefore allow the media more time to cover the story as it unfolds. Rescues are pretty straightforward, since we usually know the location of the person who needs rescuing and can plan accordingly. But with a search, we not only have no idea where our subject might be found, we don't have any idea if they will need to be rescued once they are found.

One of the most difficult aspects of searches, from a psychological stand-point, is that you never know how they will end. Or if they will ever end at all. In the Alpine Rescue Team's fifty-plus year history, there have been a handful of unresolved searches. I participated in three of them.

Now, there are entire books written on search theory. They are peppered with lots of really swell acronyms like POD (Probability of Detection—a per-centage based on how likely an alert, conscious person could be expected to be found in a specific search area), POA (Probability of Area—also a percent-age, but based on the chance that a person could be lost in a specific search area), LSP (Last Seen Point), and RP (Reporting Party) to name a few. There are also many different week-long courses that teach search theory, spend-ing hour after thrilling hour each day dissecting past examples of successful and not-so-successful searches. Even the name for this course, MLPI, is an acronym (Managing the Lost Person Incident).

But after participating in more searches than I can even count, it sud-denly hit me one day. If you want to simplify search theory, cook it down to its bare bones, you need to think of a search as a game—a game that many of us first learned as children. In RescueWorld, searches are akin to a very com-plex game of Clue. In the game of Clue, you learn the rules, you roll the dice, you play the game, you take notes, you use deductive reasoning.

Of course, here in RescueWorld, it's never as simple as discovering that Professor Plum did it in the conservatory with the candlestick (which, if you really think about it, is pretty goddamned barbaric for a professor). The board game Clue only asks you to discover who did it, what they used to do it, and where they did it. To win the game of Clue in RescueWorld, you must figure out so much more. You are playing against that ultimate gamesman— the Grim Reaper. The worst thing that can happen when you lose a game of Clue outside of RescueWorld is that you shove the game across the table in self-righteous indignation and petulantly label the winner a cheat. The worst thing that can happen when you lose the SAR version of Clue is that someone dies lost, alone, and forsaken in the wilderness.

When I search for someone, I've learned to take what little information I have at my disposal, and form my opinions as to what kind of person I am searching for. I do my best to make it my own personal crusade to find someone not only because it's my job as a dedicated SAR professional, but because I train myself to identify with the person I am looking for.

You have to come up with these kinds of mind games to keep yourself sharp and engaged as you walk around for hours, usually in the dark, shouting someone's name over and over and over. I often find myself wondering if our lost subject is a Daydreamer or an Explorer. Daydreamers usually wander off the trail, realize they are lost, and then stop moving and wait for someone to find them. Explorers tend to ignore the trail entirely, get lost, and then keep wandering around in an effort to avoid the embarrassment of a search being launched. They are the ones that end up miles away from their last seen point, often completely outside the search area.

I was used to following instructions on searches. But now all of a sudden, people were going to look to *me* for direction. And worse (at least from my perspective), they were not only supposed to listen to what I had to say, they were probably going to *do* what I said—within reason, of course.

As I frantically drove up the curvy mountain road to where the distraught mother/wife of our lost party was filling in the CCCSO deputy on the particulars (husband: middle aged, medium build, five-foot-ten, short blondish hair, jeans, and a red windbreaker; nine-year-old daughter: tall, skinny, long blonde hair in a ponytail, last seen 7 miles away at the Echo Lake Trailhead), I multi-tasked and tried my best not to straighten out a curve and drive off a cliff. And to not dwell on the fact that the description for the lost little girl eerily matched that of my own eldest daughter of the same age, Sarah.

While driving and scribbling notes and talking on the radio and reading my pager and answering calls from curious in-bound teammates, I glanced up long enough to see a middle-aged man of medium build, about five-foot-ten, with short blondish hair wearing jeans and a red windbreaker holding

Large-scale searches are a logistical nightmare, especially when they go on for more than one 12-hour operational period. Juggling dozens of searchers from different organizations, military and civilian helicopters, canines and their handlers, the media, and of course the family requires advanced skills in multi-tasking. Photo by Tom Wood.

hands with a tall, skinny young girl with her long blonde hair pulled into a ponytail walking slowly up the gravel shoulder of the road as I drove past.

I was so focused on everything but where I actually was that I was nearly a quarter-mile past them before I registered what I had seen and slammed on my brakes. I dropped into reverse and straddled the shoulder driving backward until I came back even with the two weary travelers.

Although they were more than 9 miles uphill and away from where they were supposed to be (which was one of the reasons I paid them little heed when driving past them), they were indeed our lost parties.

Score! As they climbed into the cab of my truck, I shook hands with the man, Nathan, and his daughter, Anna. This was no small feat, since I was so busy patting myself on the back at the same time. I was feeling pretty damned full of myself. And why not? I'd had my share of finds and was no stranger to that elevated state of being that accompanied a successful search. But there I was, my first callout as a Mission Leader, and I was lucky enough to also call in an MRA Code 1 (Subjects located and okay). It was like playing the lottery with Hurley's numbers from the TV show, *Lost*—and actually winning.

But the ticker tape parade in my own honor that I was orchestrating in my mind was momentarily put on hold by a simple question uttered fearfully by the nine-year-old girl I had just picked up.

"Mom is going to hurt me for this, isn't she?" she asked timidly.

I was uncertain if she was asking me or her father this question, but I took it upon myself (being the on-call Mission Leader and all) to respond.

"No, no," I replied with no small amount of certainty. "She'll be so happy to see you both, she'll forget that she was ever upset with you for getting lost."

The silence that followed could only be described as pregnant.

As I stated earlier, I had a daughter who was the same age as this little girl and felt this statement honestly reflected what *my* reaction would be upon finding my own daughter safe and sound after dialing 911 and reporting her lost.

"Uh, you obviously don't know my wife," replied the girl's father with a little laugh that belied his nervousness. I pegged his slight accent as French in origin. The closer we got to the starting point of his misadventure, the more agitated he became. I decided that his apprehension was likely founded in his elevated feelings of guilt for getting himself and his daughter lost. After all, he seemed a decent enough sort, and was very grateful for our response.

Just before reaching the trailhead parking lot where the wife/mother and a sheriff's deputy awaited our return, I passed the half-dozen or so parked vehicles along the road of my teammates who had responded from the other side of the pass and were awaiting my arrival. Tom Loebach, a fellow Mission Leader, sat smiling in his truck as I parked mine and approached his. I wanted to brief him on my good fortune (well, theirs too, I guess) before delivering father and daughter to their awaiting wife/mother.

"Congratulations on your first Mission Leader mission!" he said through a tight-lipped smile as he remained curiously immobile in his seat.

"What's up?" I asked. "Feeling a little under the weather?"

"Well, a little," Tom confided. A marathon addict in his mid-fifties and veteran of some of Alpine's most difficult missions over the last twenty-odd years, I could tell by his body language that he wasn't himself.

"I had my prostate removed yesterday. Cancer. I was hoping you didn't need me to go into the field. I'm wearing a diaper, but I leak piss every time I move and it's really annoying. But I figured I could still run the radio from my vehicle here if you were short-handed and had to go into the field."

At first, I was certain he was joking. But his pinched expression and slightly pale complexion said otherwise. *That,* ladies and gents, is the kind of crazed dedication and selfless devotion to both our fellow human beings and the cause of mountain rescue that runs rampant through the hearts of the rescuers here in RescueWorld.

I thanked Tom for his selflessness and informed the other rescuers who had made the hour-long drive to the top of the pass that the search was over (almost before it had begun). I climbed back into my truck to drive Nathan and his daughter the last few hundred yards to the spot at the trailhead where the deputy and the wife/mother awaited.

As I approached the trailhead parking lot, I spied a shiny late-model Lexus SUV that was parked next to the more utilitarian Clear Creek Sheriff's Department SUV. Just as I pulled up and parked behind the sheriff's SUV, both of its doors swung open, discharging a deputy from the driver's side and an attractive but obviously distraught blonde woman sporting a blindingly white down jacket from the other.

At that point I was flying pretty high with that heady cocktail of adrenaline and the other chemicals that tend to accompany this sort of mountain rescue success story. No matter how many times you witness these reunions, you can't help but feel moved when you've played the smallest part in its orchestration. Especially when the story's ending is such a good one, and a kid is involved.

As I've said before, every mission that you respond to as a mountain rescuer, you bring more to the trailhead than your rescue gear and the Ten Essentials stuffed into your pack. You carry around a lot of personal history. I am a parent. And I think that if one of my kids had wandered off and gone missing, I'd be falling all over myself to thank those responsible for bringing my lost progeny back safely.

Purposefully, the wife/mother strode toward us. I had on my best "Aw Shucks" grin in preparation for all the praise I was certain would be heaped upon me for "singlehandedly" locating and returning her beloved husband and darling little girl. I half stuck out my hand to introduce myself, but her eyes were focused on her family as she raced past me toward them.

I could feel the tears of happiness welling up in my eyes until I noticed the pinched look of concern on the deputy's face. His oddly ... taut body language could only be described as being way too cop-like given the present situation.

"You are fucking DEAD! I am going to fucking kill you!" spat the woman in white, as she reached her husband and gave him an angry shove that nearly knocked him off his feet. Suddenly, the birds quit singing and you could practically see the trees bending away from me as all the wind left my sails. At light speed, I went from mountain rescue savior to lowly witness in an ugly domestic dispute. *Well this isn't exactly what I expected*, I thought to myself, as the deputy made to insert himself between the two.

"Now you told me that you had calmed down!" the deputy said to her, as her eyes burned holes through her husband and smoke poured from her ruddy ears. "I meant it when I said that I would charge you with battery and cuff you if you did this," he added. Obviously, there had been some interesting discussions between the deputy and this woman before I arrived.

"Get in the goddamn car!" she said to the terrified little girl, who stood statue-like, completely unacknowledged and vulnerable beside my truck. As the poor little creature dutifully marched to the Lexus and opened the door, the husband took advantage of his chance to slink likewise to the other side of the car.

"Don't you fucking dare get in that car!" she hissed, and he let go of the car door handle as if it had been red hot. What followed was ten minutes of ugly, one-sided battle. As I retreated farther and farther away from the embarrassing debacle, the deputy had to get closer and closer to keep them from coming to blows.

When the woman in white finally promised that she would not kill her husband or hurt her child (at least until she crossed the county line and became another sheriff department's problem), she spared one last look at me as if to say "Thanks for nothing!" and angrily slammed the car door shut. Her husband barely had time to jump into the passenger seat and close his door before she dropped the tranny into drive and sped away from the trailhead, spitting gravel in her wake.

The sheriff's deputy and I exchanged bemused glances and "what can you do?" shrugs, exchanged some basic information, got in our respective vehicles, and drove off. I don't know what was going through his head, but I couldn't help but wonder if maybe getting lost on occasion was the only way that poor browbeaten husband could find any peace of mind.

I found no small amount of irony in the fact that although on paper this mission had a fairy tale ending (and they all lived happily ever after), the reality of what I witnessed saddled me with feelings of guilt and emptiness. Guilt because I had allowed my own personal feelings of self-importance and pride to take over and claim sole responsibility for what was in reality a *team* effort (and besides, I *did* just find them walking alongside the road). And emptiness because that little girl was likely going to spend a much scarier night at home than if she had remained lost in the cold darkness of the Rocky Mountains.

I guess finding someone isn't always the same thing as saving them, and sadly, even in RescueWorld, fairytale endings only happen in fairy tales.

Rescue

Teamwork is crucial when carrying out rescues in hazardous terrain. Here, a fallen climber is carried out down a scree slope in Clear Creek Canyon. Photo by Tom Wood

The Colorado Air National Guard is an invaluable asset, especially since their external hoist capabilities are required for critical patients who have the misfortune of being injured high on remote peaks. Here, the flight medic is being lowered from a Blackhawk onto a narrow ridge on Mt. Bancroft in 2012 so that we could connect the packaged subject to the hoist line dangling from the helicopter above us. Photo by Adam Perou Hermans.

Shepard's Prayer

"**Dear** God, please don't let me fuck up." I uttered this desperate prayer as I stood shivering, johnson in hand, coaxing the last few quickly freezing dribbles of urine out my freezing member while doing my level best to keep it from coming in contact with the aluminum carabiners that hung from the front of my harness. Forget about the dangers of sticking your tongue to a frozen flagpole—I was concerned with forfeiting a piece of my manhood to my frozen rescue gear.

But my efforts at urination were of course not the (main) reason for this profane but heartfelt prayer, made (in)famous by Apollo astronaut Alan Shepard as he sat strapped to a NASA rocket atop thousands of parts assembled by the lowest bidder. In fact, thanks to Tom Wolfe's book, *The Right Stuff*, it's now known as Shepard's Prayer.

"Dear God, please don't let me fuck up," I implored one last time as I zipped up and turned back to the group of rescuers huddled together a dozen feet away.

There were actually two reasons why I appealed to the Almighty that day. One was a Texan named Bill, and the other was a fellow mountain rescuer named Don. Both men needed rescue and were lying several hundred feet below us in an avalanche chute. I had just been put in charge of their technical evacuation. I was scared shitless.

It was about 9:00 p.m. on Saturday, February 8, 2003, and we were standing atop a 12,200-foot ridge on the Continental Divide in the dark. The Arctic winds that whirled and eddied around us chilled the air to a stunning minus 60 degrees Fahrenheit. Winter rescues like this are always a challenge in the Colorado backcountry, but this one was a doozy.

The story behind what would become the most physically and mentally challenging mission I'd ever participated in began innocently enough the day before. A small group of Texans were up touring the Colorado high country by rented snowmobile in beautiful Grand County. It was a bluebird day and the groomed snowmobile trails that wound from the small town of Frazier up through the trees to the top of the Continental Divide were deceptively tame for the out-of-towners. While they didn't know it at the time, they were about to contribute to America's fastest-growing demographic in backcountry rescue: snowmobilers.

We never found out why they became lost. In fact, since they were recreating in Grand County, which was not one of Alpine's primary response areas, we didn't even know that a search was initiated when the Texans failed to return their rented snowmobiles late that afternoon. The responsibility for their search fell to the Grand County SAR team, which was intimately familiar with the terrain on their western side of the Divide. A well-trained Mountain Rescue Association–accredited team, they had the situation well in hand.

After searching by snowmobile for most of the night, they spotted a thin plume of smoke in the distance shortly after sunrise and discovered the Texans huddled around its source (say what you will about the health risks associated with cigarettes, but I've yet to find a cold smoker in the backcountry because they've always got a lighter on them). The Texans were wet and hungry from their off-trail misadventure, but otherwise in pretty good shape for a bunch of guys wearing cotton coveralls and cowboy boots. Since their rented snow machines were hopelessly buried in the snow and a brutal front was predicted to race in from the north, the rescuers opted to load everyone onto the backs of their own machines and retrieve the rentals at a later time.

It was now mid-morning, and the clouds were indeed building off to the northwest. I knew this because I had made the same observation at that same moment some 30 miles to the southeast as our rescue team wrapped up an ice driving training with the Clear Creek County Sheriff's Office on the frozen Georgetown Lake. I wasn't the only Alpine member getting "my redneck on" that day as we practiced piloting our rescue vehicles across the ice while they skidded and spun sideways and backwards across the large ice-covered lake. When we finished the training, fellow Alpine member Mark Freeman and I decided to do some ice climbing on the frozen waterfall across the highway from Georgetown Lake.

Up to the north in Grand County, the jet stream dipped a little farther south and a lot earlier than predicted. The barometer plunged, the winds picked up, and the snow let loose. The resulting whiteout instantly left the rescuers with only a few feet of visibility by which to cautiously navigate their snow machines along the narrow trail on the ridge along the top of the Continental Divide before their makeshift path rejoined the main trail to the west that snaked back down through the trees to Frazier.

At approximately 1400 (that's two in the afternoon for you civilians out there), GCSAR member Don Neuman had Bill, one of the Texans, on the back of his sled as he carefully motored along the treacherous ridge. Being the lead machine, he was doing his best to link up the rare patches of snow that dotted the barren and rock-strewn terrain until he located the right spot to pick up the trail that would lead the tired band of Texans and their rescuers back down to the warmth and security of Mission Base.

At times, the visibility diminished to zero, and Don was forced to get off his snowmobile and walk in front of the idling machine. Arms out like a sleepwalker, he wanted to be certain he wasn't about to crash into a boulder. Taking tentative steps, and occasionally sticking a foot out in front—like a person testing the temperature of a cool mountain lake with one pointed toe before jumping in—he did his best to make sure that he wasn't about to drive over the cliffs that abruptly dropped away from the southeast side of the ridge.

If you are ever unfortunate enough to find yourself lost in a *true* whiteout (outside on foot, not from behind the protection of a windshield), it is an unpleasant and surreal experience, to say the least. Without any visual cues (like a horizon line) to realign your equilibrium, your brain begins to short circuit. You feel nauseated—seasick—whether you are moving or not. Your sense of balance takes a beating as well, and it's hard not to stumble around like a complete drunk, because you may not even be able to see where you are setting your feet down as you walk. Forget about walking in a straight line. You may swear on a stack of Bibles that you are walking toe to toe, in a perfectly straight line, while in reality you are making a jagged circle.

Negotiating your way through a whiteout on foot is hard. Safely steering an eight-hundred-pound snowmobile with a two-hundred-plus-pound man seated on the back through a whiteout at an elevation of 12,200 feet is so close to impossible that you may as well just go ahead and say that's what it is. Impossible.

So it was under these dire circumstances that Don drove his snowmobile (with the horrified Bill on back) over a snow-corniced cliff—tumbling, rolling, and wrestling with the snowmobile as all three plummeted several hundred feet down the steep, narrow, and snowy mountain chute (also known in mountaineering circles as a couloir).

Lucky for the riders following Don that they had momentarily gotten their machines stuck in the snow, and did not follow him over the edge like lemmings (which is exactly what happened to a group of snowmobilers from Florida one week later in Vail when two snowmobilers followed the lead machine over a cliff, resulting in death by suffocation of one of the riders who was trapped head first in the deep snow).

When the other GCSAR members freed their machines and realized that Don's snowmobile tracks ended at the edge of a cliff, they called in the MRA Code every mountain rescuer dreads to hear: MRA Code 3. In English, that translates into *Team member injured, assistance needed.*

ART RESPOND TO GRAND COUNTY,

MRA CODE 3, PLUS ONE INJURED SUBJECT NEED EVACUATED.

CODE 3 RESPONSE

Once again, my actions were being dictated by a small electronic device shouting at me in capital letters. The Alpine Rescue Team's response area abutted GCSAR's at the summit of the always avalanche-prone Berthoud Pass, and since Mark and I were climbing relatively near there, we knew that we'd be among the first to respond to this desperate call from our comrades for mutual aid.

When responding to a call for a fellow rescuer here in RescueWorld, there's always a great sense of urgency coupled with an unsettling sense of dread. RescueWorld is, after all, a small community and the chance that we might know the downed rescuer is usually pretty high.

We quickly abandoned our ice climbing and subsequent beer drinking plans and piled into my truck. My F-150 was equipped with state-approved lights and sirens, and since we had been granted permission by the dispatcher to run Code 3, I fired them up and had the red, white, and blues clearing ski traffic for us.

Regardless of what most people think, running with lights and sirens down the middle of three snow-packed lanes of bumper-to-bumper I-70 ski traffic at 90 miles an hour on the interstate is *not* fun or cool. Running code is nerve-wracking, scary, and the number one killer of emergency responders each year. I swear to God, the sound of a siren turns some drivers' brains to Jell-O, and the flashing lights strip them of any semblance of common sense. I've had people pull out and stop dead in front of me in the middle of the highway while I approached them in the left lane going 80 mph. My favorite drivers (not really) are the ones that insist on staying in front of you and don't let you pass. For *miles*. Never mind that you are only half a car length behind them with your siren wailing and lights blinding them and you are frantically waving your arms for them to get the hell over (to be fair, these drivers are usually ninety-year-old, hat-wearing little men who can barely see over the steering wheel).

So in case you slept through this part of driver training, let me give everyone out there a refresher on what to do when you spot an emergency vehicle approaching you from the rear. First of all, slow down, BUT DON'T STOP! Make your way over to the right until the emergency vehicle passes you. And by the way, for those of you out there who think that "drafting" an emergency vehicle is a great way to beat traffic, you're right. But it's also illegal. More than once, I've alerted either the county sheriff or the state highway patrol that I was being followed by some jackass through traffic as I ran code. Cops love writing *that* particular ticket.

Listening to the mobile radio in my truck as we sped over Berthoud Pass into Grand County, we did our best to piece together what was going on, and prepare ourselves physically and mentally for what might lie ahead of us. By this point in my "career," I had learned a few things about a few things. Once a mission gets rolling and you enter the field, remembering to eat and drink becomes difficult because there is so much going on. So on the drive in, you learn to chug water and stuff your body with the calories it will need to fuel your efforts.

Bonking (not to be confused with boinking—which is of course an entirely different thing) is what happens when you don't take care of your body's fuel and hydration needs while performing a calorie-sucking rescue. You simply shut down. But for those of us working in RescueWorld, one of the real dangers associated with bonking is the marked decrease in mental acuity that precedes the physical shutdown. The higher brain functions go out the window first, which means that your decision-making capabilities become compromised. Often the bonker is completely unaware of just how poorly they are doing until a fellow rescuer observes them doing something odd, like maybe sucking their sunscreen out of its tube like it is an energy gel. In a rescue situation, if you throw in some altitude, sub-zero weather, compromised brain function, and then ask someone to make life-or-death decisions, you are cooking up a recipe for disaster.

So when Mark and I rolled into the beehive of activity that was Mission

Base in Frazier half an hour later, we immediately set about addressing our own personal needs (eating even more, drinking even more, urinating, adding layers of clothing, donning our avalanche transceivers and personal radios) before alerting the Grand County Incident Commander (IC) of our presence.

The briefing we received painted a grim picture of the situation. GCSAR had about a dozen rescuers in the field, but they were spanked after already spending most of the previous night out searching. The remaining Texans that had not gone over the cliff had already been brought in safely. But as far as the situation with Don and Bill, the news was a mixed bag. Good news—a paramedic and rescuer had reached them, and they were both alive. So far. Pretty much all the rest of the news was bad.

The weather continued to deteriorate. Snow was increasing in intensity. Winds were steady now at 30 mph, gusting to 50. Air temperatures at the 12,200-foot-high ridge were struggling to reach zero. This put the windchill at values too scary to calculate.

No direct communication with the paramedic on scene was possible, since he was with the subjects on the opposite side of the ridge. The paramedic had to relay his information to a rescue member stationed atop the ridge, who in turn passed the messages to the Incident Commander back at Mission Base. Darkness would fall in less than two hours, further complicating the rescue effort.

Don's injuries, as best as could be deciphered from the chaotic radio traffic, were serious. He had an open femur fracture and a broken arm and collarbone. Bill, the Texan, seemed to weather the nearly 1,000-foot tumble down the mountain with the snowmobile better than Don. His chief medical complaint was hypothermia and frost nip (which is a less severe medical condition than frostbite in which only the top layers of skin freeze).

After a quick meeting with our own recently arrived Mission Leader, John Wells, we saddled up a couple of snow machines and awaited the GCSAR member who would act as our guide for the 9-mile drive into the scene.

On the way in, we passed many GCSAR members on their way out of the field. They all carried themselves with the head-down, exhausted demeanor of the walking wounded. Some had been out in the elements for nearly twenty hours at that point—a valiant effort to be certain. Our relief party, which was what we now considered ourselves, numbered about six members. Another group of Alpine members were on their way in behind us.

As we rode our machines up the packed trail above treeline, the winds noticeably increased. Any exposed flesh was flayed by the razor-sharp snow crystals carried on the wind. It was like being sandblasted with ice. I still have two small crescent-shaped patches of skin on the top of my cheekbones below where I wore my goggles that turn purplish when I either get too much sun or windburn from that day's frost nip.

When we ran out of snow on the scoured flanks of the ridge, we ditched the machines and hiked up to the crest of the ridge in search of the two abandoned snowmobiles left by GCSAR to mark the rescue site.

Once we gained the ridge, we decided that in order to make it easier for the inbound teams behind us to follow, we should flag our route through the rocks and over the tundra. But when I tried to unroll the bright orange plastic surveyor's flagging from its roll, it simply crumbled in my hands and blew away. It was so cold that the frozen plastic flagging shattered into little tiny pieces whenever it was touched.

Knowing that fast-approaching darkness and worsening weather would make it even harder for anyone coming in behind us, we decided to take a GPS reading on our present location. But even though we had kept our GPS devices relatively warm inside our jackets, the extreme cold still killed the batteries before units could lock onto enough satellites to give us a reading. So much for modern technology.

We broke out a compass and used it to take a bearing toward the east. We believed this would lead us to the place on the ridge where Don had gone off the edge and relayed this information back to Mission Base. Thank God they (compass manufacturers, that is) use glycol to suspend the magnetized needles in compasses, and not water, or we'd be stuck with a frozen compass to go along with the now-worthless GPS units. (As a former carpenter, it intrigued me to hear the old-timers I worked with refer to their bubble levels as "whiskey sticks," in reference to the days when level manufacturers used alcohol—not glycol—in their levels and compasses).

We stumbled a half-mile on the ridge line until we found the two abandoned snowmobiles on the ridge. We were astounded to find that that's exactly what they were—abandoned.

"Hello, anyone here?" we shouted into the howling wind. No reply. There was not a living soul in sight.

After getting on the radio on MRA 1 (a frequency nationally dedicated to mountain rescue), we were able to reach the three rescuers who were with Don and the Texan. One GCSAR member, Frank Nieto, was on his way up the couloir to our location. He had spent the last few hours digging a shallow snow cave out of the main fall line, and then he dragged Don into it. Bill joined them in the shallow cave, seeking shelter from the elements while awaiting rescue. On the verge of exhaustion and hypothermia himself, Frank made the difficult decision to leave the field before he became a liability. That left only two GCSAR members (Dan Jamison and Matt Lloyd) with the two subjects, and Site Commander Greg Foley. Greg was not with the subjects, but rather just over the edge of the cornice out of our view, seeking shelter from the brutal wind. Of the original dozen rescuers that we had been told were on scene, these three were the only ones that remained.

Greg, a former Alpine Rescue Team member, was a seasoned mountain rescue veteran. He had his doubts concerning the chances of a safe rescue of the two subjects that night. Especially given the low number of personnel on scene. A textbook version of a technical rescue of this difficulty and magnitude called for at least eighteen to twenty fresh rescuers. At this point, we had ten.

Tom Loebach, one of Alpine's Mission Leaders and strongest members, took control of the scene from Greg, who looked both relieved and tortured about passing on command. Don was a good friend of his, as well as teammate.

Here in RescueWorld, there aren't many hard and fast rules. But one of the few we follow religiously revolves around the prioritization of the person we are attempting to rescue. Although it sounds selfish, when you are out in the backcountry performing a rescue, your own safety comes first. Next is the safety of your teammates. Last (hopefully not dead last) is the safety of your subject. We follow this rule for some pretty obvious reasons. Namely, if you become injured during a rescue, you will be of no help to your original subject. In fact, you will actually be hurting them, because once you become injured, resources will have to be diverted away from the original party needing rescue. We put our teammates' safety next for the same reason.

So although we do occasionally take chances (especially during rescues like this one), we do our absolute utmost to perform accurate risk assessments and scrutinize the cost-to-benefit ratios when making our go or no-go decisions.

Even though SAR teams in many ways resemble paramilitary organizations, we differ on one key point: on a SAR mission there is no such thing as an "acceptable loss." Oh, and we don't carry guns. So make that two differences.

If we feel we can't contribute to the rescue without becoming a liability, we owe it to our fellow rescuers to man up, swallow a little pride, and do what's best for the mission. And ultimately, this is what most benefits the subject (or subjects, as the case may be).

Greg understood this, and shifted the focus of his efforts to coordinate the half-mile carry and 9-mile snowmobile evacuation that would be necessary once the subjects were hauled up to the top of the ridge.

Taking stock of the resources at hand, Tom ascertained that only six to eight more rescuers were actually in the field en route to our location. Everyone else was responding from out of county and was being delayed by the storm. We were, for all intents and purposes, on our own.

Alpine members Scott Grotheer and Mark Freeman harnessed up (with much assistance from their fellow rescuers), tied their ropes to the snowmobiles being pressed into service as an ad hoc belaying anchor, and rappelled down over the edge on a few ropes that we tied together, carrying some technical gear, space blankets, oxygen, and a litter to assist the lone paramedic below with the packaging of our two subjects.

Now if we were doing this rescue in Planet Hollywood RescueWorld, Scott and Mark would have each simply thrown an injured guy over a shoulder like a heavy sack of potatoes once they reached them and then heroically Batmanned their way up the rope, hand over hand. But being encumbered by reality as we were, we needed to come up with something less flashy and a lot more practical. So without the luxury of a script that promised a happy Hollywood ending, we had to wing it and hope that when the sun rose the next morning, we all awoke somewhere warm, with all of our fingers, toes, and noses still attached. And Don and Bill getting the care they needed at a hospital down in Denver.

Tom conferred with senior Alpine member Roy Wyatt while the other Alpine members unloaded and took stock of all the gear we had humped into the field.

"Why don't you run Site Command for the technical evac, and I'll work on overall mission coordination with Mission Base?" Tom asked me.

To buy myself a few moments to clear my head and gather my scattered thoughts on the daunting task ahead, I walked a short distance away from everyone to get rid of the extra water I'd chugged on the way in, which pretty much brings us right back to where we began this story.

Now, I've already shared my struggles with organized religion and relationships. Math, like religion and relationships, has always been difficult for me to master as well. In order to succeed at or understand any of the three, you need to pay attention to the details. I am not a detail-oriented person in the least, and this has been my undoing when it comes to religion (details = doctrine and dogma), relationships (details = remembering anniversaries and birthdays, learning the art of compromise) and math (details = *every-thing*). I'm a big-picture kind of guy, and couldn't have agreed more the first time I heard someone say that the devil was in the details. *Damn right he is,* I thought. *No fucking wonder I had been so frightened of him as a kid.*

I've always sucked at math, and the linear thought processes that are so vital to math are alien to me. That part of my brain has always had shit for brains. This almost pathological fear of math was one of the main reasons for my apprehension about being responsible for setting up this system. A safe and efficient technical rope rescue system is *all* about details. About doing the math.

"Don't sweat the small stuff," might be good advice for some situations, but not when you are in charge of setting up a technical rope rescue system, because someone's life *depends* on you sweating the small stuff. Sweating the details.

I whispered Shepard's Prayer one last time for luck, and then walked over to the pile of technical gear and ropes that were swiftly being buried by the drifting snow. *Okay,* I thought. *Here goes.*

Although I'd practiced rigging our technical systems ad nauseam in the five or so years I'd been a member of Alpine, and even helped set up several during real missions, I'd never been asked to be in charge of setting up and running anything like this. The person best suited to this task was Scott (who was and is a true wizard in technical rope rescue systems and a linear thinker in the classic sense), and he had just rappelled down over the edge.

We had about half an hour till the first subject below was packaged and ready to go, so we set about engineering the rope system right away. First off, I wasn't too terribly excited about using two snowmobiles parked in a T formation as our anchor, but there was quite literally nothing else available. There was no snow on the barren ridge top that would allow us to use any sort of snow anchors. The biggest rocks in our vicinity were only the size of basketballs, so rock anchors were also out of the question. It was the snowmobiles or nothing. As stated earlier, each machine probably weighed about eight hundred pounds. That may sound like a lot, but given the forces on the anchor we would generate with our hauling system, we needed about five times more weight than that. I was worried the whole anchor would be slowly pulled toward the edge, then over, and scatter the subjects and rescuers below like so many bowling pins. We decided that at least two rescuers sitting atop the machines while taking a break from hauling, acting as human ballast, would have to do. It wasn't much, but at least they could alert us if they felt the anchor moving.

Moving on to the ropes, thanks to Scott's and Mark's rappel down to our subjects, we now knew we would need about 900 feet of it to reach the injured parties below. We had brought one 300-foot 11mm rope, and four 200-foot 11mm ropes. Barely enough, since we would need to tie the 300-footer and three 200-footers together to make the 900-foot drop, and still have one 200-footer available up top to rig a haul system.

Now here comes the math that so terrified me. If rope porn isn't your cup of tea, feel free to skim the next several paragraphs.

I estimated that with a 200-pound subject in the litter (Don was six-foot-three and 230 pounds, and Bill was only slightly less) and a 200-pound rescuer attached to the litter to help maneuver it through the snow, that put our load at about 400 pounds. But since we would be pulling them up a roughly 55-degree slope, we wouldn't be seeing 100 percent of that load on the system. It would be more like 75 percent of that 400 pounds, which would be more like 300 pounds. My head was starting to hurt at this point.

With all the friction on the rope as it ran over the cornice and through the snow, I figured that would make the load feel about 100 pounds heavier (for all you rescue geeks out there, this is known as the coefficient of friction and it adds roughly 30 percent to your overall load). So in total, we had a 400-plus-pound fish on the line, I thought to myself. Smoke was now pouring from my ears.

Then I set to figuring out how we would haul them up. Alpine traditionally uses a 3:1 mechanical advantage system, created by an independent rope run through a few pulleys and then attached to the main line for hauling purposes. This meant that we would only see about one third of the load (about 130 pounds) each time we pulled. In order to keep from overloading a haul system by adding too many haulers, on Alpine we employ what we call "The Rule of Twelves." Basically, this means that if we multiplied the number of haulers times the mechanical advantage, that sum should not exceed the number twelve. So for a 1:1 mechanical advantage, we could use up to a dozen haulers. For a 2:1 mechanical advantage, six haulers. For our 3:1 mechanical advantage, we should have four haulers (in a perfect world). Now, this is of course assuming that each hauler is fresh and can consistently haul about 100 pounds with each pull. Even with the mechanical advantage, the load was too heavy for the haulers to pull hand over hand, so they were forced to tie small Prusik loops for handholds.

The Prusik hitch, one of the mountaineer's most versatile tools, is a small-diameter cord tied to make a loop, and then wrapped around a larger-diameter rope three times. When this loop is then pulled, the friction locks it down onto the larger rope. It can then be easily manipulated to move it up and down that larger rope.

These Prusik hitch handholds affixed to the icy haul rope allowed the haulers to use their legs to walk backward and pull. Since it was highly unlikely that each hauler could maintain the superhuman stamina needed for two separate 900-foot up-hauls, I figured we could add a couple extra haulers as needed and still be within our 4:1 safety margin—the 3:1 mechanical advantage plus the safety cushion built into the entire rope rescue system to ensure redundancy.

This 4:1 safety margin is the Holy Grail of technical rope rescue on our team. It is an oft-strived-for ratio that we use to determine the amount of "cushion" that we build into a technical rope rescue system. If we can reach and maintain this 4:1 safety margin, we should never experience a catastrophic failure during a practice or rescue. It's based on the weakest link of our system divided by our maximum anticipated load. Since we used tandem Prusiks to attach our hauling system to the main line that snaked over the edge and attached to the litter below, we knew that a set of tandem Prusiks slipped on the main line at approximately 2,400 pounds of pull was our weakest link. The maximum load we would ever put on a system was 600 pounds (based on the weight of one subject in a litter attended by two rescuers on a dead vertical high-angle rescue). So dividing 600 into 2,400 gets us four. Hence our 4:1 safety margin (fun fact: the safety margin for a commercial aircraft is 1:1).

At this point, I was just about ready to ask Tom to radio back to Mission Base to see if they could get Stephen Hawking on the horn to help walk me through the rest of these calculations, but I figured that bouncing all these numbers off my fellow rescuers on site might be a better use of time.

So back to our 3:1 mechanical advantage haul system. For every 3 feet that we hauled up top, the litter at the end of the rescue rope would be raised one foot. The limited amount of frozen and rocky real estate available atop the ridge restricted each pull to about 50 feet of rope at a time. This translated into roughly 16 feet of upward progress down below. Each time the haulers ran out of room, the system would be locked off while someone slid the tandem Prusiks back down the main line as close to the edge as possible. Then the whole process would be repeated, which is called a reset.

Since we had to up-haul both Don and the Texan 900 feet up the icy 55-degree slope of the couloir, this meant that we would have to reset that system at least 112 times in the course of the rescue. Also, every time the mechanical advantage system tandem Prusiks bumped up against each of the four knots that joined the main line ropes together, the system had to be locked off again while the original tandem Prusiks were untied and then reconnected to the rescue rope on the downhill side of the knot before we could begin hauling again. This added roughly eight more resets.

This would have been a difficult exercise to accomplish in daylight, with good weather, a fresh team of rescuers, and a solid anchor. Since we had none of those luxuries, we realized with a growing sense of dread that the envelope wasn't just being pushed, it was practically being shoved to the brink.

Also of concern was the possibility that our moving rescue rope, cutting like a hot knife through butter, would saw through the wind-loaded cornice perched atop the couloir above our subjects. Avalanche conditions were high that day and the thought that the cornice, once cut away from the anchoring snowpack that surrounded it, would tumble down the slope and trigger a massive avalanche and bury all below made me physically nauseated with worry. We did our best to "pad" the edge of the cornice and limit the cutting action by laying ice axes and ski poles perpendicularly under the moving rope. Still, once the rope was weighted and moving, it would likely cut a few feet into the cornice. Better that than cutting through it, though.

My ears were beginning to bleed with the contemplation of all the technical aspects of this rescue, so I figured maybe it was time to switch gears and worry about something else: the actual people in the system. An often-overlooked component of any rescue system is the human element. Most accidents that occur during rescues are the direct result of human error, not equipment failure or simple bad luck. If anything went wrong on this night, it would probably later be traced back to a simple unnoticed mistake that snowballed into catastrophic failure.

I think the creation of a safe and efficient rope rescue system requires a hell of a lot more than just the book-learned knowledge of the forces and physics and calculations involved. Or the quality of the gear you use (though I will stop here for a second and acknowledge my pride in the fact that every rope and piece of rescue gear we used in the system that night was made or distributed by the company I now work for: PMI). It is, after all, a system engineered and powered by human beings, and as such, the needs and capabilities of the rescuers involved in such a system must be addressed independently of the technical data. Any technical rope rescue Site Commander worth their salt keeps a wary eye on the people in the system and plays a never-ending loop of worst-case scenarios over and over in their head in an attempt to foresee any hidden monkey wrenches.

Team morale, in dire situations like this, is paramount. Often, one of the many hats (or uniforms, as the case may be) the Site Commander wears on a grueling rescue like this is that of the cheerleader. How's that for a mental picture?

If rescuers have too much time to stand around, they may succumb to the hopelessness of the situation. If they feel that they are being yelled at like little children, they will turn their focus inward and stop contributing to the overall morale of the group. These mishandled situations can devastate the rescue effort. Sometimes I swear that a positive word and a hearty slap on the back does more to warm someone from the inside out than a thermos of hot coffee and a bucket full of hand warmers.

And speaking of warmth, or the lack thereof, all rescuers on site were increasingly facing the danger of severe hypothermia and frostbite. Many of us now sported little waxy gray patches of skin on the ends of our noses, the tips of our ears, and on our cheeks. These are the harbingers of frostbite. As we tied and untied the Prusik hitches and knots, we had to remove our thick, bulky gloves and mittens. If we couldn't get the knot tied within about ten seconds, we hurriedly donned our gloves and another person stepped in to try to finish the knot before their fingers became too cold. We constantly assessed each other's state of mind and physical condition, because due to the altitude and extreme cold, we had trouble remembering even the most basic knots needed to assemble the rescue system. Everything took three times as long as it should have. Even unzipping a jacket pocket to get a sip of icy water from our Nalgene bottles was an act that required ten minutes and the assistance of a teammate.

The extreme cold was beginning to wear us down. Most of us had skipped lunch and now dinner, and our fuel reserves were being robbed by our bodies as they struggled to maintain a consistent core temperature. Many of us had been shivering uncontrollably for some time. Since shivering is external evidence that our bodies are working overtime to keep our internal thermometer as close to 98.6 degrees Fahrenheit as possible by generating heat from the repeated expansion and contraction of muscles, we could ascertain each other's proximity to hypothermia by observing each other's teeth chattering and palsied efforts at speech and motion.

Shivering is actually a good thing. It's when your body says "the hell with it" and stops shivering that you need to worry. Some of us had stopped shivering. We were running out of time. If we didn't get this rescue completed soon, we would become casualties ourselves.

And as if all that wasn't enough to worry about, the weather continued to worsen. Mother Nature was pissed. The winds were now howling so loud that we literally had to be face to uncovered face and shouting at the top of our lungs to hear each other.

As Site Commander, it was my responsibility to be sure that everyone involved with the system could hear all of the commands being given. No one could hear me if I covered up my face to protect it from the wind and snow, so I was left with no choice but to leave my mug exposed to the elements and hope that I could somehow avoid frostbite. It was so cold that my teeth hurt.

Now that all the figuring was behind us, we were ready to begin the up-haul and get some blood flowing. Our system was assembled and ready to go about the same time that the first subject was loaded into the litter below. Don selflessly refused to be hauled up first, even though his open femur fracture and other injuries pegged him as being in more need of advanced medical care than Bill.

Scott, of the dry wit and great technical abilities, attached his harness to the litter and readied his ice axe. When we needed to stop for a reset, he would plunge the axe into the snow inside of the triangle formed by the rope where it attached to the head of the litter, and this would anchor them in place until we were ready to begin hauling again.

"Top—litter here. Am I on belay?" Scott yelled into his radio from nearly a thousand feet below us.

"Litter—top here. You are on belay, ready for up-haul on your command," I barked into my own radio. "KXL 315, this is Alpine Rescue Team on a technical evacuation, a litter is on belay. Clear all non-essential radio traffic from this channel."

"Get us outta here!" Scott said.

"HAUL TEAM READY?" I yelled into the wind toward the handful of rescuers poised for action. "HAUL!!"

And with that command we set to our work, which was further complicated when several of our headlamps dimmed and finally died completely from the cold. These were the days before LED headlamps coupled with Lithium Ion batteries that could withstand the cold were readily available. The incandescent bulbs in our lights were no match for the deep, battery-draining cold that now enveloped us. We positioned the two or three rescuers with

Technical rope rescues are both thrilling and scary as hell, often prompting me to repeat the Shepard's Prayer before going over the edge. Photo courtesy of the Alpine Rescue Team.

functional headlamps at the key places in the system that needed illumination while the rest of us (myself included) toiled in the dark.

I don't remember what time we began to haul the Texan up the couloir. I was both so focused and so exhausted that it was like experiencing the entire episode through the other-worldly, gauze-like filter of a dream. Or looking at the surreal scene through a snow globe after it had been shaken up.

I do remember that when we saw the top of the litter pop up and over the cornice, I was infused with a warming rush of adrenaline that spread like wildfire from my core to the tips of my toes.

Once we had the subject and Scott safely atop the ridge, we were delighted by the arrival of a handful of fresh rescuers from Summit County SAR and the Rocky Mountain Rescue Group. Under Greg and Tom's direction, they carried the hypothermic Texan the half-mile to the waiting snowmobiles and began the long shuttle down to town.

All of us back at the rescue site were energized by the fresh team's arrival and our success at getting our first subject topside. We were now a well-oiled (if slightly frozen) machine. With two new (and rested!) haulers added to our ranks, we sent the litter, still tied to the end of the rope, back down to Don and the three remaining rescuers below.

Although the mission was far from over, we set about our business with confidence and renewed vigor. *We just might actually pull this thing off,* I marveled to myself.

We accomplished the second up-haul in about half the time of the first. GCSAR members Dan and Matt opted to remain independent of the litter, but to hang onto it for support as they followed Alpine member Mark, who had attached his safety harness to the litter. When the litter neared the top of the cornice, the haulers put some extra oomph! into their last pull, and the litter exploded through the snow and onto the top of the ridge, jerking a surprised Mark along beside it.

We carried Don to the waiting snowmobiles a half-mile away, loaded him up in GCSAR's specialized covered Cascade sled, and he was whisked away. We went back to the haul site and collected our gear, loaded it onto the snow machines we had ridden in on (which some thoughtful rescuers had turned around and lined up on the trail), and began the long, cold ride through the blizzard back down to Mission Base.

Tears of relief welled up in my eyes, then—windblown—froze to the side of my face as I maneuvered my machine down the trail, following the tail-lights of the snowmobile in front of me. All of the emotions I had kept buried quickly clawed their way to the surface, overcame me, then moved on.

It was just after midnight when we arrived back at Mission Base. There was still gear to be put away, hands and feet to be thawed, and of course the mission debrief. Most of us were too tired to drive home, so we crashed in a nearby hotel that had generously donated rooms for our use.

Nearly all the rescuers on scene that long cold night lost skin off our noses, ears, and cheeks to frost nip (which kind of makes you look like you are peeling after getting the world's worst sunburn). But no one, as far as I knew, suffered any real frostbite.

It took time and several painful surgeries, but Don made a complete recovery. Bill was treated for extreme hypothermia, miraculously kept all his fingers and toes, and went back to Texas with a great story to tell. (In fact, the story was so great that The Weather Channel re-enacted it for a segment of their popular show, *Storm Stories*.)

Postscript: A few years later, I met up with injured Grand County rescuer Don Neuman at the REI Flagship store in Denver. He wanted to make a donation to Alpine for the work we did that night, and somehow the *Rocky Mountain News* got wind of this and set up a photo shoot. Alpine member

Paul Woodward (known to all as just Woody) came down with me for the staged event and interview. In spite of the years since his accident, Don still sported a slight limp. He choked up (causing me to choke up as well) as he handed me the check. The flashbulb went off, and we shook hands.

Although the donated money wasn't mine, I can honestly say that in all the years I've worked in RescueWorld, that was the only time anyone ever handed me a check for doing a rescue.

And though I had lost my religion many years earlier, Shepard's Prayer had worked nonetheless. I hadn't fucked things up.

The Poor Man's BASE Jump
and Reflections on the Aroma of Gangrene

I strongly suspect that for many people, there is an enormous difference between just existing and truly living. Case in point: BASE jumpers.

BASE (which stands for Building, Antenna, Span, and Earth—the things these people jump from using hand-deployed parachutes) jumpers are often voted the recreational group least worthy of rescue by John Q. Public. Some might go as far as deeming them Least Likely to Survive.

It certainly doesn't help the sport's reputation when a BASE jumper (aka someone who thinks jumping out of airplanes is too boring) who survives a botched jump and lives is shown on TV being escorted away from the scene in handcuffs. Most buildings, antennas, and bridges have strict bans against BASE jumping, and many cliffs are located in wildlife areas with similar restrictions.

"BASE jumping is a highly dangerous sport that can easily injure and kill participants." This dire warning was not uttered by someone looking to condemn the sport. Rather, it was lifted from an online forum published by BASE jumpers for BASE jumpers.

But just because someone gets hurt doing something that they know is illegal, should they be left to die? If so, it follows that everyone who goes over the posted speed limit and crashes their cars should also be left to die, right?

In the SAR community, we hear this statement on a regular basis: "I don't want *my* tax dollars being spent to save someone who obviously doesn't care if they die anyway." Again, following that line of thought, do we deny further healthcare to the four million Americans who care so little for their well-being that they have become morbidly obese? The answer to all of the above questions is, of course, no. We are Search and Rescue teams, not the Risk Assessment Police or the Cost/Benefit Militia.

BASE jumpers are a unique breed of skydivers. But are they so crazy that they are willing to chance death just to sate their appetite for a rush of adrenaline? Or is there more to it than that?

Having met a few of these individuals, I wouldn't dream of pretending these folks don't have serious thrill issues. Ask them why they do it, and you're likely to get a more abbreviated response than the one given by the mountaineer who was asked why he climbed the mountain. But instead of answering with the statement *because it was there,* the BASE jumper will likely counter with another question when asked why they do it: *Why not?*

The recent high profile death of BASE jumper and extreme athlete extraordinaire, Dean Potter, did little to silence the critics of the sport.

But from what I can tell, the simple act of launching oneself headlong into the void is neither a wanton act of stupidity nor grounds for a diagnosis of insanity. From my observations, it's more an exercise in attempted aerial, life-affirming perfection among these elite daredevils.

Millennial BASE jumpers may talk a big game on camera (you'd swear that they get paid royalties every time the word "dude" is spoken), but off camera and out of the limelight, most of them look at their jumps with complete and utter seriousness. They have to. They must gauge and time their bodies' reactions down to the hundredth of a second as they plummet toward the earth at 125 miles per hour.

Back in the day (at least my day—the late eighties and early nineties), the whole notion of BASE jumping was reserved for those who operated within the realm of James Bond. And skydiving, while more accessible, was far beyond the means of a guy making $6.75 an hour as a journalist in Parkersburg, West Virginia.

The best we could do back then was what I now refer to as the Poor Man's BASE Jump. If I knew then what I know now, I'd like to think I would reconsider my participation in such goofiness. Having since seen first-hand what a few hundred feet of free-fall does to the human body, I feel as if I now choose my thrills with much more care, and treat gravity with the respect it deserves. But being young (mid-twenties), dumb, ten feet tall and bulletproof, I was immune to such bouts of common sense at the time.

Step One of the Poor Man's BASE Jump: Spend several pre-jump hours at our favorite white trash heavy metal watering hole, the Wheel (or sometimes the upliftingly downtrodden Hill House), getting shit-faced drunk while waiting for the darkness that would provide the necessary cover for our nefarious (and illegal) plans.

Step Two of the Poor Man's BASE Jump: Hop in my Jeep and head to the Lion's Den Truck Stop off I-77. The Lion's Den, an adult bookstore offering more sin and vice than any of us cared to even guess at, sold nitrous oxide. You may know it better as laughing gas or the stuff they use in cans of whipped cream. While not illegal to sell, its use as a cheap recreational drug is illegal. I can't imagine that many dentists shopped at the Lion's Den for their nitrous supply, but who can say. Dentists just might be the only people stranger than mountain rescuers and BASE jumpers.

Anyway, each pressurized little canister, when fitted with a brass screw fitting, would fill a large balloon with nitrous. For those of you who have ever been to a Grateful Dead or Widespread Panic or Phish show, you can skip the next paragraph.

When you hold the balloon to your mouth and inhale the trapped gas in the balloon, a peculiar thing happens. For about ten to twelve seconds you see stars, sound warps and distorts to match the pulsing of the blood through your ears, and you experience more than a little euphoria. It's a short-lived sensation, and makes you feel like absolute crap if you do it more than a couple times a night. Oh, and it also causes irreversible brain damage to the part of your brain that controls speech if you do it too often.

After procuring our Whippets, as they were called commercially, we would pile back into my Jeep and head somewhere high. Seeing as how we were right on the Ohio River, this usually meant finding one of the half dozen bridges that spanned the mile or so of river between Ohio and West Virginia. Since automobile bridges had too much traffic for us to effect our illicit jumps, we usually opted for the railroad bridges. Though the trains ran several times a night, they allowed us time to plan our jumps between trains.

We would set our anchors on the bridge directly above where we guessed the edge of the shore to be. I say guessed, because there were no lights below us to illuminate either the river or the shore. This, of course, was part of the fun/stupidity.

Usually we tried to bring a few 150-foot ropes with us, which we rigged in a row next to each other. After harnessing up, running the rope through each of our figure-8 style descenders and hooking them to the backs of our harnesses, we were almost ready.

Standing at the edge of the bridge, we would shake our ropes and then listen. If we could hear the ropes slapping against the rocks or scrub brush on the edge of the shore, we knew we'd probably be okay—the ropes had touched down. Probably. And although we often trusted in the knowledge gleaned from previous jumps and the sounds we heard, sometimes we just had to trust the gods of drunken stupidity that we weren't going to rappel off the end of the rope and plummet to the ground. Most of our jumps averaged 100 feet off the ground, leaving us 50 feet of extra rope.

So once we were at least pretty sure our ropes had touched down, it was balloon time. Usually we designated one person to stay up top and untie and drop the ropes to us down below after we'd completed our jump. But before then, this individual was known as the Balloon Master. His duty was to fill each of our balloons (the huge ones that had a rubber band on them that kids use for punching—you know, the ones that smelled so strongly of rubber and left that weird white powder on your lips when you blew them up the correct way) and then hand them to us. We then held the end of the balloon closed between our tightly clenched teeth and inched our way to the edge of the abyss.

By attaching our descent devices to the backs of our harnesses, we could adjust the tension on the device by both our grip on the rope and how much friction we added by running the rope tighter to our chest. To go really fast, you simply relaxed your grip on the rope and extended your arm out straight. To slow down and eventually stop, you squeezed the rope tighter and brought it into your chest. It's commonly known as "Aussie" or "Australian-style" rappelling.

SWAT teams sometimes like to rappel down buildings and out of helicopters in this fashion, as it allows them to face down the rope (instead of the traditional rappelling stance in which they must look back over their shoulder to see below) while they train their weapon held in their free hand on the enemy below.

By locking your legs shoulder-width apart, if you lean forward, you can keep your body perpendicular to the edge until you are looking straight down, with your head level to your feet. Think Spider-Man. Once we were all lined up in this fashion, looking straight down into the inky blackness with a balloon full of nitrous held between our teeth (which was actually very difficult, given our tendency to giggle uncontrollably at this point), the Balloon Master's countdown would begin.

Looking back, it's amazing and amusing to me that nearly all of my ridiculously pointless and dangerous stunts were preceded by a countdown of some sort or other. When he reached zero, we would inhale the entire contents of the balloon, then launch ourselves into space. The race was on.

Now, let's take a moment to dissect this idiocy from the perspective of the well-trained and disciplined mountain rescuer. We were trespassing on and rappelling off of an active railroad trestle. We were at least somewhat ability impaired. We weren't wearing helmets. We weren't 100 percent sure our ropes reached the ground, or if they were even over terra firma at all. We were dangling a hundred feet in the air, inhaling a substance that—if inhaled too quickly—usually causes the inhaler to pass out.

Dropping like a stone down the rope in complete blackness, with your pulse reverberating wildly off the inside of your skull from the nitrous, and the wind bringing tears to your eyes as you try to maintain enough of your wits about you to guesstimate when you needed to slow your descent as the ground rushed up to meet you was probably as close as I'll ever get to an out-of-body experience.

Incredibly, the worst injury that I ever suffered was a twisted ankle. That was 1991. Eight years later, on a cold September night above treeline in Colorado, I came to realize just how lucky I had been to survive our Poor Man's BASE jumps.

Earlier that same evening, our Wednesday night Alpine Rescue Team board meeting was mercifully interrupted by the jangling of the phone in the adjacent communications room. The call was from a Clear Creek County sheriff's deputy who wondered if we'd mind fielding a call from someone who was worried that their friend might be missing.

Requests of this sort are not uncommon. But, not all who wander are lost, as J.R.R. Tolkien famously proclaimed in *The Fellowship of the Ring*. Here in RescueWorld, though, it's more like, not all who are reported as missing are lost.

I have learned that in the Rockies, a young Colorado male who tells his wife that he is "going for a hike in the mountains" sometimes has the same illicit intentions as a young Kentucky male who told his wife he was "going out fishing with the guys." Often, after a little detective work, we locate the "missing hiker" at a nearby cheap hotel, sharing a room (and bodily fluids) with a woman who is obviously not his wife. Or buying a bus ticket to Mexico. Or in an ambulance with a cracked skull after falling off a barstool (all true stories).

The Mission Leader who handles these types of calls must weigh a lot of factors before deciding to send out the troops to beat the bushes. The "lost" party's age, physical fitness, mental status, experience level, the local weather (current and pending), amount of time overdue, and the suspected area to be searched are all factors that come into play when an ML makes a go or no-go decision.

After speaking at length with the reporting party, Ron Bookman, our on-call ML that night, didn't have much to go on. Our potentially missing subject, Wayne Crill, hadn't been seen since the previous Saturday (it was now Wednesday night). But that in and of itself was not especially remarkable. Wayne was new to the area and had been sleeping on the couches of various friends until he could find a place to rent. He was unattached, somewhat of a free spirit and given to frequent unexplained absences.

So at that point, we had no search area and no proof that Wayne was even missing. But there was one important piece of information relayed to the soft-spoken, always bearded Ron that did set his spider-senses a-tingle and inspired him to dig a little deeper. Wayne was a BASE jumper (a real one, not my poor man's redneck version) who had a thing for sneaking off and jumping alone. His new favorite place to jump? The thousand-foot-tall series of granite cliffs known as the Black Wall on nearby Mount Evans. On a hunch, Ron called the Forest Service to see if they had recently ticketed any vehicles for being parked too long at any of the Mount Evans pull-offs.

As it turned out, they had ticketed an illegally parked car on Labor Day, that past Monday morning. After running the plates with the sheriff's office, it was determined that the vehicle belonged to a young transplanted Texan by the name of—you guessed it—Wayne Crill. The ticketed car provided Ron with enough evidence to launch a search effort. Many Alpine members were already gathered at The Shack for our board meeting, and we were more than happy to cut it short in preparation for our late-night search for Wayne.

Now, Mount Evans is a huge mountain, and having twenty to thirty rescuers storm its flanks in total darkness without targeting a specific search area first could be an enormous waste of time and resources. With the help of the reporting party (and a few sheriff's deputies), Ron located three of Wayne's friends. Two were pulled out of a movie theater by deputies and another was located at

The late Ron Bookman, the Alpine Rescue Team Mission Leader who had a hunch about BASE Jumper Wayne Crill's abandoned car being reason enough to initiate a large-scale search that ultimately saved Wayne's life. Photo courtesy of the Alpine Rescue Team.

a girlfriend's house. To save precious time, Ron wanted these friends (who were all BASE jumpers themselves) to meet us on Mount Evans and lead us to the landing zones below Wayne's favorite jumps. This was especially important given that we had no definitive last seen point from which to base our search.

An hour and a half later, we arrived at Mount Evans and established dual locations for our bases of operations. The Summit Lake base would serve as the entry point for two teams, and the Camp Schwayder base, 2,000 feet below and the standard trail out of the cavernous cirque on Mount Evans' north side, would serve as the ingress point for all other field teams.

Our first team in the field usually goes in fast and light. Comprised of our most savvy and strongest members, their goal is to cover as much ground as possible and search the areas of highest probability. The Team Leader for Team One that night was Alpine veteran Scott Grotheer, a man of few words and a sense of humor dry enough to use as kindling. He and his team entered the field from the Camp Schwayder base of operations. Their assignment: to make the 4-mile trek up to the base of the Black Wall on the remote and rugged northwest side of Mount Evans and use vocal attraction and line search techniques to locate Wayne.

We all skeptically prayed for the best-case scenario of finding a hypothermic, slightly injured, but still conscious Wayne. Any alternative scenario was too demoralizing to contemplate for very long.

Team Two was loaded into a team truck and driven to a lower trailhead in the hopes that they would find him at a lower elevation. My team, Team Three, waited for one of Wayne's friends to join us at the Summit Lake base before we entered the field. He would accompany us and hopefully provide some insight as to possible places that Wayne could have launched himself. Summit Lake base was located below the Black Wall, but still a couple thousand feet higher than the Camp Schwayder base below.

Alpine doesn't typically escort non-Alpine members into the field on searches that might unexpectedly turn into body recoveries. But sometimes their backcountry skills and important knowledge of our subject's habits and possible location make them too valuable a resource to leave behind back in the parking lot.

We set out into the moonless mountain night. Our goal: the east side of the nearly thousand-foot-high Black Wall, which was the favorite jump site of our missing parachutist, Wayne Crill. Our headlamps cast each other's distorted silhouettes on the house-sized boulders littering the north side of the mountain. None of us held much hope that the outcome of this particular mission would be a happy one.

Wayne's friend was understandably on the verge of tear-filled hysteria, certain that his friend was dead. Alpine member Rachel Emmer did her level best to ply him with lots of questions. What was Wayne like? When had they last jumped together? How had they met? I knew what Rachel was up to. If she could keep Wayne's friend talking, it would give him a chance to focus on something constructive and perhaps give us a clue as to where we should look for what was left of the man we were all certain was beyond our help.

The presence of Wayne's close friend within the ranks of our field team added a level of complexity to the situation. He anxiously lit a smoke almost every time we stopped to do our vocal attraction. His perspiration smelled faintly of nervousness and beer. I could not fault him for smelling of either, as he hadn't asked to be yanked from the routine of his life to scramble around a two-square-mile field of rocks in the dark at an elevation of 13,000 feet. I admired him for his dedication to his friend and for volunteering to partici-pate in the search.

If we did stumble across Wayne's battered corpse, I was seriously wor-ried about his friend's reaction to the grisly discovery. I could tell from the sideways glances Rachel and I shared in the light of our headlamps that her concerns mirrored my own. In my (at the time admittedly limited) SAR ex-perience, a shovel and wheelbarrow and multiple body bags were usually the only tools needed once you located someone who fell hundreds of feet.

In all honesty, I felt kind of foolish for walking around in the dark shout-ing "WA-AYNE … WA-AYNE …" over and over till we were all hoarse. At this point, we knew that his chute was not in his parked car, and that he'd been missing for days. He was definitely somewhere on the mountain, and he had definitely jumped off of something. But to stop yelling on a search like this, regardless of how hopeless the situation, is to admit defeat.

Sometimes this means stumbling around in the dark screaming the name of a man who, if alive, had somehow survived a horrible fall of hundreds of feet, likely landing in the rocks above treeline with no food, water, shelter, or proper clothing to protect him from the temperatures that were nightly plummeting to zero degrees Fahrenheit. The phrase "snowball's chance in hell" kept running through the back of my mind.

When interviewed before we began our search, Wayne's friends detailed his fondness for waiting till the last millisecond to deploy his chute and I morbidly wondered if we had the flimsy blue or the more sturdy-handled black body bags on our rescue truck.

I also tried to imagine the horrible bloody mess we would likely find. For just as champion figure skaters visualize their routine in their mind's eye before performing it to prevent any surprises, I've found that when faced with the possibility of finding a corpse on a search, conjuring the absolute worst carnage I've seen in horror films or combat still photos diminishes the shock. That way, when I find the body, it's not as bad as what I've pre-imagined. Usually.

I think you could attend a hundred funerals or memorial services and still be unprepared to witness death in this fashion. For the mountain rescuer who comes face to face with the deceased in the backcountry, death is a visceral and quite earthy experience. There are no artificial arrangements of sweetly scented flowers. We are greeted with the cloying and sickly sweet smell of flesh succumbing to the natural processes that eventually reclaim us all.

There are no morticians to make the deceased look life-like (which I've always found an ironic play on the eulogizing words "Even in the midst of life we are surrounded by death"). Our Western proclivity for prettifying our dead makes it seem to me that even in death, we seek the outward appearance of life. The only makeup (usually varying shades of red, blue, or the worst—green) on our deceased subjects is either from natural decay or the result of the accident that ended their life.

There are no soothing hymns here. The closest we get to a hymn is the sound of the wind whistling over the snow and between the rocks. There are no sounds of the softly uttered prayers for the deceased. In fact, the only epitaph you are apt to hear is the one pronounced over the two-way radio each field team carries: "MRA Code 4," which is the shorthand rescue-speak used by mountain rescuers to alert everyone who might be listening that our subject is deceased. We use it as a kind of warning to the Mission Leader to clear the family or media away from a radio, so we can transmit the bad news. This was the pronouncement I fully expected to hear when our radio crackled to life.

"Our subject has been located," Scott announced in a clipped and controlled voice over the radio. Several minutes ticked by. We all stopped what we were doing and waited breathlessly (quite literally, as the air is pretty thin at that altitude) for information that would point us in the right direction to meet up with the find team and begin what we suspected would be a body recovery.

"Mission Base, We have an MRA Code 2." I could hear the stunned silence of disbelief both over the radio and in our own group.

"Team One, this is Mission Base, please repeat that last transmission?" He did, and we *still* didn't believe what we had heard.

MRA Code 2?!? Surely this must be Scott's quirky sense of humor at play. He could have casually announced that they came across the Dalai Lama and Elvis shooting beer cans with a 12-gauge out there and it would have seemed more plausible. MRA Code 2 means that the injured subject has been located, and assistance is needed to get them out of the field. Injured. Not dead—injured. Wayne Crill was alive.

This changed everything. Smiling, we commenced to high-fiving. In the previous forty years, the Alpine Rescue Team had never found someone alive and then had them subsequently die during the evacuation. We felt pretty damned confident we could keep that streak going, and we were flush with the excitement that only a life-saving rescue provides. We were going to save someone's life tonight! This kind of high was clean, pure, and fulfilling on a spiritual level that I would imagine religious zealots must surely experience as they encounter the divine. It's that powerful.

We spied a cluster of headlamps below us that we assumed belonged to Team One, so we set off in that direction. Twenty or so minutes later, we rounded the corner of a monolithic, Stone Henge–like boulder. Peering over the shoulders of the rescuers encircling the downed BASE jumper, our headlamps illuminated a scene that brought all celebratory thoughts to a screeching halt and nearly caused me to wretch.

The pitiful shape illuminated in the circle of light from my headlamp barely looked human. My first impression, after revulsion, was that someone was mistaken. There was no way this thing was alive.

My practiced technique of pre-visualizing worst-case scenarios didn't prepare me for what lay at the foot of that giant rock. The fact that this mangled mess of a man lying at my feet was alive somehow made it more difficult to cope with than if he'd been dead when we discovered him. It somehow seemed … unnatural and wrong that someone could be so horribly disfigured, yet still draw breath a full three days after his accident.

His colorful chute (and some of the colors weren't from the parachute manufacturer, they originated from Wayne) was partially draped across his body. At first, I couldn't put my finger on what looked so out of place about his bloody visage. Then I realized with a start that his entire face was smashed flat as a board, with both eyes swollen completely shut. His mouth, partially open, revealed the jagged pieces of the few teeth that survived the impact.

His arms, legs, hands, and feet were frozen at impossible angles. Akimbo is the word, I believe. At each bend, splintered, yellowish-green knobs of bone poked out through tattered and blood-encrusted clothing.

We guessed that his chute had partially deployed after the jump and slowed his fall enough to allow for survival. Based upon his injuries, it was likely that he had smashed into the colossal tombstone rock that now loomed above us with his arms and legs out in front of him, as if to ward off the tremendous and inescapable impact. His chute had covered him after he fell to the ground, keeping his core temperature high enough to prevent him from freezing to death. But the same freezing temperatures that threatened to kill him by hypothermia had paradoxically prevented him from bleeding out. His body had reserved most of his circulation for warming his core, thus robbing his arms and legs of blood that would have simply run out of him and onto the frozen ground.

His friends (there were now two of them on scene) huddled close to Wayne and spoke hushed and tense words of encouragement in his bloodied ears that still oozed what looked to be cerebral-spinal fluid. Occasionally their heartfelt exhortations elicited a weak, gurgled moan of pain-wracked acknowledgment from Wayne.

Stepping back from the halo of light encircling Wayne, the enormity of what now lay ahead of us struck me full force. It hadn't even occurred to me (or anyone else) that we might have to devise an evacuation plan for a living, breathing human being. I expected we would find his battered body at the base of the cliff, take some photos for the coroner, scoop him into a bag, and carry him out.

Wayne needed a paramedic with a bag full of drugs, a litter, and lots of oxygen. We had none of those things on-site, so we requested them via radio. We were about a four-and-a-half miles uphill from Mission Base, so we didn't expect the cavalry to arrive anytime soon.

It was now approaching one in the morning, and the night sky was crystal clear. We guessed temps were in the teens. Many of us, expecting that we could be out searching for the entire night, had brought bivy sacs and sleeping bags. We huddled together under them, and took turns monitoring Wayne's condition. All we could offer him was a space blanket and choked words of encouragement.

Taking my turn at his side, it was impossible to detect the rise and fall of his chest under the silvery space blanket. I was genuinely concerned that he would simply stop breathing while I knelt there, and I'd never know. So every ten minutes or so, I nudged his shoulder lightly and called his name. He responded by letting a low moan escape his clotted throat, and slightly turning his head toward me.

It was also impossible for me to escape a creepy sense of guilt-ridden déjà vu. My own poorly planned but luckily executed thrill-seeking endeavors should have ended like this. *That should be me lying there*, I thought guiltily.

The fact that it wasn't me filled me with both gratitude and the inexplicable groundless fear that I was probably meant to get run over by a bus instead.

Brian, the paramedic from Clear Creek County EMS, arrived after three in the morning. He quickly assessed Wayne's condition and determined there was no way in hell he would survive the jostling and lost time that a four-hour carry-out down the steep and rocky trail to an ambulance would entail. This left a helicopter evacuation as the only viable option for Wayne's survival. But Flight For Life did not fly into the mountains at night back then. It was simply too dangerous without the night vision goggles they now use. We would have to find a way to keep Wayne alive till daybreak.

To that end, Brian would give Wayne low-flow oxygen and get an IV set up to administer pain meds. Once the meds had dulled his pain, we would begin moving and repositioning his limbs. Then, we could pull traction on one of his legs to straighten it out. The leg might need to be amputated if we didn't get the restricted blood flow issue to his foot resolved. Pulling traction involved holding Wayne's thigh in place while Brian positioned himself at his foot, and, grasping his ankle, pulling with all his might till the leg was straight. The exposed bone could then be temporarily tucked back inside the wound. It seemed to me like some medieval torture technique akin to the rack. Although the danger from infection is serious when this action was performed, Brian estimated the potential consequences for leaving the problem uncorrected were much greater.

As two of us knelt and prepared to hold Wayne down, Brian crouched over Wayne's waist to reposition his leg. When he grasped the limb, lifted and rotated it, we heard a slight ripping sound—like two pieces of Velcro being pulled apart as the leg broke free from the clotted and frozen blood that held his leg fast to the ground. A noxious wave of trapped gas, released from the wound by the injured limb's movement, caught the three of us fully in the face. Imagine a hundred pounds of raw hamburger left out for a week in the

Texas summer heat, and that might come close to describing the rotten stench of what clawed its way down our nostrils and into our throats. Brian, overcome by the hideous and unexpected attack of odor, leaned off to one side and unceremoniously added the scent of vomit to the hit parade of other smells (like urine, old blood, and fecal matter) that wafted through the chill air.

Quickly regaining his composure, Brian took his trauma shears and carefully cut away the clothing from the area around that particular wound. More bad news—gangrene had set in. The smell of it would be on my clothes, skin, hair, and in my nose for days afterward. And yes, it was actually green.

Seeing that we would be unable to get Wayne strapped into the litter and onto the chopper unless the leg was straightened, Brian made the tough call to proceed. With two of us holding Wayne down (getting more than a little of the fluids that had already escaped from his wounds all over us in the process), Brian gave a mighty tug. In spite of all the pain meds now flowing through his veins, Wayne gave a scream, muffled though it was from the remains of his swollen tongue (he had bitten clean through most of it on impact). With a slight, wet popping sound, the leg did indeed straighten out. Wayne sagged a little, either from exhaustion or a feeling of relief at having his leg straightened out after being bent 90 degrees out of joint for three days.

After that, there wasn't much else any of us could do. It was just too cold to really sleep, so we ended up shuffling around in a circle swinging our arms and occasionally hopping up and down to generate some heat.

About forty-five minutes before the chopper was due, we gently loaded Wayne into the litter. We wanted our arrival at the landing zone to coincide with that of the helicopter, in the event that the sudden movement of Wayne sent him into cardiac arrest. The bird would be equipped with an automatic external defibrilator and an experienced flight nurse. The helicopter ride to the hospital in Denver would be quick, less than twenty minutes. If we had opted to carry Wayne out and sent him to the hospital in an ambulance, it would have taken several bone-jarring hours.

The short trail carry through the maze of boulders to the LZ was uneventful, and I think we were all grateful for the opportunity to get some of our own blood flowing.

We heard the chopper before we saw it. It arrived just as the sun peaked over the east ridge. I'd bet that I was not the only rescuer who heard the virulent and robust strains of Wagner's "Ride of the Valkyries" playing in my head as the chopper crested the orange ridge and landed a short distance away. Minutes later, Wayne was on board and flying directly into the sunrise.

It often seems as if no one ever needs to be rescued in daylight or in good weather. But regardless of the time or place, the Alpine Rescue Team has never charged anyone one single penny for their rescue. Photo by Dale Atkins.

It's always a strange feeling of letdown after a subject is evacuated by helicopter. All of the urgency instantly disappears. You are suddenly bereft of any further responsibility for your subject's care. The adrenaline wears off, leaving you feeling a bit shaky and edgy. No one says much as you pick up the gear that is strewn around, sling your pack on, and begin the long walk back to the mundane world of McDonald's, Facebook, traffic jams, and talk radio.

On this particular walk back to civilization, I borrowed gum from someone to get the taste of decay out of my mouth (it didn't work) and wondered absently, *What kind of life would Wayne have if he survived? Would he spend the rest of his life in a wheelchair? Drinking his pureed steak through a straw?* Surely, I mused, a complete recovery was impossible. Right?

Just goes to show how much I know. Wayne did indeed survive. With a vengeance. All the King's doctors and all the King's surgeons found a way to put Humpty Dumpty back together again.

Not only was his recovery a complete success, but one year later, Wayne was rock climbing again and we ran into him at a parking lot near his accident site on Mount Evans. He was still in need of some dental work, but for the most part, he looked pretty damned good. He was very appreciative of our efforts to get him out of the backcountry.

As he walked over to his car and began chucking his climbing gear into it, I marveled that neither Icarus nor Evel Knievel had anything on Wayne Crill.

A year after our run-in with Wayne at Summit Lake, I heard that he had taken up BASE jumping again, had broken both legs again, and would be flying the friendly skies again as soon as he was healed enough to do so. He had also taken a wife, who was, of course, a BASE jumper herself.

Sadly, in 2014, gravity reasserted its dominance over Wayne when he suffered a 60-foot fall from a climb in Eldorado Canyon. In spite of the helmet he wore that day, Wayne suffered from a traumatic brain injury that, at the time of this writing, has forced him into assisted living.

I guess I should feel put off that Wayne seems so hell-bent on destroying himself. That he may have a death wish (especially in light of the fact that the man arguably most responsible for saving Wayne's life, Alpine Rescue Team Mission Leader Ron Bookman, was so unjustly taken from us in 2005 when he suffered a seizure, fell off his mountain bike, and broke his neck—leaving his twelve-year-old-daughter fatherless).

But I don't, because I don't think there is any way that Wayne would have survived those three solitary days of torture, and all his subsequent battles with gravity, if he didn't have an almost superhuman will to live.

Paradoxically, I think Wayne's drive to live, and not to simply exist, is what propelled him to the brink of death time and time again.

But that's just a guess. And as the immortal Ulysses Everett McGill once said, "It's a fool who looks for logic in the chambers of the human heart."

Couldn't agree more—especially if that human heart beats in the chest of a BASE jumper and climber like Wayne Crill, the (nearly) Indestructible Man. May you never give up or give in, Wayne.

Recovery

An unfortunate part of SAR work, recoveries often push our members to their physical and emotional limits. Photo by Tom Wood.

Suicide: The Low Side of
That Rocky Mountain High

I think Colorado is a great place to live. Aside from the stunning natural beauty of its purple mountain majesties and plentiful amber waves of grain, there are many, many reasons why Colorado's population has exploded over the last three decades.

If you are a wealthy, wannabe hippie, we've got Aspen. If you are a real hippie, we've got Crestone. If you are a religious conservative, we've got Colorado Springs. If you are hankerin' for the cowboy life, we've got that statewide.

Outdoor sports enthusiast? Pick any recreational activity under the sun (except maybe surfing) and there's probably a group or club somewhere in the state dedicated to introducing like-minded fanatics. You're a hipster? You can rent a chic loft in Lodo and drink mojitos all night while Twittering and texting all your friends till your fingers bleed. Professional sports fan? Got all those bases covered as well.

But for some, that Rocky Mountain High (you didn't think you'd escape a book about anything that takes place in Colorado without at least one John Denver reference, did you?) lifestyle has a darker flip-side. Colorado is also a popular place to kill yourself. Year in and year out, more Coloradans die by their own hands than from automobile accidents and homicides combined.

And Colorado is not the only mountainous western state with this problem. Arizona, Colorado, Oregon, Washington, Utah, Idaho, Wyoming, Montana, New Mexico, Nevada, and Alaska lead the U.S. in per capita suicide rates (according to the American Foundation for Suicide Prevention). Suicide is now the tenth leading cause of death in the U.S., according to the Centers for Disease Control and Prevention, and the World Health Organization reports that world-wide, suicide rates have increased by 60 percent over the last half century.

As a result, more and more backcountry rescuers and first responders are coming face to face with an issue that in 1999, the Surgeon General deemed, "a national public health problem." Suicide.

Increasingly, the rescuers and first responders who are repeatedly tasked with handling death and tragedy are finding themselves susceptible to the very same emotional and mental issues that plagued the suicides they recover.

"First responders are a culture in and of themselves ... Most people think first and then act. First responders are trained to act without hesitation. To do that, they can't consider their feelings. They're taught to think and not feel or they'll make a mistake and someone might die. The normal human mechanism in a crisis is to feel. But we try to keep those feelings to ourselves because otherwise we'll be perceived as weak," said Pete Volkmann, social worker and veteran of the Ossining, New York, Police Department in an article in *EHS Today*.

Mental health agencies that track suicide rates for first responders, professional rescuers, and law enforcement officers are reporting some sobering statistics. One study that examined North Carolina firefighters reported, "Compared with professional firefighter line-of-duty deaths, suicides occurred more than three times as often." (Fire Engineering, December 2012)

The Chicago Fire Department states that they have lost thirty-seven firefighters to suicide since they began tracking this method of death, and the Chicago Firefighters Union Local 2 Employee Assistance Program extrapolated from what data they could find that, at least in Chicago, the suicide rate for firefighters was roughly double the national average.

And though we as a society now recognize that U.S. military veterans struggle with suicide (a controversial and widely referenced media report based on statistics gathered by the Department of Veterans Affairs reported in 2013 that on average, twenty-two military veterans *a day* take their own lives), most people are unaware that per capita suicide rates for law enforcement officers and first responders are approaching those of returning war veterans.

I have lived in the shadow of the Rocky Mountains for a quarter of my life now, and been involved with mountain rescue as a member of the Alpine Rescue Team for almost the same length of time. I think of the mountains as a beautiful, vibrant place to call my home. And apparently, I am not alone. Many national surveys rate our country's mountainous states as some of the happiest, healthiest, and most desirable states in which to live (the Gallup-Healthways Well Being Index ranked three mountain states—Colorado, Montana, and Utah—as being in the top ten happiest U.S. states for 2013).

So how is it possible that some of the happiest states in America are simultaneously the same states with the highest per capita suicide rates? Here in Colorado, for example, the year 2014 posted the highest-ever total number of suicides at 1,058, according to the Colorado Department of Public Health and Environment. Suicide beat out homicide (172), car accidents (486), influenza and pneumonia (668), and diabetes (826) as the number one killer. So even though Colorado does have one of the lowest obesity rates in the nation and roughly three hundred days of sunshine per year, there's apparently much more to staying mentally healthy than being skinny and having a good tan.

So why does that Rocky Mountain High lifestyle have such a dark flipside? I've asked myself that question over and over since 2006. Because, in one disheartening stretch that year, the Alpine Rescue Team was paged for eight consecutive suicides over a twelve-week period. No less disconcerting than the volume was the total lack of any recognizable pattern to this bizarre string of tragedies. Young, old, male, female, single, married—each demographic segment was equally represented. The only thing that they all had in common was that they were all white. Hanging, self-inflicted gunshot wound, overdose, asphyxiation, jumping off a cliff—there was not even one consistent method used for completing a suicide.

Utilizing gallows humor (a common, crude, and often effective coping mechanism), some of us on the Alpine Rescue Team began to jokingly refer to ourselves as the Alpine Recovery Team.

That seemingly random string of grisly, tragic deaths made no sense, left the whole team demoralized for weeks, and was mentioned as the main reason some team members hung up their helmets and walked away from mountain rescue.

As a way to cope with and try to make sense of those eight suicide recoveries, I set out to write an article about suicide recoveries and how mountain rescuers could better deal with their psychological aftermath—but quickly shelved what I'd written. As hard as it can be to deal with suicide as a rescuer, I came to realize it was even harder to *write* about suicide as a rescuer.

In my previous life, I was a West Virginia journalist (no wisecracks please—we used words as well as lots of pictures) working at the *Parkersburg News* back in the early '90s. In those days, we were strictly forbidden from covering a suicide in the newspaper unless it somehow crossed over into the realm of newsworthiness. Therefore, it went against my ethics in journalism training (again—no wisecracks please—there really used to be such a thing) to publicly broach a topic that was typically banished from open discussion and only spoken of in whispered, hushed tones behind closed doors. And to be honest, information on suicide statistics was hard to come by in 2006, especially in relation to mountain rescue. Most mountain rescue teams did not separate suicides from the recoveries they listed in their annual reports (if they even had annual reports), and they certainly didn't record the suicides of their own members.

I quickly realized I could usually handle responding to suicides as a mountain rescuer, but felt ill-equipped to write about such a complex—and controversial—subject. I feared that I would say the wrong thing, or callously reopen the wounds of either rescuers who had dealt with a suicide recovery or those who'd lost their loved ones to suicide. And God knows I had no intention of discussing anything personal relating to suicide. And not because I had previous suicidal thoughts that I feared to share. Quite the opposite.

I can honestly say I've never entertained a suicidal thought in my life. Not even for a millionth of a second, even in my darkest, lowest hour. This is not a boast, or something I say to put myself above those who have struggled with that dark impulse. I make this admission because I don't want to insult those who have had those thoughts by pretending I feel their pain in an article focusing on suicide. I just couldn't understand why anyone would want to end their own life, and this made the task of writing about suicide doubly hard for me.

Not to say that I don't feel indescribable sadness that some people have that turn of mind. I sometimes wish I could experience that kind of pain—just for a fleeting moment—if for no other reason than I could then say, "I know exactly how you feel," to those who've confided to me this desire to be rid of the world. But that admission sounds condescending and hollow even to me.

So I gave up, and pushed it out of my thoughts. *You're not supposed to talk about that kind of stuff anyway. It's TOO PERSONAL,* my inner critic scolded me.

But in spite of my reticence to write about suicide recoveries in the mountains, this troubling trend continued. For both the Alpine Rescue Team and our neighboring team to the north, the Rocky Mountain Rescue Group, suicides are the number one category of fatality we recover from the mountains. Not rock climbers. Not skiers. Not hikers. Suicides.

"We have had some members take suicide recoveries pretty hard. We are making sure that everyone who goes on one is contacted within a day or two, particularly support members," said former RMRG member Dan Lack.

So the longer I thought about my failed attempt to write about suicide, the more I realized that it was this persistent reluctance to talk openly about suicide that fostered its growth. By giving up on my article about how the first responder community could better cope with the aftermath of suicide in the backcountry, I felt that I was doing a great disservice to both the people who struggle with suicidal thoughts and the first responders who come to their aid or bring them out of the backcountry to provide closure for the loved ones they've left behind.

The contagion of suicide thrives on silence like a cancer. And according to mental health professionals, it's treatable, just like measles or polio. But while there is no vaccination for suicide, there are strategies that help contain its spread. There is a catch, though; in order for these strategies to work, they have to be *shared. Talked about. Written about.*

That's how they work. And although presenting charts and graphs and facts and statistics in an article on suicide seemed all good and fine (and safe), I felt that if I tackled this subject, I wanted to take a personal, conversational approach, since initiating open discussion on suicide is the first step to its prevention.

And also, since suicide recoveries in the mountains aren't likely coming to an end anytime soon (if ever), I wanted the ability to offer more useful advice than that which I received as a rookie rescuer in those difficult times: "Be sure to let someone know if you are having a tough time coping." I've always felt that that kind of crap advice is about as useful as telling a rock climber, "The best way to stay safe when climbing is not to fall."

I came to the conclusion that I needed to finish what I started, but I knew I was in over my head. I had to get answers from someone who could educate me and help me approach the subject matter with sensitivity. An expert who could help make sense out of something that, to me, seemed so senseless.

"Suicide should be treated as the public health issue that it is, and not as a religious or criminal issue," said psychologist Sally Spencer-Thomas. Sally would know. A nationally recognized psychologist who specializes in suicide prevention, she learned firsthand how to deal with suicide and its devastating aftermath when she lost her own brother, Carson, to it in 2004.

As both a way to find meaning in Carson's death and hopefully provide others with the means to prevent or cope with a similar loss, she founded the Carson J. Spencer Foundation, a nonprofit organization that deals in the workplace and at schools with suicide, devises public health strategies for the workplace and educational institutions, and provides bereavement support for those dealing with the aftermath of suicide.

I contacted Sally because, unlike many psychologists who approach the subject of suicide from a purely academic, scientific, and objective perspective, she used humor and first-hand experience to approach suicide from the viewpoint of both a mental health professional *and* someone who has been out there on the front lines. Also, she happens to be my neighbor.

When we first sat down to discuss the cheery subject of suicide a couple days before Christmas in 2011, I immediately asked her why suicides were most common around the holidays. Like so many other things, it turns out I was grossly misinformed on this topic.

"December is actually the lowest month for suicides," she said, as we sat in her living room next to her family's enormous twinkling Christmas tree. Citing the increased presence of family members and the hectic schedule of the holidays, she explained away that common suicide misconception with a wave of her hand. "April and May are statistically the highest months," she said.

As we talked, her son Tanner practiced Christmas tunes on his guitar. Her eldest son Nick did his best to show his youngest brother Jackson how to blow up the Death Star on the family Xbox. Midway through our conversation, her husband Randy came home from Christmas shopping, stomped the snow off his boots, and chucked the take-n-bake pizza he'd brought home into the oven while we continued our chat on the couch a few feet away from their kids. I mention the setting for our discussion about suicide because it perfectly exemplifies Sally's message about suicide prevention. It's a topic that should be discussed out in the open, without hesitation, and sometimes even in front of the kids. She practices what she preaches. Unfortunately for those in need of help in the western U.S., there are not enough people like Sally being encouraged to preach this gospel.

"As a state, we're just not willing to treat this as the real health issue that it is. In Colorado, there is simply no culture of help-seeking for those who are struggling," she said.

Sally noted that in 2006, Colorado was ranked dead last in state-allocated funds for substance abuse awareness and prevention. It was hard for me not to correlate that fact to the string of suicides that Alpine had dealt with in the course of that same year.

"So why do western U.S. mountain states consistently lead the pack in per capita suicide rates?" I asked.

"There are many studies out there that indicate altitude plays a significant role in an increased per capita suicide rate worldwide, but mountain states with high suicide rates have several other factors that contribute to their disproportionately high suicide rates," she said. "The geographic isolation that so many people in the mountains must deal with, a high rate of firearm ownership, a high rate of alcohol consumption, and a pervasive pull-yourself-up-by-your-own-bootstraps cultural attitude all play a part.

"The very same active lifestyle that contributes to the high levels of overall fitness in western mountain states also carries with it the built-in expectation that seeking early help for mental issues such as bipolar disorders and depression is a sign of weakness. It's an unwritten rule that everyone should *power through* their problems. Alone," she said.

I'd seen this single-minded determination to remain untouched by the tragedies swirling around them in many rescuers. Myself included. As if reading my mind, Sally said, "First responders are especially vulnerable to the after-effects of suicide. There are certainly painful but normal responses that first responders go through after dealing with a suicide. But when they go unresolved, they can grow into a disorder. How first responders walked into that event can affect how well they cope with it later," she said.

Even the way we talk about the topic of suicide is important, Sally explained.

DON'T say: Someone "committed suicide." This phrase carries many implied negative religious and criminal implications—*someone committed a crime*, or *committed a sin.*

DO say: Someone *completed* a suicide.

DON'T say: There is a suicide "epidemic." This can encourage at-risk individuals to see themselves as part of a larger story and may elevate suicide risk.

DO say: There is a suicide contagion.

DON'T say: A suicide attempt was "successful," "unsuccessful," or "failed" when speaking of suicide. It's hazardous to suggest that non-fatal suicide attempts represent "failure," or that completed suicides are "successful."

DO say: There was a *suicide death* or an *attempted suicide.*

The longer Sally and I talked about suicide (the sounds of an exploding Death Star and slightly out-of-tune guitar chords in the background), I realized with a start that more and more of my questions were coming from Tom the Regular Person and not from Tom the Writer or Tom the Mountain Rescuer.

It began to feel like I was in therapy; that I should be laying on the couch while *she* took the notes, asking me about my relationship with my mother and charging me $100 an hour.

"What should you say to someone who's expressing suicidal thoughts?" I asked.

"What *shouldn't* you say to someone expressing suicidal thoughts?" I asked.

"What are the warning signs of someone contemplating suicide?" I asked.

"How seriously should you take someone who mentions that they have thought of killing themselves?" I asked. These questions weren't just part of my research for an article. They were questions that needed answers for much more personal reasons.

And as I sat in Sally's living room scribbling my notes by the light of her family's Christmas tree, I suddenly realized why my article on suicide in the mountains wouldn't allow me to keep it locked in my brain. It was trying to speak to me, to tell me something. It was trying to tell me that I needed to finish it so that in the future, I could arm myself with the proper tools and methods to respond not to my own thoughts of suicide, but to those shared thoughts coming from others near and dear to me—people in both my biological and rescue family.

Even though I've never entertained a suicidal thought in my life, I know people who have. I've had three situations in my personal life (outside of my involvement with mountain rescue) when I've dealt with someone contemplating or attempting suicide. I mishandled all three situations miserably.

As I've said, I don't feel that mountain rescuers ply their trade in a void. This was one of the core reasons I wanted to write a book about my experiences in RescueWorld in the first place. God knows that those of us who work in that environment don't walk in as a tabula rasa. We all wander into these searches and rescues and recoveries carrying around a lot of personal history. And it seemed to me that the recoveries we performed tugged at old repressed memories more than the searches or rescues did.

The recovery missions for people who completed suicides (for me anyway) are always more difficult than the "typical" recoveries we see in Rescue-World. For it was not simple bad luck, bad weather, an avalanche, a falling rock, a sudden heart attack, or a bolt of lightning that stole the breath from this person; it was their own hand that wrenched the unwanted spark of life from their bodies and cast it away.

One of my goals in writing about how we as first responders handle suicide was to spark discussion in the SAR community of ways we could better arm ourselves when combating the residual effects of a suicide recovery. Or discover ways we can avoid succumbing ourselves. Or in the rare occasions when we are called in to help reason with a suicidal person in the backcountry, have at least a few more arrows in our quiver.

I know I sure could have used a few of those arrows back in the winter of 2003. Around 2:00 a.m. on a cold March night, we received a page from the Jefferson County Sheriff's Office requesting assistance with the evacuation of a critically injured, suicidal patient in the Windy Saddle area of Lookout Mountain (so named because it looks down on the city of Golden below).

It was snowing as we arrived at a scene that looked more like a hostage standoff than a simple rescue of an injured subject in the backcountry. There were two fire engines blocking the road, a couple of ambulances, and at least a half dozen squad cars blocking the road. Everyone had their lights flashing, which made the area look more like a disco than a lonely mountain road.

Parking was at a premium, as there was no real shoulder on either side of the road. To the east, the lights of Golden twinkled hundreds of feet below. Off the west side of the road, the only light visible was a single winking turn signal a couple hundred feet down the steep hillside below us. Apparently, this was to be an up-haul of some poor motorist who took a turn a little too fast and slid off the road. Happens all the time in Colorado.

Funny thing was that this was just about the only straight stretch of the road on Lookout Mountain. The light dusting of snow on the road clued us in on another peculiarity. The tire tracks still imprinted in that snow on the road indicated that our happy motorist had driven straight off the edge of the cliff. Judging by the trees and scrub brush that remained untouched directly below these tires tracks where they left the road, this person had been hauling ass.

Hmmm, a(nother) Thelma and Louise *wannabe?* I wondered as I readied my gear. Ending your life by driving off a cliff was not an unusual choice for despondent Coloradans.

As we awaited further instructions, we scanned the wreckage below. No EMS personnel could be seen down there working to extricate or treat an injured driver. In fact, the wreckage site was completely abandoned. And all the EMTs and paramedics were seated inside their nice warm ambulances.

We are taught to congregate away from the center of activity at Mission Base while awaiting a field assignment, so we were out of earshot from the communications vehicle. Even so, I could sense frustration and anger in the tone and body language of the Jefferson County deputy who limped around our communications van as he relayed the situation to our Mission Leader, Ron Bookman. Shortly thereafter, Ron waved us over and filled us in on the situation. Apparently, a life was at stake. The briefing was brief.

"Our subject is way down below the wreck in the woods somewhere. He's dying, we need to get him up here as quick as possible, and the cops are royally pissed at this guy," he said. "Oh yeah, take lots of rubber gloves with you," he added.

Being the good soldiers we were, we didn't ask for any additional explanations that would delay us. Five minutes later, a half dozen of us set out loaded down with a litter, ropes, and medical gear. A single deputy and a paramedic accompanied us (since the Alpine Rescue Team is considered a Basic Life Support agency, we were not allowed to carry or push drugs for our patients—hence the Advanced Life Support paramedic from the Highland Rescue Team Ambulance). The deputy in our party was in touch with the other law enforcement officers who were already with the subject. They talked us down to their location, about a mile below the crash site.

At that point, we were too winded and busy mentally planning our route back up and out to ask any of the questions we were dying to ask. Why were the deputies so pissed at this guy? What were his injuries? And most importantly, how—and why—the hell did he end up more than a mile below the wreck of a car that he had just driven off a freakin' cliff?

When we finally arrived, breathless and sweating despite the low temperatures, it was to a decidedly surreal scene. A few law enforcement officers were huddled around a small, hastily prepared and smoky fire. They were warming their hands, and waved casually at us as we emerged from the gloom, clinking and clanking and huffing. Were it not for the fact that they were in full uniform and the firelight glinted off both their shiny patent leather black shoes and holstered weapons, we could have easily assumed we stumbled upon some guys sharing a few laughs and beers around the campfire on a cold late winter's eve.

As we took all this in, we realized there was something missing. Namely, our injured subject. When we asked where he was, one of the deputies waved distractedly over his shoulder to a small stand of scrub brush at the edge of the flickering light provided by the fire.

"He's over there," he said with undisguised disgust.

In the foggy gloom, our subject's slumped and still form was nearly indistinguishable from the large and rounded rocks that punctuated the snowy scrub brush—until he shuddered. As we approached him, donning our rubber gloves, he again shuddered violently, like someone had just walked over his grave, as they say in the dime store detective novels. And in this case, the analogy was apparently not too far away becoming literal.

While a couple of our members with more medical training knelt down and set about the business of assessing his condition with the paramedic, our Site Commander John Wells interviewed the deputies so we could piece together just what in the Wide Wide World of Sports was going on.

I busied myself assembling the litter we would use to carry our subject, Tim, all the while keeping my ear cocked to John and the officer. I wanted to hear what events led to this bizarre situation. After hearing what preceded our arrival, I scoff no more at Hollywood's exaggerated portrayals of the incredible amount of abuse the human body can endure and still perform physiological *Die Hard* movie-style miracles.

Let's back up a little bit here, and take a moment to explain the circumstances that brought Tim to his present desperate and dire situation.

A couple hours before we received our page from the sheriff's office to respond to Windy Saddle, a routine traffic stop occurred on nearby Interstate 70. A state trooper had pulled over a small sedan for driving erratically. No big deal, I'm sure he thought to himself. This was likely yet another case of someone who'd had a few too many Coors Lights and refused to turn his keys over to his buddies. But after speaking briefly to the driver, it likely became obvious that the driver might be a lot of things, but inebriated wasn't one of them. Jittery and talking nonsense, he acted more like an escapee from a mental institution.

While the officer was in his patrol car running the California plates, Tim slammed the transmission into drive and took off like a bat out of hell. After calling in for backup, the officer gave chase as Tim exited the Interstate and headed straight for the treacherous and winding road that climbed up and over Lookout Mountain.

Near the summit of the mountain, the officer stated that in a burst of speed, Tim hit the straightaway and launched his speeding vehicle into space. I was right! Another *Thelma and Louise* wannabe!

Screeching to a halt, the officer jumped from his vehicle and trained his vehicle-mounted spotlight on the wreckage that came to rest a couple hundred feet below. After scrambling down the icy, rock-strewn mountainside, he approached the still-running vehicle in time to see Tim stumble from the wreckage. The smashed car's taillight was still blinking and added an angry red strobe effect to the goings-on. By this time, more officers had arrived and watched the scene unfold from above.

As the officer neared the wreckage, an obviously deranged and bloody Tim turned and pulled out a knife when he caught sight of the approaching officer. He waved it menacingly at the officer, who still couldn't believe that Tim hadn't been killed from the impact of the crash.

I wasn't present to watch this drama unfold, but I know exactly what went through that officer's head at that point. *Oh shit, he's gonna attack me with the knife!* Instead, Tim did something much stranger. He stabbed himself in the chest. Repeatedly. Then he went to work slitting his own throat, from ear to ear. Then he turned, stumbled away at a run down the hill and was swallowed by the trees.

Now, let me just interject right here and say that I completely empathize with this officer's plight at that moment. I'd been in his shoes. Adrenaline pumping. Heart in my throat. Staring down a man armed with a knife. But in my case, it was not a spotlighted stranger on the side of a mountain who brandished a knife, squared off, and then started hacking away at himself.

No, for me, my flashback transported me back to a warm summer's afternoon in 1993 in my sister's front yard in Vienna, Ohio, facing down my kid brother who had pulled a knife from his pocket and, in full view of his family, began to hack away frantically at his forearms.

Now, when I was a dyed-in-the-wool Southern Free Will Baptist child, I had a near-pathological (and almost comical) fear of going to hell, of coming face to face with Old Lucifer himself. My brother, on the other hand, seemed to have no such fear of the devil. No, for him it wasn't a red-skinned guy with a pointy goatee, horns, and a pitchfork he feared, but rather his own personal band of demons that were always nipping at his heels.

I mentioned earlier that I had dealt with suicidal pleas for help three times in my personal life and responded poorly, without fail. This was the first episode.

This desperate act was one of many pleas for help that my beloved brother made, but the only one we'd taken notice of. Fortunately, his wounds (at least the physical ones) were not deep, and he recovered fully from those. But even after more than twenty years, I still look back at how I'd ignored all the warning signs that led up to that horrific moment on my sister's front lawn, and wish that I knew then what I know now about the proper way to respond to someone exhibiting suicidal behavior.

My goals in writing about suicide are twofold. I want to both encourage mountain rescuers and first responder's to talk about the difficulties they face when dealing with the aftermath of suicide recoveries in the backcountry, and I want to arm the leaders of mountain rescue teams with the knowledge to better respond to their members who exhibit signs that they are struggling with suicidal thoughts. Thoughts that may be the result of a Post-Traumatic Stress Disorder (PTSD) associated with the sometimes tragic work they perform as mountain rescuers.

Given the extended amount of time we spend with our lifeless cargo when we perform body recoveries in general, and suicide recoveries specifically, it should come as no surprise that they can cut such a deep groove into our psyche. For in contrast to other urban EMS agencies that perform recoveries—and whose contact time with their patients can be measured in minutes—as mountain rescuers, it is not unusual for us to spend *hours* with those we bring out of the backcountry.

But what about the hapless Tim, who, ten years after my kid brother cried out for help on a sunny Rustbelt lawn in 1993, had just made himself a human pincushion on a snowy Colorado night?

As Tim ran through the darkness at incredible speed down the steep embankment and away from the wreck, still stabbing himself and shouting unintelligibly, the state trooper called in for backup and gave chase. More officers scrambled down the slope to assist, armed with mag flashlights and getting more and more pissed as the chase stretched from feet to yards to a mile. One officer turned his ankle (all the officers were wearing footwear better suited to a night spent behind the wheel than scrambling down a snowy hillside over rocks and deadfall), and had to hobble back up the hill. I guessed him to be the one who'd given our Mission Leader Ron the heated briefing upon our arrival.

No one was sure just *what* Tim was on, but whatever it was, it powered him through the darkness ahead of the police as if the hounds of hell were nipping at his heels. When the crazed man had reached the small clearing where we now stood, he simply collapsed face first in the snow and wouldn't get up.

"Well I'll be gotohell," marveled Alpine member John Wells in his characteristic Texas drawl.

Deciding that perhaps the bitter cold temperatures might keep Tim from completely bleeding out, the officers on scene opted to leave him shivering in the snow and muttering to himself while they started a fire and awaited the arrival of a paramedic to sedate him and some rescuers to come and cart his sorry ass back up the hill.

What's that, you say? Cold-hearted treatment? Inhumane? Police brutality? Don't judge a man till you walk (or run) a mile in his shiny patent leather shoes. Especially after you discover why Tim went postal on himself in the first place.

I snuck a peak over at Tim, whose shivering had graduated to violent convulsions—his body's last-ditch effort to keep itself warm. I could see that the huge gash across his neck had exposed his trachea, narrowly missing his jugular. He looked like a male version of Carrie after she had been doused by a bucket of pig's blood at the prom. And not just because of all the blood (which had by this time soaked into the snow around him and looked a lot like the chalked outline of a murder victim you'd see on TV). It was because the crazed look in his eyes (when they were open anyway), confirmed that this man was not presently occupying the same mental plane as the rest of us.

In an effort to rewarm him, we removed as many of his wet clothes (soaked through with sweat and blood) as was practical, and replaced them with some of our own dry clothing. Though I was happy to pitch in, I silently bemoaned the fact that I was forfeiting my $30 Gore-Tex wind stopper hat and $70 Gore-Tex vest. Not because I feared I'd need them on that bitterly cold night, but because I did not want to have a blood-soaked bio-hazard wardrobe handed back to me at the end of the mission. Thanks Tim, but no thanks.

When we were finally ready to roll, Alpine member Scott Grotheer took control of the litter's movement back up the hill. As Litter Captain (sounds kind of regal, almost British, doesn't it?), Scott's job was to run the on-site evacuation and radio our progress back to Mission Base, several hundred feet in elevation above and a mile away.

With the help of the cops on scene (told you they weren't being cruel—just human), we carried Tim back up the hill, leaving a thick trail of blood behind us.

It was now about 4:00 a.m., and a paramedic had administered a powerful intravenous cocktail of saline and pain meds to help Tim weather the inevitable jostling that occurs when being up-hauled in a litter. Although I doubted our paltry jostling could have possibly roughed him up worse than his earlier crash landing or bloody foot race down the mountain, it was nevertheless a concern in his weakened condition.

Since we rested often (we were short-staffed for such a long slog up the mountainside in the early hours of the morning), we checked Tim's condition (blood pressure, respiration, pulse, pupil dilation, mental status—for what *that* was worth) at each stop.

About an hour into the evacuation, we noticed a distinct drop in his pulse and breathing. Scott, sensing that perhaps Tim was finally crashing out, hurriedly relayed this disturbing news to our Mission Leader back at the road while the paramedic whipped up an intravenous concoction intended to perk up Tim. After quickly injecting it into the IV that we were trying desperately to keep from freezing, the paramedic gave us the thumbs-up. Tim's vitals jumped right back to where they should be, and we resumed the agonizingly slow ascent over the deadfall and ice-rimed rocks that conspired against us.

A short time later, Scott checked his watch and realized that we might actually finish the evacuation in time for him to clock in at work by nine.

Now, let me cut in here to explain a curious protocol Alpine follows here in RescueWorld. As I mentioned earlier, an MRA Code 4 is radio-relayed rescue-speak for a deceased subject. But sometimes, the friends and family or media listening in to our radio traffic are familiar enough with mountain rescue to know what that means. Dropping that bomb over the radio might incite hysterics for friends or family members still harboring hopes of hearing good news as they sit huddled around the radio at Mission Base. Or the media, eavesdropping on our transmitted conversations by scanning the police and rescue frequencies, might prematurely release tidbits of unconfirmed information about a fatality in order to scoop their competition. Neither possibility is very desirable.

So what we do when we are preparing to transmit sensitive information about a fatality (sneaky devils that we are) is to transmit a nonsense message back to Mission Base. Once the Mission Leader hears this nonsensical message, he knows to clear the family and all non-essential personnel from the vicinity of the radio and prepare for some bad news.

And just what would this nonsensical transmission sound like? Perhaps something like, "Mission Base, this is Site Commander, can you call my office and tell Marcia that I would like a gallon of yogurt and a pound of granola for my breakfast?"

Which was Scott's first radio transmission following his previous announcement to Mission Base that our subject's vitals were dropping. I looked over at Scott and asked if he was serious. He said he was, and asked why wouldn't he be? He was starving, and would need to eat as soon as he arrived at work after the mission.

As non-paid professionals in RescueWorld, our working life and our rescue life often overlap at inconvenient moments like this. Scott, a very deliberate and linear-thinking scientist who studied microorganisms in water samples for the government, didn't see what anyone would find unusual about a request for breakfast at work. Scott was just very hungry, and knew that Ron up at Mission Base would have his work number listed on the call roster and could arrange for Scott's breakfast to be ready and waiting for him when he got to work.

Unfortunately, Ron interpreted Scott's breakfast request as an esoteric and nonsensical message that would soon be followed by a pronouncement of Tim's death.

Now, I was not at Mission Base when they received Scott's request for copious amounts of yogurt and granola, but I later heard that it caused quite a little stir as ML Ron Bookman hastily began shooing media and nonessential personnel away from the radio, rummaging around in our rescue vehicles for a body bag, and informing the Jefferson County dispatcher via radio that bad news was on its way.

This was a first. Not once since the Alpine Rescue Team's 1959 incorporation had a living subject died on us after we initiated their evacuation (unfortunately, it has happened a couple of times since Tim's rescue).

Five minutes later, Ron radioed dutifully back to Scott that he was ready to receive his radio traffic.

"Uh, what radio traffic?" replied Scott, swapping hands on the litter to key the mike on his handheld radio.

When Ron radioed back to Scott that he was ready to receive the MRA Code 4 information, Scott looked to the rest of us who surrounded the litter in confusion. For the life of him, he couldn't figure out how a breakfast request for a pound of granola and a gallon of yogurt could be construed as Tim's obituary.

From both exhaustion and the absurdity of our situation, I couldn't help but laugh, and attempted to stifle my amusement behind the back of my hand till I realized it was still slicked with Tim's blood. The unrestrained laughter was contagious, and even the cops who were helping us drag Tim's bloody (but still breathing) body up the hill couldn't help but chuckle when we explained the mix-up to them.

Shortly after Scott reiterated to Mission Base that Tim was indeed critically injured but still alive, we arrived at the road. Tim had survived his evacuation, which ended at about the same time the sun came up.

Scott did make it on time to work at the Federal Center, where his requested pound of granola and gallon of yogurt awaited. His mis-communicated nonsensical communication that morning later earned him the Alpine Rescue Team's Windy Peak Airplane Magnet Aw-Shit Award, which is bestowed upon the team member guilty of the team's biggest fuck-up of the year. He still contends to this day that there was nothing unusual in his request.

As for the eventual fate of the crazed Tim, I can only guess that he is languishing in prison (or an institution) somewhere. We were told that later the same day, law enforcement officials ran his California plates and tracked down his address in the hopes that they could figure out the reason for his … irrational behavior.

When California authorities checked his residence there, they were more than a little surprised to discover the already decaying remains of his murdered roommate/partner. Apparently that same personal demon that sometimes nipped at my brother's heels when he was down had completely possessed Tim. By driving cross-country, off a cliff, and tearing through the woods on foot, Tim had not been running from the authorities at all. He only sought to outrun himself.

We were later notified by the Jefferson County Sheriff's Office that Tim's blood tested positive for AIDS, and that we needed to be sure that all protocols for dealing with blood-borne pathogens had been followed by our team.

Thank you God for rubber gloves and bleach.

Upon later hearing all the disconcerting news about Tim, I asked myself if I would still have made the same efforts to rescue a murdering, suicidal maniac had I been armed with this knowledge when the chirping of the pager woke me at 2:27 that morning.

Tom Loebach (one of our team's senior members) likes to say that everyone has a mother, and it's for the mothers out there that he does the rescue. Similarly, I believe that even when one of our subjects doesn't want (or maybe even deserve, depending on who you ask) to be saved, there's gotta be someone, *someone*, out there who loves that person and wants to see them returned safely. I do it for them. I would feel horribly saddened to know that someone lived the whole of their life without endearing one single human being to them—even in spite of perhaps their terrible and damning deeds.

So I would say yes, I would do it all again, if for no other reason than that. We're here to rescue people, not to judge them.

The marines had a particularly vulgar, unofficial slogan that has found its way to uncounted numbers of T-shirts and even (partially) onto a Metallica album: "Kill 'Em All and Let God Sort 'Em Out." If we had a similar, more PC T-shirt here in RescueWorld, it would probably say something more like: "Save 'Em All and Let the Sheriff Sort 'Em Out."

Now, let's talk about JT.

I never knew John Thomas Fielder when he was alive. I met him when he wasn't.

All that I know about this young man from Colorado was what I learned the days, weeks, and years after my field team discovered his lifeless body atop a snowy, windblown 12,000-foot peak in Clear Creek County on March 21, 2006. And I want to say right here and now that the only reason I am willing to speak of JT's demise and his subsequent recovery is because of what his father had to say to the world after his only son chose to end his own life.

This grieving father, the well-known, best-selling Colorado nature and wildlife photographer John Fielder, courageously defied convention after his son's suicide. The elder Fielder broke free of the silence that typically clings to suicide like a cold that just can't be shaken. He took action and spoke publicly about a painful topic that most people choose to internalize when faced with its aftermath.

His openness gave me inspiration to both address the role SAR plays in the recovery of those who lose their struggle, and to better deal with my own personal difficulties in understanding those around me who fight this lonely battle against self-extinction.

John Fielder's public response to the loss of his son taught me that just because I dealt with the aftermath of suicide on a depressingly frequent basis as a mountain rescuer, this didn't necessarily prepare me for the times I dealt with that same topic on a more personal level.

But if there's one thing you can say about the work we do here on the front lines of mountain rescue, it's that it often forces us to deal with issues that we'd otherwise try to bury. Issues like suicide.

I will not go into the reasons why JT took his own life out of respect to his family. Suffice it to say, he had decided to end his life while taking in the beauty of a lonely peak in the very same breathtaking backcountry that his father had captured so many times on film and published in his books.

When we received the first page to respond to a search for JT because he was potentially suicidal, a storm was forecast to dump a fair bit of wind-driven snow onto the already avalanche-prone peaks in the search area.

My field team consisted of Alpine members Todd Holmes, Bryan Osburn, and one of JT's close friends, Chris. On our rescue team, it is highly unusual for a "civilian" to accompany a field team into the backcountry in the face of an impending blizzard through avalanche territory. Especially when searching for someone who might be suicidal. But Chris, by chance, had worked as a counselor for Paul "Woody" Woodward, one of our Mission Leaders who owned a young adult adventure hiking/guiding company. Woody vetted Chris' backcountry experience.

Chris was our best bet in finding JT. He seemed certain of JT's location, based on the number of times they had skied this particular area together in the recent past.

Our small search team located his abandoned skis just before 8:00 p.m. a few hundred feet below the summit of the 12,000-foot peak. We could not find many footprints in the windblown snow leading away from the skis, but we found enough to deduce that JT had gone directly uphill. He was heading for the summit. We followed.

The temperature had dropped dramatically, and we knew that when we crested the exposed ridge, we would be blasted by jet stream–strength winds. The snow had also begun to fall, limiting our visibility to 20 or 30 feet.

We were now about 4 long miles up the mountain, and the nearest rescuers were over a mile away, searching another likely area.

Half an hour after finding the skis, we found their owner, lying on his back, covered with a few inches of snow. He was still wearing his ski goggles. The snow that had landed on his face had not melted. His open mouth was also full of unmelted snow. Although we suspected that his heart must have stopped beating hours earlier, we did our level best to check for signs of life. Any sign at all.

Were his pupils responsive to light? No. Did his breath fog our goggles when we held them in front of his mouth? No. Could we detect even a faint heartbeat with the stethoscope we had brought? No. Did we get even a faint autonomous reaction when stroking the bottom of his bare foot? No. Did the painful stimuli of a hard-knuckled sternal rub elicit any response? No.

We were praying for any indication that we should initiate CPR. That was when we discovered all the gashes on both wrists and the frozen blood that had been already covered by the fresh snow that had fallen.

It appeared that JT had completed his suicide several hours before our arrival. Bryan, being Outdoor Emergency Care certified, was designated as lead medical. He was tasked with the difficult job of relaying all our efforts to find JT's vitals back to Mission Base. Our Operations Chief below (also ironically named JT) then conveyed this info via cell phone to our Physician Advisor on call back at St. Anthony's Central in Denver. Since Bryan was not a coroner, paramedic, or law enforcement officer, the responsibility for pronouncing JT deceased would ironically rest on the shoulders of our Physician Advisor, a man located 50 miles away.

Given all of the information we presented, the PA felt it was too late to initiate CPR. Bryan noted the time over the radio and JT was officially pronounced dead.

Moments earlier, we had discovered a blood-soaked note stuffed into JT's pocket. I tasked Chris with delivering JT's hastily scrawled last words to the sheriff below. JT's father, John Fielder, was now in the command post communications van, and we felt that having Chris deliver this note would give him a reason to leave the mountain and perhaps provide some measure of comfort. We felt it might be difficult for Chris to witness the evacuation of his friend. Especially since the only evacuation gear we had with us was Bryan's thin bivy sack.

We decided that Todd, the strongest of our group, should accompany Chris down the mountain while Bryan and I awaited further instructions. After they disappeared into the snowy fog, Bryan and I were left to hunker down against the increasing winds and biting snow. We could not begin the evacuation until we were given permission by the sheriff's office to move JT's body. So we waited. And waited.

We had no way of knowing what was holding up the show down below. We just knew that we wanted to get a move on before the hellishly brutal weather forced us to abandon JT. We did not want to leave him, because this meant that we would need to enter a second operational period at some point after the weather broke and the avalanche danger lessened. That might happen in a day. Or maybe a week.

While we waited for their response, we shut our headlamps off to save precious battery power.

It was not a pleasant feeling to sit on top of a mountain in the middle of the night in a whiteout with a dead man staring at my back. This was one of those rare times when the frenzied pace of a search or rescue grounded to a halt. A stolen, quiet moment when the dull roar of life was turned down to zero. A chance to un-shoulder the emotional baggage you carted up the hill with you so you can rifle through it to see if there's anything in there that might help you cope with your present situation.

Bryan, seated on a rock a few feet away, peered silently into the night as well, lost in his own thoughts, probably sorting through his own baggage.

I stared into the snow blowing sideways past me (the orange glow of the large industrial mining complex a couple thousand feet below gave the night an alien-like orange haze), my mind wandering. I blamed the howling wind for the tears leaking from my eyes that were quickly freezing to the side of my face before I could wipe them away.

I couldn't help but recall my own brother's bouts of depression and his thinly disguised cry for help on my sister's sunny summer lawn so many years earlier. JT was the same age and build as my brother was all those years ago when he mutilated himself in front of us, and this further deepened my identification with the young man who lay in the snow a few feet away.

And as much as I tried to push it out of my head, I could not help but recall my second, and much more recent, bungled response to a loved one's admission that they were struggling with suicidal thoughts. An admission that came from someone whom I considered to be a rock solid pillar of emotional strength.

This second incident took place only four months earlier, and struck much closer to home. As my wife and I were on our way home from a Christmas party that previous December, my festive mood had instantly turned to rage when, out of the blue, she informed me that she had recently found my loaded pistol on the top shelf of the closet at home, and toyed (though that's not a very good word to describe the situation) with turning it on herself.

I was so dumbstruck by this statement that I slammed on the brakes and pulled off to the side of the road. I do not recall the self-righteous and indignant things I said, but I'm reasonably certain that not one of my words were the right ones. I had known that my wife was still struggling with some post-partum issues after the birth of our last child, but had no idea that her feelings of sadness or depression ran so deep. Or why.

My incredulous disbelief was compounded by my own feelings of emotional inadequacy that sprang from my failure to recognize any suicidal warning signs from the woman who was my life partner. The woman who was the mother of my children. The woman who was my friend. (After that night, I don't think we spoke of the incident again until years later when my renewed efforts to finish this piece on suicide brought the whole incident, kicking and screaming, back into the light.)

Returning back to that frozen peak with my brother's lifeless doppelganger lying in the snow beside me, I tried to imagine how JT's father felt right at that moment. Was he blaming himself, too? Was he also angry at his son? With himself?

At that moment, the implications of these thoughts were too deep to plumb. If I continued this dark reverie much longer, I was going to become a liability to the mission at hand. I needed to keep a clear head until we were off the mountain, so I derailed that train of thought and keyed the mike on the radio.

"Mission Base, this is Site Commander. Once AGAIN, any instructions?"

At long last, they gave us the thumbs-up. Bryan and I readied ourselves for the evacuation. I offered up the only words that came to mind as an appropriate eulogy for JT in a husky, apologetic whisper. It was a eulogy that I've unfortunately spoken more than a few times before and since then. "I'm so sorry JT."

We zipped JT into Bryan's thin bivy bag, and did our best to get him over the quarter-mile of frozen rocks to the snow a few hundred feet below. It was hellishly hard work, and not a pleasant thing to recall.

After reaching the snow below, we met up with the other Alpine team members who would be assisting in the evacuation.

After much sweat and about 1,100 feet of elevation drop, we had JT back down to the snow machines. Although it was late and we were all tired from swimming through the three-plus feet of fresh powder, not a single complaint was registered. JT's body was treated with a dignity and care and respect that belied the difficult circumstances surrounding his evacuation.

I was so proud of my Alpine family for their skill, professionalism, and humanity that night. But deep in my heart, I felt troubled that I was walking away from this recovery without a better understanding of how to respond to a suicidal person's pleas for help.

Since that cold and difficult night many years ago, I did have one more episode when a very close, very young family member (less than ten years of age!) spoke to me of suicide. But given the age of the person, at first I mistakenly thought her too young to take seriously. It wasn't until this young person began to explicitly describe to others the way in which she wanted to take her own life that I finally realized that this was not just a way to get some extra attention. Not just some brief but passing phase. This little person was suffering. Thankfully, she was able, through therapy and lots of family support, to come to terms with the internal struggles that plagued and frightened her.

I have come to the conclusion that I'd mismanaged my attempts to help my loved ones through their darkest moments because I was talking when I should have been listening. Projecting when I should have been absorbing.

My first response to the whole notion of suicide was also one that sprang from a deep well of anger. It wasn't so much that I was angry at anyone personally for thinking suicidal thoughts or exhibiting suicidal tendencies. It was more that I was angry with myself because I simply did not know what I should do or say in response. This frustrated the living hell out of me. It infuriated me. And my anger was compounded by the fact that I was on a fool's errand—always in search of the perfect response to something for which there *was* no perfect response.

My belief that suicide was an act of selfishness was all wrong, too. I was actually the one exhibiting selfish behavior in response to my family's confessions and demonstrations of suicidal impulses. And as most mental health professionals are quick to point out, suicide is a desperate act carried out by a person experiencing intense pain, and they just want that pain to stop. That is a *natural* response to pain, and not a selfish one. Using the word "selfish" in conjunction with suicide only serves to perpetuate the stigma associated with it.

"A suicidal action that manifests from intense, excruciating, unbearable pain associated with a serious mental illness has nothing to do with selfishness. Period," wrote Kevin Caruso on the suicide.org website.

As Sally confirmed years after JT's suicide when we talked on the matter, I was mistakenly treating this mental health issue as an "us" and "them" type of problem. It should always be a "we" issue when dealing with the mental health issues that 90 percent of the time preclude suicide, she said.

"About one in five of us will experience the death of a family member to suicide and about sixty percent will know someone who died by suicide over the course of our lives. We don't appreciate how common the life and death struggle is because of the secrecy that shrouds suicidal behavior," Sally said.

Often in mountain rescue, we hear the word "hero" bandied about. Sometimes I think we hear it so much that we forget just what it means when someone is truly heroic. But in speaking with Sally on the topic, she said that's the word she likes to use for those who survive their darkest moments.

"Most [survivors] have experienced unimaginable psychological pain, and have had to fight their way back to life, usually horribly misunderstood and often completely on their own. Just as we think of cancer survivors as heroes in their fight for life, so I think of those who have conquered the life-threatening mental illnesses they have faced."

I couldn't agree more, and though it might sound maudlin, I just want to say right here and now that I finally recognize the heroic nature of the people in my life who once looked to me for help, and somehow found enough courage to carry on when all I had to offer them was either a deaf ear or displaced anger.

You are *my* heroes and the inspiration for me to do all I can to help my fellow mountain rescuers and first responders avoid the mistakes I've made.

To Touch the Face of God

"The crew of the space shuttle Challenger honored us by the manner in which they lived their lives. We will never forget them, nor the last time we saw them, this morning, as they prepared for their journey and waved good-bye and 'slipped the surly bonds of earth' to touch the face of God."
—President Ronald Reagan, addressing the nation after the Challenger Shuttle Disaster on January 28, 1986

CHALLENGER POINT, 14,080+'
In Memory of the Crew of Shuttle Challenger
Seven who died accepting the risk,
expanding Mankind's horizons
January 28, 1986
Ad Astra Per Aspera (To the stars through adversity)
—Inscription on the plaque placed atop the renamed Challenger Point in Colorado's Sangre de Cristo Mountains on July 18, 1987

"The Columbia is lost; there are no survivors."
—President George W. Bush, addressing the nation after the Columbia Shuttle Disaster on February 1, 2003

Columbia Point, 13,980'
In memory of the Crew of the Shuttle Columbia
Seven who died accepting the risk
Expanding humankind's horizons
February 1, 2003

"Mankind is led into the darkness beyond
Our world by the inspiration of discovery
and the longing to understand. Our
journey into space will go on."
President George W. Bush
  —Inscription on the plaque paced atop the renamed Columbia Point in
  Colorado's Sangre de Cristo Mountains on the weekend of August 7, 2003

Like many Americans born in the sixties, I grew up right alongside our country's space exploration program. One of my earliest memories of watching television consisted of me shoving leftover birthday cake (mostly) into my mouth while watching live black and white broadcasts of the lunar landing while strapped to my high chair in July 1969. I was two years old.

I watched the live launch and subsequent explosion of the Challenger Shuttle from my cramped dorm room in Dunbar Hall at Kent State in 1986. I was eighteen years old.

I did not learn of the Columbia Shuttle explosion from the television. I learned of it over the radio while on an overnight winter survival training exercise with Alpine in early February 2003.

Shortly thereafter, I spent two-and-a-half weeks in east Texas (as did six other Alpine members) helping NASA with their efforts to recover as many of the parts of the shuttle as we could find and try to figure out just what had caused this tragedy. Foot by foot, we helped conduct what would become the largest grid search in the history of the United States, with more than 25,000 searchers covering an area 10 miles wide by 240 miles long (approximately 2.28 million acres). We recovered 84,800 pounds of debris—nearly 40 percent of the shuttle.

While there, I met many of the surviving shuttle astronauts. They occasionally stopped by our base of operations in East Palestine around dinner time to say thanks to all of the searchers. They had lost their co-workers and friends, and their sense of loss and the seemingly endless depths of their grief were palpable. I approached them one evening, thanked them for their service, and asked them to sign the cover of that day's dog-eared and wrinkled Search Briefing pamphlet as a memento of Alpine's small role in the massive recovery effort. Signed by several of the astronauts, it hangs in a frame on the wall of The Shack to this day. I was thirty-five years old.

When Alpine first received a page requesting assistance with the recovery of a fallen climber from the recently renamed Challenger Point in southern Colorado on Thursday, August 18, 2011, I felt duty-bound to participate. I was forty-four years old.

Two, eighteen, thirty-five, forty-four. I'm sure there is some sort of pattern, some sort of relevance there, but I just can't seem to connect the dots to discover what it is. I like to find the patterns that seem to connect such tragically random events such as these. To do so seems to impart some sense of order to impossibly unrelated events. It helps me to hold onto the flimsy notion that our lives are not governed or ruled by the oily fist of chaos—but rather some sort of sentience that has a sense of fair play and order. I guess you could call this sentience God. But minus all the mysticism, righteousness, and tithing, thank you very much.

Perhaps, for me, the common thread connecting all these events together like decorative Christmas popcorn on a string is the deep sense of reverence and sadness I've always felt toward the men and women who lost their lives striving to boldly go where no one has gone before. I do not care one bit how corny that sounds.

Like astronauts, mountaineers are always pushing the envelope, struggling to survive in an unforgiving and harsh environment, and I feel the same sense of reverence and sadness at their passing. Mike Lepold was one such mountaineer. The missing fifty-two-year-old Glen Ellyn, Illinois, resident was the reason we were paged out that Thursday.

Rewinding to the day before Mike was reported missing, we later learned that on that fateful day, Mike awoke early near Willow Lake in the Sangre de Cristo Mountains, strapped on his Camelback, and set off for Kit Carson and Challenger Peak. He hoped to bag two fourteeners for the price of one, since only a narrow ridge separated the two peaks. Although he lived in Illinois, the mountains were his passion, and he had scaled more than forty of Colorado's fifty-four fourteeners over the last decade.

Mike must have been making good time, because he was able to call his wife, Lori (back in Illinois), from the summit around noon. He took a quick photograph of himself with his phone and sent it back to her before starting his descent. Wearing his Cubs hat, sunglasses, and a victoriously boyish smile, it was his last photo.

Exactly what happened to Mike after that, we'll never know. In any event, when he didn't check in with his wife later that evening as he promised to do, she called the Saguache County Sheriff from Illinois to report her husband as being overdue.

The next morning, Cindy Howard and Linda Brigham, two members of the neighboring Custer County Search and Rescue Team, happened to be hiking in that same remote area near the summit of Challenger Peak. Being good citizen rescuers, they had brought their radios with them out of habit, not knowing that there was a search going on. When they were notified by the Saguache County Sheriff's Office that a hiker was missing, they soon spotted something suspicious below the saddle connecting Kit Carson and Challenger. The object, hundreds of feet below them, appeared to be that of an unmoving, unresponsive person lying on his or her side. They took a couple of photos and headed back to the trailhead.

A military helicopter fly-by later that day confirmed that the object in the photos hadn't moved since that first photograph taken many hours earlier, and a thermal image from another Air National Guard aircraft fly-by confirmed that whatever was on that ledge was no longer warm enough to be alive. Given that this object so strongly resembled a fallen climber, that it was only a short distance from Mike's last known point, and that no one else had been reported overdue on the busy peak, Saguache County Sheriff Mike Norris concluded that Mike Lepold's body had been the one photographed, and made the difficult decision to switch from search mode to recovery mode.

It was now late Thursday afternoon, and most of Saguache County's SAR members had been searching for more than twenty-four hours. The small county's resources were just about tapped out. Sheriff Norris put in a call to the Colorado Search and Rescue Board (CSRB) for additional resources.

CSRB is a group of seven to ten individuals—all volunteers with various Colorado SAR teams—who take turns each week being on call for statewide requests for SAR mutual aid. So when a SAR team in Colorado needs help, they don't call Ghostbusters, they call CSRB. The CSRB then contacts the various sheriff's departments in Colorado to formally request the assistance of their respective SAR team.

When the Alpine Rescue Team received the Saguache County request for mutual aid from CSRB via our pagers, it was nearly 8:00 p.m. on Thursday night. Lights a-blazin' and sirens a-roarin', we were speeding up the twisty paved road that climbed to the flanks of Mount Evans for an injured and cliffed-out seventeen-year-old female. It was our third call of the day.

As fate would have it, I was Alpine's on-call Mission Leader that day, and thereby obligated to attend all of them.

As the on-call ML, it was my responsibility to notify the CSRB state coordinator regarding the availability of our team for the recovery effort on

Challenger that next day. But first we had a rescue to finish. Luckily, as rescues go, this one was pretty routine. A young lady visiting from New Jersey had wandered away from her family on the Mount Evans summit and became trapped on a narrow ledge below when she twisted her knee and darkness set in.

By the time we rescued the stranded girl from a rocky ledge on the northeast side of Mount Evans, it was 11:30 p.m., and we needed to decide if we could allocate any resources to Saguache County for their ongoing search the next morning on the recently renamed Challenger Peak.

Feeling the way I did about all things NASA-related, I quickly volunteered to go if we could scrape together a response team in the middle of the night. But as we drove back down the mountain and into cell range, my phone blew up with the texts and voicemails I didn't receive while on the mountain. These texts and voicemails informed me that my wife Maren—a dedicated home-birth midwife—had been called to a birth an hour earlier, the kids were asleep and home alone, and I needed to get back to the house pronto.

By volunteering to take off for what was surely going to be a two-day mission, I was violating an unwritten rule in our relationship—I didn't check in at home before promising to respond. This turned out to be a poor decision on my part, since I knew when we received the first of our three pages that day that I had left my wife with a very pregnant client who had been rumbling for the past few days, and no one to get the kids on and off the bus or feed them if she was called away to attend the birth.

Just as my wife's schedule is altered when I respond to a search or rescue for complete strangers, my best-laid plans are sometimes at the mercy of the hormones and contractions of the pregnant women in my wife's care. I sincerely believe that our complete absence of any 9-to-5 expectations of normalcy is what allows us to be so supportive of each other's chosen profession.

I had no choice but to back out of the recovery, and without any other Mission Leaders volunteering to head up our team's response, the radio-communicated consensus reached between myself and the two others Mission Leaders leaving the mountain was to cancel our response to Saguache County.

Steve Wilson, one of Alpine's newer Mission Leaders, began his shift at midnight, so he was tasked with the unenviable chore of calling CSRB state coordinator to tell him that Alpine, one of the largest SAR teams in the state, could not spare anyone to send to Challenger Point in Saguache County to search for the fallen climber. As much as we hate to say no, when a mutual aid call comes in during the week, sometimes that's what we have to do. If we can't get at least one senior member to supervise the handful of rescuers who volunteer to leave the confines of our counties—we don't send anyone.

I was fuming that I could not respond to the call for mutual aid, but deep inside I couldn't help but admit that I was in the wrong. It was unfair of me to expect my wife to ignore all of her responsibilities *again* (and saddle her with a handful of mine to boot), while I took off in the middle of the night to pursue the siren call of my mistress Alpine. And let me tell you, Alpine can be one greedy bitch. She's ruined more than few marriages in her now fifty-plus years of existence.

I knew I was already in hot water for being gone most of that day and half of the night, but if she found out that I had volunteered to take off again, I would be lucky if she didn't take a hammer to my pager. Luckily, I couldn't speak with her much since she was at that moment coaxing her client to breathe, *breathe* through contractions and then push.

I got home around 1:00 a.m., and thankfully the house hadn't burned to the ground and no one had stolen our children from the safety of their beds. Just before dawn, my wife came home from the birth and fell face-first into bed, asleep before she even hit the mattress. As she began her sleep cycle, I ended mine and called Steve, Alpine's on-call ML du jour. Although we didn't send a team of rescuers to assist with the search and recovery effort on Challenger, I was relieved to hear that several other counties from across the state had answered the Saguache County sheriff's call for help.

Western State SAR, Douglas County SAR, Summit County Search and Rescue Group, and El Paso County SAR all sent members to assist Saguache County SAR that day.

Since summer was winding down, I took (yet another) personal day off from work so that we could take the kids to one last afternoon movie before school started. Halfway through the movie, the trill, annoying beep of my pager interrupted the stereophonic sound of cowboys battling aliens. It was immediately followed by the sound of me cussing out my chirping pager (which I had forgotten to mute) as I fumbled to unclip it from my belt and silence it while simultaneously warding off the hateful stares of the couple seated next to me.

MISSION LEADER CALL DISPATCH

RE: MORE HELP NEEDED TOMORROW FOR

THE SAGUACHE CO RECOVERY

Oooh boy. Now what? It was now late afternoon, and though I wasn't the on-call ML, I knew that if Alpine sent a team down for the following day, they would be leaving in a matter of hours. I wanted to be in that group.

But the kids were really into the movie, and we promised to take them to the bookstore after the movie. I had also promised my son Seth that I'd watch him at fencing practice up the hill in Evergreen after our family trip to the bookstore. On top of that, I committed one of RescueWorld's cardinal sins: I had left my truck at home and ridden with my family in my wife's car.

Now, there are days when I am more than happy to escape my daily routine and trade in "normal reality" for "mountain rescue reality." This was *not* one of those days.

I was by then acutely aware (thanks to the Internet) that the subject of the ongoing search and recovery effort on Challenger left behind two children and a wife back in Illinois. This strengthened my guilty resolve to fiercely defend my pursuit of a normal afternoon with my family, in spite of my desire to help with the search and recovery effort. And to tell my family how much I loved them waaaay more than they felt comfortable hearing. It's one of the by-products of bearing witness to tragedy over and over again. You learn quickly to appreciate the people you love in your life, and to let them know it. Especially when you get reminded on a semi-regular basis how suddenly and unexpectedly they (or you) can be taken away forever.

As I struggled with the conflicting desires to spend more time with my family and also leave them to help my SAR comrades perform a potentially dangerous recovery, I realized just how fleeting and fragile our lives are here on this crazy planet. Working in RescueWorld has taught me to truly appreciate how quickly the things I hold dear can be taken from me. Or how quickly we as rescuers can be taken from our loved ones.

When it comes to preparing to face matters of life and death, I often err on the side of ritual and superstition. It makes absolutely no sense whatsoever, but sometimes I feel that if I can somehow utter the magic words "I love you" to my kids and wife as I hustle out the door on the way to a call, we can all somehow cheat fate and duck and cover while the Grim Reaper swings his blade.

It's completely ridiculous, and a belief that has as much basis in reality as the pro baseball player who wears the same unwashed socks every game to keep a hitting streak alive. But it makes me feel like I have at least a little control over my own fate. Like I've got control over my own lucky streak of living long enough to help create three amazing little people.

I didn't have to explain to my wife what the pager was asking me to do. She could read my expression and sense me fidgeting around anxiously in my seat for the rest of the movie.

"So what are you waiting for?" she asked me, as we filed out of the movie and she caught me reading my pager for the third time since the movie credits started to roll. She knew me all too well.

The rock stars in RescueWorld are not just the folks who go out and beat the bushes or sometimes put themselves at risk to help others. Often, the real rock stars in RescueWorld are the spouses and families of the rescuers who not only allow, but *encourage* them to respond. My wife Maren is one of those kinds of rock stars.

The next few hours were a blur to me as I split my attentions between my promised duties to my family and my efforts to put together a response crew. I learned that the rescue teams dispatched to the mountain that day were unsuccessful in their attempt to locate and recover Mike. They had cached some rescue gear on the mountain and then retreated.

Through a non-stop series of cell phone calls (as we herded the kids through Barnes & Noble, then into the car, then up to Evergreen for Seth's fencing lessons, then to The Shack to pick up Rescue 2, then to the pizza place to pick up dinner for the family, and finally home with only forty-five minutes available to pack and prepare for a two-day recovery effort above treeline in another part of the state), I helped put together a team of folks to make the four-hour drive to southern Colorado.

Something about those peaks down there breeds the type of high drama that most people in the world associate with mountain climbing and the rescue or recovery of the climbers who test their mettle on the vertical slopes.

I've always felt that the remote, jagged peaks of southern Colorado tend to look more prehistoric and therefore more picturesque than their northern cousins in the Front Range. Here in the Front Range, most of our mountains look like great mounds of rocks piled randomly by bored children. The Sangres and the San Juans, on the other hand, tend to look more like the classic peaks of the Dolomites in Italy. Or the lesser peaks in the Swiss Alps. Not that I've ever been to either, mind you. But that has always been my impression of the difference between the peaks in my backyard and the peaks of southern Colorado.

When we receive a call for mutual aid in southern Colorado, it's always a scramble to get ready before we rendezvous with our teammates and pile into a car or truck or SUV packed to the ceiling with rescuers and all their stinky gear.

After making a quick pit stop at a convenience store to pick up all the Red Bulls, 5 Hour Energy shots, Slim Jims, Reeses Pieces Fun Packs, Clif Bars, Gu Double Espresso Energy Gels, and peanut butter–flavored Luna Bars we'd need for fuel, we were off.

Rescue road trip! It's like your best memory of a college road trip minus the beer, acne, and usually pointless hopes for sex.

When we arrived at Crestone (a smallish village located on the western flanks of the Sangre de Cristo mountain range), it was nearly midnight and the unlit streets were empty and silent. We knocked on the back door of the volunteer firehouse, but no one answered. A quick peek through a side window revealed several rescuers who'd arrived earlier fast asleep on the floor. Rather than wake them, we quietly retreated to the rescue truck, grabbed our sleeping bags and stumbled through the well-lit parking lot and into the inky blackness that surrounded it. It was a beautiful night, and we made our beds among the cactus, piñon pines, and yucca plants that competed for moisture from the sandy soil.

I suppose it's possible that *somebody* actually slept in the hour and a half we had between the time when we laid down and the time we had to wake up and begin our pre-arranged briefing at 2:00 a.m., but I can't say it was me. But I did try really hard to appear asleep so as not to disturb anyone. When the alarm on my phone played its programmed little tune to awaken me, I was happy to end my sleep-charade.

Like sleepy-eyed little zombie children, we shuffled into the gaping maw of the enormous garage bay door of the firehouse for our briefing just as the other rescuers in the firehouse were rolling up their sleeping bags. Two members from the previous days' recovery attempt (Jesse from Douglas County and Scott from Western State) were to guide us to the place on the mountain where they had cached the gear.

Looking around the garage bay that smelled faintly of diesel fuel and past fires, I noticed it was cluttered with equal amounts of fire rescue and mountain rescue gear. I recognized many faces from RescueWorld. Five members from the Rocky Mountain Rescue Group in Boulder had also made the long drive down south.

As we choked down some coffee, Ben, the fire chief/search manager, introduced himself and explained all that had transpired up to that point. This was to be the third and final push to locate and get our subject down from the mountain. We could forget about air support from the military, since they crashed a Chinook helicopter the previous year in a similar attempt to airlift a body off of Little Bear Peak. Flight For Life appeared to be out of the question as well, since they won't usually transport a deceased subject from the backcountry unless the sheriff is willing to pay them to do so.

With no small amount of restrained emotion in his voice, Ben informed us that if today's efforts at locating and recovering Mike's body was unsuccessful, Mike's body would remain on the mountain until the winter avalanche cycle swept him down to the valley floor below where he would hopefully be found late next spring.

It was obvious that the efforts of the last three days had taken their toll on Ben. He admitted, running his hands over the stubble on his head and chin in one motion, that over the last few days, he was surviving on fewer hours of sleep than most people got in a single night. His sleep-deprived, stream-of-consciousness briefing made it very clear that in spite of his fatigue, he was still determined to see this mission to a safe and successful end if he had any say in the matter.

Ben had every reason to be punchy and irritable, but he chose a different tack. In spite of his very nearly catatonic state, he managed to conduct himself with the utmost patience and an irreverent, dry wit. As he paced back and forth a couple times during the briefing, slightly bent over and with one hand behind his back, I couldn't help but chuckle when I realized who he reminded me of at that moment—Groucho Marx. All he lacked was the greasepaint moustache and the big cigar.

I fully appreciated his efforts at levity, and not just because they created a much more relaxed and open atmosphere. They spoke volumes as to the depth of his character, and the lengths to which he was willing to go to appear upbeat in a supremely unpleasant situation.

We devised our plan of attack, and then set off at 4:00 a.m.

We were loaded down with enough technical rock, steep snow and ice climbing gear to rescue the entire Dallas Cowboys cheerleading squad from the summit of Mount Everest. We also had enough food, water, and emergency shelters to survive for two days above treeline, but we sincerely hoped that it wouldn't come to that.

Although I had been designated Site Commander, all thirteen members of our team were seasoned mountain rescue veterans—and solid mountaineers to boot. So pretty much the main responsibility imparted to me was the mundane job of informing Mission Base of our progress via radio.

It was a very bright moon that occasionally checked in on our progress through gaps in both the clouds and high mountain ridges above us as we wound our way up the steep and snaking trail by headlamp. As we marched single file up the trail, my thoughts turned to the fallen climber. Lying alone, his body broken and lifeless on some cold mountain ledge. Right now.

And of his cruelly widowed wife, Lori. Also alone, her spirit broken and unable to help her husband. Right now. Did she have any internal warnings or premonitions that day she said goodbye to him when he left Illinois for Colorado?

How did he fall? Did he suffer after the fall? What were his last thoughts? Were they of his wife? His children, Melanie and Adam?

My mind traveled back to my own childhood-era religious pamphlets of Jack Chick–inspired visions of hell. My fear of dying unexpectedly and being punished in perpetuity by the devil for sins that I was unaware of even committing. I came to the sudden and abysmal conclusion that for me, death followed by an eternity spent in hell with that red-skinned, goatee-wearing fallen angel named Lucifer poking my ass with a pitchfork would be a walk in the park when compared to living for five minutes after the loss of one of my kids.

French existentialist and life of the party Jean-Paul Sartre once famously proclaimed that "Hell is other people." I not-so-famously contend that hell is sometimes losing other people.

And just what kind of living hell were Mike's now-fatherless children going through? Right now.

With these troubling thoughts and unanswered questions bouncing around in my sleepy head, I did my best to keep pace with my fellow rescuers. And as if the contemplation of the gruesome task that lay ahead of us wasn't depressing enough, I got stuck behind a rescuer suffering from HAFE.

Not to be confused with HACE (High Altitude Cerebral Edema), or its deadly cousin HAPE (High Altitude Pulmonary Edema), HAFE is a sometimes silent (but rarely deadly) condition familiar to all mountaineers. HAFE (High Altitude Flatulent Emissions) is the bane of all who venture into the high country. For reasons as yet unknown to modern science, it only strikes the person directly in front of you on the trail. And brother, let me tell you, when oxygen is already in short supply (and you have asthma like I do), it really *sucks* that what little oxygen you *do* inhale tastes and smells like rotten ass. I do not know if it is the result of the mountaineer's built-in gauges trying to equalize the body's internal pressure, or if the decreased oxygen intake results in increased methane output, but the amount of passed gas always seems to increase proportionately with altitude. You'll never hear *that* particular aspect of mountaineering discussed in all those really swell, pristinely filmed IMAX Everest epics. Only here in RescueWorld, ladies and gentlemen.

Anyway, we arrived at the gear cache just as the sun's warming rays crept over the east ridge and painted the opposing west ridge a brilliant orange hue above us. We had hiked about 6 miles, gaining 4,300 feet of elevation to reach 12,500 feet in about four hours. Not bad, considering our heavy packs and lack of sleep. Somewhere above us, a victim of the mountain waited.

As I dropped my pack, donned my ridiculously yellow Gore-Tex Alpine Rescue jacket and switched from trail running shoes to crampon compatible mountaineering boots, I took a moment to survey our surroundings. We were on a large grassy knoll in an enormous cirque, surrounded on three sides by granite walls several hundred feet high. The toe of the snowfield that we needed to climb was still about a quarter mile away, a couple hundred feet above us. Consulting the creased photocopy of the grainy photograph taken from the air the day before, we guessed that the fallen climber's body was somewhere above and to climber's right of the snowfield, on a sloping grassy ledge near the middle of the 400-foot cliff.

As previously agreed upon, our four strongest climbers (Mark, Brian, Scott, and Jesse) would ascend the 30–45 degree snowfield (which was actually a bullet-proof field of ice at that early hour), cache a plastic litter and body bag at the top of the snow/ice field, then figure out the best way to climb up the steep, rock-strewn face to the ledge system that we guessed was Mike's final resting place.

Frank took the spotting scope, climbed up the opposite side of the valley, and tried to locate the body from that vantage point. He would also act as spotter to notify us over the radio of any rock fall headed our way. The rest of us below the lead climbers would work on anchors until we were notified that Mike had been found.

Since I was supposed to be in charge, I figured that I'd better do something leaderly before we began in earnest. After a few hits on my inhaler, I gathered everyone together for an impromptu pep talk/safety briefing before we split up. The clinking and clanking of all the climbing gear being racked and readied for action continued as I began to speak.

"So before we split up, I just want to let everyone know that if you are uncomfortable with this body recovery, it is a thousand percent okay if you want to hang back," I wheezed. After a couple more gulps of oxygen, I continued. "Mike is dead. Nothing that we can do today will make him *less* dead.

We are here to help the family achieve some peace of mind and afford them the chance to begin the grieving process."

The longer I talked, the more aware I became of just how difficult it was to talk to my fellow rescuers without sounding like some cardboard cutout caricature of a cigar-chomping general from some B-grade war movie. The clichés continued to pour unchecked from my mouth. It was like I was channeling George C. Scott's Patton or something.

"We don't need any heroes here today." Oy.

"The clock is ticking." Oy. Somebody please shut me the hell up.

"Has anyone here *not* done a body recovery before?" I asked. Not one of the thirteen veteran rescuers raised their hands.

"Good. Because if we find him and it's getting late, you won't be surprised when I tell you to just kick him off a ledge. We are the last hope for getting him off this mountain for the rest of the year. If we are forced to collect him in pieces down below, that's just the reality of a recovery in the mountains." And right about that time, I noticed that I was being videotaped by some stranger who had infiltrated our group.

Now, I vaguely recalled someone saying on the hike in that a filmmaker was camped out on the mountain, but was astonished that I hadn't seen him approach our group.

"Hold on," I said to the group, as I abruptly abandoned my ridiculous speech and approached the stranger who subsequently lowered his camera in alarm at being noticed.

In the few seconds it took to walk across the spongy green tundra, I fully intended to take the Sean Penn approach to handling pesky photographers. I was going to grab the camera from the startled man and hurl it to the ground, then maybe punch him in the face for having the audacity—the nerve—to just start filming a body recovery without asking for anyone's permission to do so (altitude can really magnify your emotions).

And then the startling irony of the situation washed over me like a bucket of ice water dumped on my head. I used to be that guy. That guy with a camera glued to his cheek, documenting the trials and tribulations of others and then trading those captured/stolen moments for a paycheck. Holy shit.

Talk about a flashback. But this was a flashback experienced through a mirror that reflected me not as the neophyte journalist (spouting aped catchphrases from journalism ethics classes like "The public has a right to know" and "It's a newsworthy event"), but more like the angry parent who didn't want his kid's twisted and lifeless body to be photographed as it is pulled from a car wreck. I suddenly felt very protective of Mike's privacy (and dignity), which I felt would be violated by someone filming us dragging him off the mountain.

Christ, I thought I had left all these First Amendment moral dilemmas behind me two decades ago on the steps of the *Parkersburg News* in West-By-God Virginia, but here they were again, back to haunt me.

I opted to go with choice number two and play the good cop first (at least until I ascertained the photographer's motives and intent), reserving the right to play the bad cop later on, should the situation call for that.

"Hi, my name is Tom, I'm with the Alpine Rescue Team," I said with (what I hoped looked like) a genuine smile as I stuck out my hand.

"I'm Darin, I'm a filmmaker," he said, as he switched the expensive-looking HD camera to his left hand and shook mine with his right.

Darin looked to be in his mid to late forties, with a thick moustache and thick-lensed glasses. He was wearing a baseball cap embroidered with what I guessed to be the name of an aircraft carrier.

"I've been camping up here all week, and I heard about the fatality. I feel kinda connected to this guy, even though I don't know if I saw him before he fell. So I thought I'd shoot you guys in action. If you don't mind, of course," he added.

I knew good and well that I had absolutely no *real* authority to tell Darin to cease and desist. True, I was acting on behalf of the Saguache County sheriff, and I could've played the Authority Figure card and tried to prohibit him from filming. But this was a public place (National Forest), and as long as Darin's filmmaking didn't compromise anyone's safety, there wasn't much I could legally do to stop him from filming.

Although it might be in poor taste for him to record us shucking Mike's body off a ledge, poor taste is still legal in the U.S. And besides, my gut was telling me that this was not the kind of guy who would put something out for the world to gawk at on YouTube just to make a name for himself. He seemed genuinely moved by what was going on. I could hear it in his voice and see it in his eyes.

I explained to him that as long as he kept his distance, he was free to shoot whatever he saw fit. But I also pleaded in earnest with him to think long and hard about the footage he actually released before doing so. I felt as if I were acting in the interest of Mike's family to warn Darin that any controversial footage he chose to release might forever scar Mike's loved ones if they saw it.

Darin agreed to both keep his distance and to be mindful of the sensitive nature of his subject matter. I had no concrete reasons to trust that he would keep his word. But I did anyway. I then turned my attention back to our efforts to find and recover Mike's body.

As our four lead climbers began their climb up the 45-degree snow slope, aided by their crampons and ice axes, we climbed to the base of the snowfield above. I planned on having the rest of us below the lead climbers work to establish the anchors we'd need once Mike's body was located and lowered down the steep snow to us. The nearest place we could land a helicopter (if we could even convince one to come) was nearly half a mile and several hundred feet below our current elevation of 12,800 feet.

But the mountain didn't agree with our plan. For in all the years I'd worked in RescueWorld, I never dodged more rocks than I did on that day. It didn't matter where we tried to hide, rocks of all shapes and sizes assailed us. It was like we were soldiers pinned down by enemy fire.

"ROCK! ROCK! ROCK! ROCK! ROCK!" we all yelled, despite that we were all very well aware that rocks were indeed falling toward us. We yelled it so many times, in fact, that I thought if we just had a set of drums and three guitar chords we could have been the Ramones singing, "ROCK rock rock rock rock 'n' roll high school ..."

But not all of the rocks we dodged were the ones kicked loose by the four climbers above us. By then, the late morning sun was melting the snow and ice that cemented some of the more precariously perched loose rocks to the side of the mountain. It was as if the mountain would shrug imperceptibly, thereby flinging random rocks free of its shoulders, sending them whistling down slope in search of some nice juicy skulls to smash.

"Here comes a microwave!" Jesse screamed over the radio from several hundred feet above us. After diving for cover, we peeked over the top of our own respective hiding places and spied Jesse's block of stone (which was indeed square-ish and roughly the size of an old microwave from the early eighties). It caromed off one side of the rock wall above us, and then the other as it gained speed, heading directly for the hiding place of the five Rocky Mountain Rescue Group members.

This hiding place was in the center of the chute behind a narrow, waist-high chunk of granite right at the bottom edge of the snowfield. About a hundred feet away from the rest of us, the rescuers from RMRG were attempting to hand drill some anchor bolts in the boulder. This would serve as our main anchor point for the lower once the body was off the snowfield.

Though the rock was hurtling toward them, it seemed to be falling in slow motion from my vantage point off to the side of the chute, since I had so much time to watch it fall. Andrew, Darin, Mike, Ian, and Page were lined up single file behind the boulder. They reminded me of worried prairie dogs, each of them popping their heads up above the protective boulder every couple of seconds to track the progress of the two-hundred-pound projectile that seemed to sense their location. It was like watching a game of Whack-A-Mole, only with much higher stakes than a few arcade tokens.

When the rock was only a few feet from impact, one of the rescuers chanced one last quick peek over the top, and nearly had the top of his head taken off as the microwave-shaped cannonball exploded into their pillbox-like boulder. We were showered with the debris a hundred feet away. The anchor they had hand-drilled had suffered a direct hit, and the webbing on it was shredded, but everyone was safe.

In spite of ourselves, we all burst into laughter at surviving the near miss, and I was relieved to see that Darin the filmmaker was too far below us to capture our relieved fit of laughter on video. The last thing I wanted Mike's family to see on film was a bunch of rescuers yucking it up on a body recovery.

The rock fall abated somewhat, and we got back to business. Jesse and Scott were now at the top of the snowfield 500 feet above us. After ditching their crampons and ice axes, they switched to rock climbing mode and tried to pick a route up the cliff face. Based on the photographs from two days earlier, they were trying to access a prominent ledge 200 feet above them, off to climber's right. As we watched from below, Mark and Brian had also reached the top of the snowfield and were working to set the ice screws and snow pickets we would need if Mike was located above them and then lowered down the cliff to their location. Luckily, they discovered a small snow cave at the base of the cliff and it offered them some measure of protection from all the rocks that Jesse and Scott kicked loose (in spite of their best efforts not to) as they carefully traversed the loose, rocky face above them.

Due to the nature of the traverse, they had to make their way across the rock face un-roped. From our vantage point below, it appeared as if they were clinging to the rock face like flies to a wall, 100 feet above the snow, but they assured us over the radio that altthough their route was exposed, it was relatively safe. The key word being *relatively*, of course. My stomach was in knots.

It was now about 11:00 a.m., and I knew that if we didn't locate Mike in the next few hours, we would have to either spend the night on the mountain and try again tomorrow, or abandon our attempt completely. By this time, I felt a fierce sense of ownership over this recovery. Although I admonished my fellow rescuers that no dead body is worth risking a live one in my cliché-ridden briefing only a couple hours earlier, I was now bound and determined to see this thing through. I didn't plan on leaving that mountain unless Mike was coming with us. I could sense that same iron resolve in all the rescuers on the hill, and I was proud to be working with a group of guys so dedicated to a cause that, on paper, would seem so utterly unworthy of our efforts.

If we followed the course dictated by common sense, and not our hearts, we wouldn't be up there in the first place, and Mike's family might never be granted the closure that we were working so hard to assure for them.

At that point, Jesse and Scott disappeared from our view as they picked their way across a narrow ledge that angled up and to the right toward the area where we expected to find Mike. Until they located him, there wasn't much the rest of us could do except pray that the clouds building to the west did not unleash the rain and lightning that would bring the recovery to a screeching halt.

"We've got lightning!" Frank relayed over the radio from his position as spotter across the valley. Frank had a lightning detector with him, and he relayed that it recorded three strikes within a couple miles of our position. Not good.

Within minutes of Frank's warning, Jesse radioed down to me to stand by for important information. How strange it is to say that we were all longing for the grim news that a dead body had been found.

"Site Command, Jesse here. We have an MRA Code 4." Code 4 was of course rescue-speak for a discovered fatality. I won't say we rejoiced at that point, but this was welcome news indeed.

I communicated this information to fellow Alpine member Eric, who had arrived at the firehouse shortly after we set out on the trail. He was acting as our radio relay below us at the trailhead in the hopes that it would buy the sleep-deprived fire chief Ben at least a few hours of rest. It was good to have a familiar voice on the other end of the radio miles below us.

"Any chance of getting a helicopter up here to us?" I asked Eric, who said he would get with Ben and the sheriff to see if anyone could be coaxed into flying Mike's body off the mountain (provided, of course, that we could successfully accomplish the difficult technical evacuation ahead of us).

I knew it would be an uphill battle to get anyone—military or civilian—to put their bird and its crew at risk to fly a body off a mountain. This was something that required no small amount of begging and pleading. And sometimes money.

When the public balks at the high cost of a backcountry rescue, it is usually the cost of a helicopter that they are seeing, since all of us ground pounders volunteer our services and equipment free of charge. Most civilian helicopters are owned by for-profit medical entities, and there is always a price tag attached to their use (usually in the neighborhood of $1,000 per hour). Think of them as flying ambulances. And since most insurance companies will not cover the costs associated with the helicopter evacuation of a deceased policyholder, that means someone has to pay for that service.

In Colorado, that someone is usually the county sheriff. Each county typically sets aside a small part of their annual operating budget to cover the use of helicopters in the backcountry. But all too often, the use of a helicopter for one big mission can wipe out these meager funds.

Although our search on the mountain was now at an end, the search below us for a helicopter was just beginning. Jesse and Scott photographed Mike's body for the coroner, while Brian abandoned the safety of his snow cave to carry up the body bag and rolled-up plastic SKED litter to the two rescuers above.

A light drizzle began to fall, but focused as we all were on what was going on above us (and dodging the hail of dislodged stones that once again rained down from above), I don't think any of us down at the edge of the snowfield even noticed.

About an hour later, we helped Mike begin his long journey back home. I won't go into the grisly details of how we packaged and evacuated Mike's battered body. Because—as crazy as this might sound—sometimes discussing certain particulars of a body recovery are a lot like discussing one's sex life, in that both situations beg for some measure of discretion and only the people involved need to know the intimate details. This was indeed one of those kinds of recoveries.

I will say that we used every single high-angle rope rescue trick we could come up with to get him down the 200-foot vertical rock wall; 600-foot-long, 45-degree snowfield; and finally the 900-foot-long, 30-degree talus field to the landing zone (LZ).

Frank abandoned his post as spotter and joined us, and two members from Alamosa County SAR arrived and pitched in as well. We needed them desperately, because the lead climbing team (Brian, Mark, Jesse, and Scott) were completely spanked from their efforts to locate Mike and lower him from the 13,200-foot-high ledge where they found him. It was all they could do to down-climb the snowfield bearing all the gear they carried up hours earlier.

Mike and his litter weighed over 200 pounds, and it took no small amount of grunting, sweating, and swearing to move him down the hill given the number of rescuers we had on the mountain. An evacuation like this usually required more than double the number of rescuers at our disposal, especially given the altitude.

But the clock was indeed ticking, and if we didn't get him to the LZ before the storm settled in or darkness enveloped the mountain, Mike would be spending a fifth lifeless day on the hill.

When I gave the word to Eric and Ben down below that we were about an hour out from the LZ at 12,200 feet, they replied with a thoroughly disheartening query. "Don't suppose anyone is willing to spend the night with the body up there if we can't get a chopper today, is there?" they asked.

Knowing that a storm was forecast for that evening (and it was definitely on its way, as Frank's lightning detector reminded us on a regular basis at that point), I hastily conferred with the rescuers at hand and replied in a matter of moments.

"No," I replied.

I told them that if a helicopter couldn't make it up there that day, we would put Mike's body high on top of a boulder near the LZ, festoon the area with orange flagging that would make it easily visible from the air, and then everyone would beat feet down the mountain.

Although they didn't know it, I was lying to them. Whether a helicopter came or not, Frank and I had already decided to stay with the body after sending everyone else down toward the trailhead. This was the third body recovery in a month that Frank and I played a role in, and we took a morbid sense of pride in the fact that we had become pretty goddamn good at treating each recovery with the sense of dignity it deserved while still accomplishing our mission: to get the deceased home to their loved ones. We were like the Dynamic Duo of Death.

We didn't decide to stay because we worried that animals might ravage his body if it was left alone that night. We didn't decide to stay because we might be commanded to do so by the sheriff (this is one of the beauties of being a volunteer in RescueWorld—you can always opt to say not just no, but hell no to such requests).

The reason that the two of us volunteered to spend a cold, wet, miserable night with the dead man's remains on the side of a mountain was quite a simple one—it was just the right thing to do.

I did not relay this part of the plan to Ben and Eric out of the fear that if those responsible for dispatching a helicopter knew that someone was willing to stay with the body, it might negatively influence their willingness to fly Mike off the mountain on that same day. It was a gamble, a teeny tiny white lie, that we hoped wouldn't come back and bite us on the ass.

We were all hoping and praying that the begging and politicking going on miles away and thousands of feet below us would result in a helicopter meeting us at the LZ to fly Mike off the hill. If no helicopter arrived, we estimated that it would take a fresh crew of rescuers and packhorses at least another full day to carry Mike down to the trailhead in Crestone.

"Site Command, Saguache County operations here, you'll be seeing Flights landing at your LZ's coordinates in two hours."

All of us within earshot of a radio cheered loudly in response to this good news. As it turned out, when the Flight For Life crew out of Breckenridge learned that members of Rocky Mountain Rescue, Douglas County SAR, and Alpine were on the mountain, they agreed to make the long (for a helicopter) one-hour flight to our LZ and pick up Mike since they worked with all of our teams on such a regular basis up north. Though the sheriff would have to pay for their service, everyone involved agreed that it was a safer option than risking another long day on the mountain with another crew of rescuers.

Soon after, we arrived at the LZ, which was a flattish area on top of a knoll at an elevation of 12,200 feet.

Even though we were assured by Ben and Eric that the helicopter was on its way, Frank and I remained skeptical. We decided to stick around while everyone else headed back down the mountain just in case the helicopter decided it was too risky to land. We'd seen it happen before.

After the lower team of rock-dodging rescuers relieved the exhausted lead climbing team of all the heavy gear from their packs and stowed the extra burden in their own, the rescuers set off down the mountain, leaving Frank and I some extra food just in case we did end up spending the night.

Frank, knowing that we could at last take a breather, lay down on the spongy green tundra and promptly fell asleep. I curled up on the cool ground next to an enormous, 15-foot-tall boulder a few feet from where Mike's body lay. From my ground-level vantage point, my ear to the moss, the bright blue bag that served as Mike's temporary resting place, nested in the bright orange plastic SKED litter, looked disquietingly beautiful there among the wildflowers. In my oxygen-deprived and exceedingly weary brain, it some-how seemed like it belonged there. It was a surreal moment.

Out of the corner of my rapidly closing eye, I caught movement. It was Darin, the filmmaker, capturing our collapse. I had completely forgotten about him. At that point, I was too tired to give a damn what Darin might be filming.

Darin put his camera down and slowly walked over to Mike's body. I could see the tears in his eyes. "What happens to him now?" Darin asked.

I rolled over, sat up and explained that a helicopter was hopefully on its way, and once Mike was off the mountain, he would be flown down to the Saguache County coroner, then released to his family back in Illinois. Darin wanted to know the fallen climber's name and address so that he could pres-ent his edited footage to his family. At first I slipped back into my author-ity figure voice and began spouting off catchphrases like "not at liberty to divulge ..." and "patient confidentiality laws in Colorado state that ...," but then I gave up.

"Mike was his name," I said. "You can find out the rest from the sheriff."

An hour later, the Flight For Life helicopter arrived. As I said earlier, we work with Flight For Life on a fairly regular basis, and place a lot of trust in them—with good reason. Based out of Denver, they were the country's very first civilian hospital-based air ambulance service way back in 1972, and their safety record is outstanding. In the now highly competitive air ambu-lance business, the Flight For Life pilots refuse to make any of their go or no-go decisions based on the almighty dollar during a rescue. Quite simply, they are the best in the biz, in my humble opinion.

After making their picture-perfect landing, shutting down the rotors, and exiting the helicopter, I was pleasantly surprised to find that I recognized the entire flight crew, having worked with them on two other missions the previous weekend back home.

We solemnly loaded Mike into the helicopter, then Frank, Darin, and I watched the powerful AStar B3 helicopter lift off the knoll and then turn down toward the valley, the whirling rotors and their winged heart logo on the side of the ship catching the last few rays of sunlight. As the distinctive whupp-whupping sound of the helicopter faded into the distance, it was re-placed by an eerie cacophony of coyote howls that arose and filled the cirque, echoing off the sides of the encircling cliffs. It was a chilling sound, and one that seemed a more fitting sendoff for Michael Lepold than the playing of "Taps."

We exchanged contact information with Darin and headed back down the mountain.

Many of the recoveries that take place in the high and remote corners of RescueWorld require the use of rotary wing aircraft. Photo by Charley Shimanski.

The stressful nature of our work combined with our exertions at altitude had robbed us of all earthly desires but one: to sleep. Forget about food or dry clothes. Everything else paled in importance. Struggling to put one foot in front of the other, I started to fantasize about sleep in much the same way a teenage boy might dreamily fantasize about the opposite sex. I wanted it that bad.

Sleep: It can be maddening to crave something so very simple, so very basic, yet so unattainable.

When we finally reached the trailhead, it was 9:00 p.m. and dark again. We had been in the field for seventeen straight hours on an hour's rest. After a quick debrief with a visibly relieved Ben and the county coroner, we packed up our gear and stumbled across the street to crash on the floor of a friend's house. Bliss.

Some weeks later, Darin sent me a link to the edited footage he had assembled for Mike's family. True to his word, it was a moving piece that he dedicated to the memory of the perished shuttle astronauts, Mike, and the mountain rescuers who helped to bring him home. He titled the film "To Touch the Face of God," in honor of the eulogizing words from President Reagan engraved upon the plaque atop the very mountain on which Mike had lost his life.

While viewing part one of Darin's short film, which condensed the four-day-long search and recovery for Mike down to forty-two minutes and seven seconds, I came to the realization that if I were so inclined, I too could condense the entire written narrative of Mike Lepold's recovery. I could go as far as shrinking it down to a single sentence: Someone fell off a mountain in Colorado, died, and then some people got him off the mountain.

But this brief sentence, and the similarly abbreviated headlines that alert the world when an accident befalls someone in the backcountry, does a disservice to both the deceased and the pall bearers/foot soldiers (and their supportive families) in RescueWorld who sacrifice so much to ensure that, dead or alive, everyone makes it home eventually.

The Army Rangers have a saying they like to recite before going into battle, "No soldier gets left behind." But as we fight the never-ending battle with the forces of Darwinism here in RescueWorld, we expand the Army Ranger's creed to include not only our fellow soldier-rescuers, but *all* who venture into the wild.

"No one gets left behind."

Debrief

Photo by Tom Wood

A Fool's Circle: Learning the Hard Way— Again and Again

Sometimes I feel like the world's biggest fake. Not because I've somehow sold out (selling out involves making gobs of cash, so if I *have* sold out, I've done a piss-poor job of it). Not because I've started a family and settled down (though living a single and nomadic lifestyle might sound exciting in theory, I've found it to be grossly overrated in practice myself). No, I sometimes feel like an imposter because I am guilty (repeatedly) of doing almost every single thing that I now rail against as a mountain rescuer and industrial safety trainer.

Me, the idiot who used to play with dynamite. Me, the moron who used to get high off nitrous oxide while illegally rappelling Aussie-style off railroad trestles. Me, the genius who used to drink a twelve-pack of Milwaukee's Best and then free solo an 80-foot cliff in the dark.

As the current Field Director of the Alpine Rescue Team, I'm now supposed to lead one of the largest, busiest, and most respected mountain rescue teams in the United States through the busiest four years they've ever had.

As the Training Manager for PMI's Vertical Rescue Solutions, I'm now supposed to preach safety to the guys who climb 1,500-foot-tall cell towers. I'm tasked with educating them about things like why OSHA insists that they establish a Managed Fall Protection Plan so that they can stay in compliance with ANSI Z359.2 (2007) and that they should remain attached to the tower with their fall arrest lanyards 100 percent of the time—when I used to be the thrill-seeking goofball who would go free climb a 200-foot-tall cell tower after a night on the town.

I'm now expected to be the voice of reason and chastise the guys hanging off ropes fifty stories in the air to change the light bulbs on a high-rise building because they used a bowline knot to tie off their main line instead of a figure eight retrace knot because the retrace knot is about 8 percent stronger.

Me, the guy who only fifteen years ago struggled to tie his own shoes. Seriously.

Instead of writing preposterously plotted porn for *Penthouse* and sophomoric science fiction, I now pen articles on less titillating but much more important and relevant subjects like Grain Bin Rescue, The Importance of the Rescue PrePlan and Tower Crane Evacuation Procedures.

Instead of being the roofer who has to tie his electrical extension cord to an air conditioning unit and body rappel off a roof when the wind blows his ladder down after everyone else has left the jobsite, I'm now the guy tasked with teaching self-evacuation and companion rescue techniques to cell tower climbers, wind turbine techs, window washers, and other at-height workers. In short, I've been forced to grow up. To wise up. Oh, the glorious irony.

Well, I've heard it said that criminals make the best cops. And former patients make the best doctors. I can only hope (and fervently pray) that (semi) reformed rednecks from the Rustbelt also make the best non-paid professional mountain rescuers and paid industrial rope rescue instructors.

Is that selling out? I hope not. I don't think so.

I guess after all those years of doing really, really stupid shit and watching people fall off roofs, get electrocuted, shot with nail guns, set on fire, and otherwise injured in ways that, when videotaped, get millions of hits on YouTube, it was time to get wise and take all the hard lessons that I'd learned and put them to good use and actually help some people.

So now, the line between my day job and my duties in RescueWorld has blurred, and I find myself in the once unfathomable (at least to me) position of getting paid to teach others how to be safe while working at height and hanging off ropes.

Even though I love my paid position as an industrial safety-at-height and rescue trainer for PMI (how could I not?), my heart still belongs to the mountains. For it was the lessons I learned from my years of involvement with the Alpine Rescue Team that led me to my job as an industrial rope rescue trainer in the first place.

So I guess I've traded my Rustbelt steel for Rocky Mountain stone, but I still cling to my industrial roots.

But I do have a confession to make in regards to my involvement with Alpine. I am guilty of breaking one of our most steadfast rules. I have repeatedly violated that sacred mountain rescue mantra that was tattooed into my brain that very first day I stepped into RescueWorld nearly eighteen years ago.

When we were warned about keeping our priorities straight upon joining the team, our team's elders (like high school guidance counselors) prophetically implied that an unhealthy preoccupation with mountain rescue was like some kind of gateway drug that led to more insidious addictions down the road. I was under the impression that after the first time I let any other aspect of my life take a back seat to mountain rescue, soon after I'd find myself out on a street corner turning tricks to support my mountain rescue addiction.

That "Family first, work second, religion third, and mountain rescue last" chant, like a necklace of garlic cloves, was supposed to ward off that life-sucking vampire known as volunteer mountain rescue.

It didn't. And still doesn't, at least for me. As a mountain rescuer, I have chosen missions over family get-togethers. As a mountain rescuer, I have called in sick to work because I was out beating the bushes in search of a total stranger who turned out not to be lost at all. As a mountain rescuer, I have, for the most part, "lost my religion," as they like to say in the South.

Many, many times over the last several years, I have put mountain rescue first. I do not regret these transgressions one bit, and may lightning strike me where I stand for daring to utter such blasphemy. And I do not make such a bold and seemingly inconsiderate statement because I am a selfish bastard. Well, I guess the selfish label might sometimes be appropriate, but let me plead my case on the bastard part.

When I set out to write a book about my involvement with SAR, one of my secret goals was to use the book as a chance to publicly apologize to my wife and kids for all the times I put mountain rescue first.

Like the time I missed my oldest daughter Sarah's sixth birthday because a one-day search on Blanca Peak in southern Colorado for an overdue hiker (on the day *before* her birthday) morphed into a two-day body recovery for which I was asked to function as Incident Commander.

Or the time when we were on the way home from our daughter Hannah's fifth and her brother Seth's seventh birthday party (they were born on the same day two years apart, just as my wife and her older sister share the same birth date with five years in between) in Denver when a climber took a fall on Lover's Leap just before we drove past it on the way home. At least they both had plenty of leftover birthday cake to munch on in my truck parked at the base of the rocks while they watched us through binoculars rescue the climber with a shattered foot until their mom and sister could swing back by and pick them up.

Or the multitude of times when I abandoned (boy *that* word keeps popping up) my wife, Maren, to heed the siren call of my mistress, Alpine.

Balancing family life with the demands of SAR work can be difficult at times. Seth, Hannah, and Sarah are my three favorite reasons for coming back down off the mountain in one piece. Photo by Tom Wood.

But while mapping my journey from Rustbelt Refugee to Rocky Mountain Rescuer, a funny thing happened. I had an epiphany of sorts. I discovered that maybe I wasn't guilty of heresy after all. Because while I sorely missed my family every single second that I was away from them, I discovered that I had *not* violated the family first, work second, religion third guideline handed down to me by my RescueWorld elders.

For how can I truly say that I have put mountain rescue above my family when mountain rescuers *are* my family? And when I say family, I am not talking a "Kumbaya," "Leave It to Beaver," definition of family. I'm talking about the very real, not-so-perfect definition of family.

These are the people I've called in the middle of the night to bail me out of more than one jam. These are some of the people that my children call aunt and uncle (even though they don't completely understand that the relationship is not biological and we've repeatedly tried to explain the difference). These are the people who introduced me to my wife and six months later stood by our side on a cold December morning at 10,000 feet as we were married. The people who have loaned me money (sometimes donated) when times were tight. The people I have cried with, drank beers with, and trusted my life to. The people I love.

While they will never replace my biological family, they have become the dysfunctional surrogate family I was denied as a child. Whether they adopted me, or I them, I still can't be sure.

Over the years, the Alpine Rescue Team has developed some very close relationships with the sheriff's offices that we work with. Here, Clear Creek County Sheriff Rick Albers receives a token of our gratitude for all the years he's served and protected both the residents of Clear Creek County and the folks who've had the misfortune to need our help in its mountains. Photo courtesy of the Alpine Rescue Team.

The second aspect of life that we are supposed to value above mountain rescue is that of our work. What we do to pay the bills. For how could we afford to spend all of those thousands of dollars on gear for mountain rescue if we have no jobs?

The first job I held as I entered RescueWorld was that of roofer (and part-time liquor store cashier on nights and weekends). Though my roofing employer at first sang the praises of my involvement in mountain rescue, that tune quickly changed once it became apparent that I sometimes left my post as a crew foreman, raced down the ladder, and disappeared into the mountains when the pager commanded me to do so.

When I said mountain rescue saved my life, this is one of the ways it accomplished that feat. If not for my yearning to devote more time to RescueWorld and find a line of work that better suited my deepening involvement, I might well have continued my career as a roofer and ended up carting around an iron lung with me up and down the ladder. Or been pushed off the roof by a disgruntled fellow roofer. I think both were equally possible.

Last but certainly least, there is religion. As members of the Alpine Rescue Team, we are told to value our chosen religion over our commitment to mountain rescue. But what if, again at the risk of a lightning bolt being hurled down upon my head from above, the mountain rescuer's devotion to the humanitarian cause of mountain rescue becomes their de facto religion?

To be honest, religion and I weren't exactly on speaking terms when I first moved to Colorado and joined mountain rescue. When I still lived back in Ohio in my parents' basement back in the mid-'90s, my parents had rediscovered their faith and were regulars at the Bristolville Free Will Baptist Church, which was one of the many churches that Preacher Click helped to found, and he had married my mother and father in that same church three decades earlier.

I had been out of the Marine Reserves for a good while by that time, had shoulder-length hair, a couple of big hoop earrings and a beard. So although I looked a lot different from the clean-cut little Tommy Wood (complete with clip-on tie) that sat in those wooden pews twenty years earlier, I was still pretty much the same person on the inside as I sat beside my mother and Grandma Click (who was at that time widowed and battling Alzheimer's while in the care of my parents) that warm summer Sunday morning. Being a typical muggy Ohio day, I had worn a button-up, short-sleeve shirt that allowed the tattoos on my arms to peek past my sleeves as I leaned forward.

I wasn't jumping up and down happy about being there, but felt it my duty to go since it was so important to my mom, who was scheduled to play piano and sing that morning. It was a typical Free Will Baptist service, with lots of tear-filled testimonials, high-volume preaching, and off-key but heartfelt hymns sung by the same people I had known all my life. Like the members of the now-defunct Niles Free Will Baptist Church, many of these folks originally hailed from Olive Hill, Kentucky, and some had been friends of my recently deceased grandfather, Preacher Click, since the 1930s.

After the service, as we all filed out down the middle aisle between the pews, I made to reach down and give a goodbye hug to a sweet old woman (let's just call her Sister McGee), who had looked just as old and just as sweet to me when I was knee-high to a fly.

"You know you're not welcome here looking the way you do," she said, her mouth twisting into something I had thought her incapable of producing—a snarl. I leaned back as if I'd been slapped, completely taken aback by the venom in her voice.

"If I was your mother, I wouldn't even let you wash your socks in my house!" And with that, she turned from me and limped away, leaning on her rubber-tipped cane as she went.

Although it might sound silly and shallow to cite the utterance of two condemning sentences from a "sweet" little old lady as the main reason I walked away from organized religion on that day, it was. Hell, I've seen people walk *toward* organized religion for more flimsy reasons than that.

I gave religion one last chance when my first wife and I were in the throes of our divorce, shortly after we moved to Colorado but before I joined Alpine. My boss at Western Roofing, Sandy Sanderson (yes that was his real name), was a devoutly religious man who knew I was struggling to find answers as my marriage to my first wife was disintegrating before my very eyes. I looked up to Sandy, who had been a good boss and a good mentor. He convinced me to attend a Promise Keepers meeting in Colorado Springs. Promise Keepers, he explained, was basically a non-denominational, faith-based support group for Christian men. I was so full of self-doubt, and desperate for some answers, I figured that it couldn't hurt to go and hear what flavor of salvation they might be offering.

At the end of the session (which I had by then realized to be a recruitment seminar), the motivational speaker addressed the hundreds of men seated in the enormous hall and encouraged them to stand up if they wanted to accept Jesus Christ as their savior. A layperson would then be dispatched to hear us recite the Promise Keeper's Pledge, hear our testimonial, and collect any donations if we were so moved to give them. I looked around nervously (sweating like a pig in a bacon factory) and noticed that nearly everyone around me was standing, receiving and giving manly hugs as they all wept manly tears.

Sandy, who was already a Promise Keeper, stood at my side and motioned for me to stand beside him. I took a deep breath, put my hands on my knees, stood up ... and then immediately changed my mind and sat right back down. At the very moment that I stood, several things became crystal clear to me in the blink of an eye.

This was no simple "support group for Christian men." This was a fiscally driven ministry/church (the home page of their website uses the word donate twice and has a link to their shopping cart) masquerading as a support group, with the motivational speaker standing in for the role of pastor, a mission statement taking the place of doctrine, and an Expo Center substituting as a house of God. This was a hip, '90s twist on organized religion.

I felt both elated and more than a little sad when I suddenly realized that it was now up to me, and me alone, to get my act together, quit feeling sorry for myself and get back on my feet.

Truth be told, I somewhat envied the men around me who had found something they believed in. I wished them well, but knew in my heart that their path was not to be mine. I felt no closer or further away from God than I did as a child, but realized, once and for all, that I wanted no part of organized religion.

Besides, I really didn't want to belong to an organization that frowned upon Catholics, Mormons, same-sex marriages, a woman's right to choose, and actor Gary Busey (yes I'm dead serious).

Sandy never asked me why I sat back down, but I could see the disappointment in his eyes.

On the walk out of the Expo Center, I half feared the ghost of Sister McGee (for surely she'd have to be at least a hundred if she was still kicking) would appear like an apparition from Christmas past and warn me to get right with Jesus before it was too late. And to wash my own darned socks.

So I thanked the God that I remembered from my distant youth that this didn't happen, and prayed that I would someday find something to fill that universal human need for spiritual community. As they say, be careful what you wish for, because someday you might just get it.

When I was accepted into the ranks of the Alpine Rescue Team some months later, my boss' church, the Evergreen Fellowship, wanted to support my decision to help others through mountain rescue, and bought me my first pair of mountaineering boots. The boots were Italian, and at $300, they were easily the most expensive item of clothing I'd ever put on my body.

I wrote the church a heartfelt letter of thanks, promising them I'd put the boots to good use as a mountain rescuer. That I would work hard to make them proud and save lives. Two months and half a dozen blisters later, I came to the painful conclusion that the boots were too small for me. But by that time, they were too worn to return, and I didn't have the heart to ask them for another pair. Instead, I gave the ill-fitting boots away, disappointed to find that once again, religion and its trappings proved to be a poor fit for me.

So one last time: Family. Work. Religion. Mountain Rescue.

After all the years of fretting over what was taking priority over what, I've come to realize that a goofy little acronym I first heard in Marine Corps Boot Camp could have saved me years of frustration. K.I.S.S.—Keep It Simple Stupid.

If I would have just thrown that whole mess into a pot and stirred it on day one, I would have saved myself a lot of heartache.

Mountain rescue *is* my family, my work, and my religion. It's as simple as that.

Acknowledgments

First and foremost, I want to thank my wife, Maren, and my children—Sarah, Seth, and Hannah—for their unwavering, unconditional, and much-needed support. I couldn't and wouldn't be able to do this if not for each of you. You give me reason to come back down off the mountain in one piece and not in a blue PVC bag.

Thanks to my pal Jerome, who has remained a steadfast friend through thick and thin.

Thanks to my brothers and sister (John, Cathie, and Dan) back home in the Rustbelt for giving me the best possible childhood friends a kid could ever hope for. Thanks especially to my dad, who sold his childhood baseball card collection and original Beatles 45 rpm records to help put me through college (and who never said a discouraging word when I nearly flunked out that same semester). Mom, thank you for showing me how to truly care about and for the human race—I wish you could still be here with us.

I'd like to thank Best Boy (or was it Key Grip?) David Tillett for his excellent copyediting skills and manuscript suggestions; Sally Spencer-Thomas for her wisdom and insight on a topic that scared the hell out of me; P. Craig Russell for demonstrating that high-falootin artistic talent and a blue-collar work ethic are not mutually exclusive; Hollis Gillespie for convincing me that even a semi-reformed redneck like myself could get published; Carey and Suzanne, Rich and Eva, Spencer and Leslie, Grandma Julie, Scott Amdur, and the Mountain Resource Center for helping our family when we needed it most; Alpine Proofreading Team members Angie Lucht, Howard Paul, Jerry Petrilli, and Paul (Woody) Woodward for helping to keep me on track.

I owe a huge debt of gratitude to Mira Perrizo at Big Earth Publishing for agreeing to publish the book you now hold in your hands.

And last but not least, I would like to thank all the past and present members of the Alpine Rescue Team (listed below). Your dedication to the noble cause of mountain search and rescue is truly admirable, and it's been an honor and a real privilege to work alongside so many amazing and inspiring people like yourselves.

Bob Abbot
Ellen Abramson
Barb Adams
Jim Adams
Rod Adams
Sue Ahrend
William Alexander
Chris Allen
Adrienne Alston
Elden Altizer
Scott Amdur
Jack Ament
Larry Anderson
Demsy Andrews
Glen Andrews
Byron Angevine
Ruth Angevine
Melissa Archey
John Armstrong
Adam Arnold
Andy Ashby
Jeff Ashby
John Ashby
John Ashby Jr.
Dale Atkins
George Aucoin
Pete Ayers
Mike Bachorowski
Deborah Baldwin
Robb Ball
Randy Bangert
Martin Barnett
Dave Baroch
John Baroch
Bill Barwick
Richard Bates
Todd Bauer

Diane Bauer-Felix
Steve Baumgartner
John Beale
Shane Becker
Bruce Beckman
Craig Behreat
Wayne Belohlavy
John Belt
Kathryn Bennet
Kelly Bethe
John Biewener
Noah Bigwood
Paula Bindrich
David Binkley
Beth Bittel
Candace Bittel
Andrew Blainey
Keely Blair
Harry Blakeman
Chris Blakeslee
Merritt R. Blakeslee
Daniel Bobalek
Dave Boeshe
Darlene Boettler
Russ Boley
Ray Bondi
Mark Bondurant
Ron Bookman
Casey Boone
Keith Boone
Michael Boone
Eric Bottjen
Jeff Bowden
Mark Bower
Jack Bowles
Larry Bowles
Lloyd Bowles

Alan Bowman
Sam Bracken
Lynn Bradfield
Glenn Brand
Jim Bredar
Dave Brewer
Mark Bricker
Marc Brideeau
Elizabeth Brignac
Becky Brock
Richard Brohl
William Brohl
Curtis Brown
Michael Brown
Roz Brown
Wes Brown
David Bruce
David Bryan
Rick Bucklew
Bill Bunting
Chuck Burdick
Jim Burge
Jeff Burke
Terry Burke
Pete Burlingame
Ralph Butler
Tim Butler
William Butler
Suzanne Cabral
Mike Callicrate
Ken Campbell
Tom Candlin
Allen Carlson
Dave Carty
Larry Caruuci
Jeff Case
Rand Case
Cheryl Cassily
Gary Cassily
Trevor Chabinski
Pat Chandler

Mark Chittum
Butch CM Clark
Doug Clark
Mike Clark
Rossi Clark Jr.
Rossi Clark Sr.
Tracy Clevenger
Scott Cliff
Joel Cline
Casey Cloud
Paul Cockrel
Don Cohen
Rick Cohan
Harold Cole
Dave Collett
Dr. Robert Collier
Tim Commans
Chris Cook
Kirk Cooper
Mike Cooper
Wayne Cooper
Betsy Copeland
Rick Corbin
Ted Cotton
Fred Coyle
Brad Craig
J.D. Crais
Alex Crane MD
George Crane
Mike Crane
Tim Cristello
Norm Crosby
Keith Cubbedge
Steve Curry
Mike Czyzewski
John Daddario
Wayne Dake
Rick Darden
Mark Davidson
Caren Davis (Plain)
Drew Davis

Pete Davis
Rick Davis
Gene Day
Michael DaBell
David Deen
Mike Deen
Ray Delahoy
Scott Delahoy
Kyle Delaney
Chris Delnero
Guy DeLuca
Margaret DeLuca
Lin Denham
Ken desGarennes
Lisa Desmaris
Chuck deWoody
Douglas Dinsmore
Randy Doane
Sam Donahue
Steve Donahue
Michael Doe
Sue Donaldson
Herb Dorn
Aaron Dover
Bruce Dreger
Dick Dreith
Scott Duke
Doug Duncan
Kurt Duncan
Michael Dunkle
Hal Dunn
Kerry Dunn
Kevin Dunn
Mike Dunn
Rick Dunn
Susan Dunn
Tom Durram
Angela Eaton-Snovak
Conrad Eckstein
Harris Economou
Linda Economou

Scott Edwards
Brian Elliott
Donna Elliott
Kenneth Elmgreen
Rachel Emmer
Danae Engel
Mike Erickson
Leilani Espinoza
Calvin Estap
Mike Everist
Anthony Fagan
Denise Fair
Bill Farrington
Jim Felix
Jason Fellmer
John Fellows
Bob Feroldi
Paul Ferrant
Scott Fetchenhier
Larry Fidler
Mechele Fillman
Melanie Findling
Tom Fiore
Kyle Firestone
Judy Fisher
Donna Fix
J. Fleming
Brett Foehner
Greg Foley
Hannah Foley (Seibel)
Anthony Frabbiele
Greg Fradsen
Scott Franey
Cathy Fraser
Mark Freeman
Greg Frost
Tama Funk
Tiger Funk
Charlie Gadeken
Gary Gaebel
Wallis Gamble

Laura Garrett
John Gates
Tom Gebhart
Dave Gendron
Steven Gerber
Mark Gerteis
Richard Glasscock
Skeet Glatterer
Lee Glivar
Anvay Goda
Kim Goldberger
Joel Gorder
Kim Gordon
Steve Gosselin
Fred Goth
Robert Gowder
Chuck Graham
Mark Graham
Sudie Graham
Rod Grainger
Rich Grange
Robin Gray
Charles Greely
Rodney Green
Steve Greene
Norman Greenwalt
Larry Greenwoold
Michael Greer
Frost Gregg
Mike Griffin
Eric Grosskreuz
Scott Grotheer
Eric Gudem
Bryon Gunnerson
Brian Guvenir
Melanie Haban
Mike Hale
Alan Hall
Cathy Hall
Michael Hall
Ramon Hall

Kreg Hamburger
Carrie Hamm
Dan Hamm
Josh Hammond
Scott Hammond
Chip Hane
Walt Hane
Nathan Hankins
Ed Harrington
Edward Harris
Erich Harris
Stanley Harris
Steven Harris
Scott Harrison
Bill Hauer
Peter Hauer
Ken Hauser
Steve Haver
Ed Haynes
Edi Head
Matt Henderson
Roger Henry
Bob Hershberger
Sarah Hesse-Bruhl
Gary Hessling
Paul Hicks
Jack Hightower
Chris Hill
Dave Hill
Mike Hines
Steve Hinson
Rick Hoadley
Gary Hoffmann
Hunter Holloway
Jamie Holloway
Todd Holmes
Curt Honcharik
Wally Hopkins
Ike Horodyskyj
Harry Howard
Larry Howes

Eric Howland
Larry Huckaby
Ken Hukari
Peter Hunker
Margaret Hunt
Jeremy Jackson
Will Jackson
John Jenkins
Carl Jensen
John Jensen
Lou Jensen
Roger Jensen
David Johns
Eric Johnson
Jim Johnson
Larry Johnson
Leif Johnson
Martin Johnson
Roy Johnson
Bruce Johnston
Cindy Johnston
Craig Johnston
Gary Jones
Scott Jones
Dave Jurich
Stanley Kalahar
Troy Kananen
Stephen Kaspar
Bill Kastner
Brian Kehe
Scott Kehe
Steve Kelleher
Brad Keller
Mike Kellogg
Ron Kelly
Cliff Ketcham
Jack Kigerl
Jeff Kimmel
Chris King
Dr. Chuck King
Rod King

Todd King
Gregg Kinnes
Doreen Kinsella
Joshua Kirk
Eric Kirkhofer
John Kleb
Alex Klein
Doug Klingbiel
Valori Klingbiel
David Knoblach
Randy Knowles
Laura Kocol (Pierce)
Mike Koepke
Daniel Kolb
Rob Kolter
Roger Krautkremer
Gary Kress
Bill Krieger
Frank Kucler
Joseph Kuhach
Peter Kula
Mike Kullman
Tom LaBudie
Dan Lafaver
Buck LaGrange
Dale LaGrange
Harold LaGrange
Tim LaMacchio
Al Lambert
Ted Lams
Turner Lang
Scott Lange
Sabrina Langner
Ben Lantow
Leo Lavender
Larry Ledwick
Harry Ledyard
Jamie Lee
Dave Leeds
Paul Lein
Rex Leiner

Christiane Leitinger
Gene Lines
Joanie Lines
Hal Link
Pam Link
Tom Loebach
Zach Loescher
Lee Lucas
Angie Lucht
Dana Luethy
Phil Luethy
Dave Lynch
Bill Lytle
Trevor Madden
Sean Mahoney
John Maisonave
Jim Mallory
Joe Marcus
Dean Marino
John Marshall
Todd Martens
Bob Mathews
Kris Mattivi (Scott)
Mark Mattivi
Kevin May
Dan McCord
Tom McCourt
Bob McCurley
Loui McCurley
Tom McElderry
Scott McIntosh
Danny McKercher
Jerry McKercher
Sandra McKinney
Connor McLaughlin
Don McNair
Bruce McQueen
Eric Meade
Doug Meer
Mike Mellor
Traver Metcalf

Harold Metzler
William Meyers
Tad Millard
Greg Miller
Sutherland Miller
Charles Moffat
Gail Moffat
Rob Molacek
Kevin Montague
Dan Moore
Dave Moore
Terri Moore
Jennifer Morris (Sarah)
Katie Moser
Dick Mueller
Bob Mulholland
Jay Mullen
Karen Murphy
Rich Nagler
Lexi Neisler
Jamie Nellis
Arti Nelson
Brian Nelson
Mark Nelson
Randy Nelson
Tony Neri
Jon Neufeld
Martin Neunzert
Mike Neunzert
Pete Nim
Larry Nix
Allen Nordin
Amy Norton
Larry Norton
Todd Norton
Tom Nowell
Eva Noworytta
Craig O'Connell
Shane O'Brien
Mike O'Leary
Pete Olsen

Steve Olsen
Ric Ondrusek
Ruth Ondrusek
Ralph O'Neill
Bryan Osburn
Margo Osborn
Robert Owen
Jackie Padgett
Gerritt Padgham
Brian Page
HP Paisley
Kim Palmer
Mike Parker
Mike Patterson
Howard Paul
Mike Paul
Suzanne Paul
Dave Paulson
Bill Payne
Mike Payne
Toni Payne
Justin Peacock
Kelly Pearson
Craig Pedigo
Phil Pedigo
Mark Peesel
John Peleaux
Mark Pelner
Hollis Pence
Dick Perkins
Rick Perkins
Scott Perlick
Al Petrick
Betsy Petrick
Jerry Petrilli
Loren Pfau
D'ann Pickering
Walter Pickett
William Picket
Rachel Picon
Chris Pierce

Gordon Pierce
Michael Pierce
Shannon Pierce (McCort)
Mike Piwowarczyk
Dave Plume
Rick Pollack
Kyle Poos-Benson
Dave Porta
Kelly Porter
Ed Portoro
Wayne Potter
Bob Powell
Dow Powell
Jim Powell
David Pratt
Diana Pratt
Jim Price
Valerie Price
Dave Pritkel
John Putt
Mike Putt
Tom Putt
Steve Raber
JJ Radinsky
Robert Ramsey
Michael Rasser
Pandora Reagon
Garry Reed
Jeff Rehman
Craig Renkert
Dave Reynolds
Tom Rhodes
Marcus Rice
David Richards
Roger Riggs
Roy Riggs
Stuart Riggs
Richard Rincoe
Mark Robertson
Phil Romero
Bjorn Rommel

Jeff Rosenbach
Eric Rosenquist
Carla Rossby
Steve Rossman
Roy Roux
Ira Russianoff
Mark Ryan
Kirt Salisbury
Cheri Sanek
David Schmoker
Robin Schmutzler
Robin Schmutzler II
George Schoenecker
Mark Schroeder
Angela Schultess
Barb Schwendler
Cliff Scott
Steve Searles
Dave Seibert
Mike Selka
Greg Sexton
Stephen Shanley
Peter Sharer
Bob Sharon
Brian Sheetz
Bruce Sheetz
Steve Shelafo
Tim Shepard
Mark W. Sheveland
Charley Shimanski
Marcia Siebenmann
Chris Silkwood
Mark H. Sims
William Sims
Andy Skaff Jr.
Orion Skinner
Greta Sloan
Magie Smiley
Andrew Smith
Bill Smith
Dave Smith

Doug Smith
Dwight Smith
Ray Smith
Mike Snovak
Craig Snyder
Don Sokolnicki
Rich Solosky
Jared Spears
Mike M. Speck
Jeff Spinzig
Rick Stearns
Robert S. Stelzer
Phil Stevens
Al Stevenson
Gordon Stevenson
Reid Stewart
Robert Stewart
Greg Stiller
Jerome Stiller
Doug Stone
Rod Strandel
Gordon Stucker
Joanne Stucker
Brian Stuebe
Duane Stutzman
Bill Sullivan
Christine Sullivan
Todd Sullivan
Richard Swanson
Heather Swenson
Frank Tadeo
Barry Teitelbaum
Patrick Terry
Joe Thinnes
Ann Thomas
Bill Thomas
Denise Thomas
John Thomas
Jeff Thompson
David Thorson
Morry Thorson

Jeff Toohey
Tom Trask
Kurt Traskos
Brian Traugh
Chris Tremlett
Howard Trueblood
Edward Trujillo
Tony Trumbly
Tim Tufts
Eve Uhing (Maas)
Janine Underhill
Lindsay Van Buskirk
Luke Van Horn
Rod Vanderwall
Richard Van Landingham
Dave Varbrick
Steve Vetas
John Villachica
John Vincent
John Voden
Carl Volk
Curt F. Von Fay
Marilyn Von Fay
Paul Von Fay
Linda Wacht
Bob Wagner
Brian Wainner
Patrick Walsh
Andy Ward
Bonnie Wasli
Kevin Wasli
Bob Watson MD
Carol Way
Steve Way
George Weaver
Richard Webb
Rich Weber
Bill Wedgewood
John Wellington
John Wells
Adam Wendling

Jason Westra
Tim Whitley
Len Wieczorek
John Wilbur
Mark Wiley
Chris Wilkinson
Rich Willhardt
Rod Willhardt
Ted Williams
Dawn Wilson (Mazzagetti)
Jack Wilson Jr.
Laurie Wilson
Marshall Wilson
Steve Wilson
Kezia Windham (Skinner)
Bill Wintle
Richard Wise
Joelle Witmer
Dale Wood
Les Wood
Linden (Woody) Wood
Mike Wood
Scott Wood
Tom Wood
Shawn Wooden
Mark Woods
Paul (Woody) Woodward
Pete Woroniecki
Brian Wrenshall
Diana Wrenshall
Rob Wright
Steve Wright
Matt (The Dude) Wroblewski
Joe Wrona
Roy Wyatt
Mark Yakoushkin
Rick Yegge
Dave Youngblood
Steve Zaiontz
Linda Ziccardi

Tom Wood is the Field Director of the Alpine Rescue Team in Evergreen, Colorado (one of the busiest non-paid professional mountain rescue teams in the country), and writes curriculum and teaches industrial rope rescue and safety to cell tower climbers, wind turbine workers, and just about anyone else who wears a harness and works at height, for Vertical Rescue Solutions by PMI. A regular speaker and presenter for the Mountain Rescue Association, the National Association for Search and Rescue, and the International Technical Rescue Symposium, he is also a U.S. delegate for Terrestrial Rescue to the International Commission for Alpine Rescue. He presently serves as the chair of the Safety Reporting Committee for both the Mountain Rescue Association and the Society of Professional Rope Access Technicians. A 1990 graduate of Kent State University's photojournalism program, he served as a Combat Photographer for the United States Marine Corps Reserve. He lives at an elevation of 8,500 feet in the foothills west of Denver in a house that is much too small for a family of five with two cats and two turtles.